No, we don't do miracles

—

But God STILL does!

Lyle and Kay Carbert

Dedication

————⸰❦⸰————

W e dedicate this book to God for His Glory! This book could not have been possible without those that have accepted the Word as the truth. Throughout all the years that we have accepted the Word, it has proved itself over and over again. To be able to live by faith takes simple faith. Because it is a simple faith, we have been able to share this faith with others.

We dedicate this book to all the people that we have met and shared the gospel with, for without you this would not have been possible.

You will soon notice all the miracles. May we be so bold as to ask the reader to take the time to read it slowly and deliberate, every word, so that it will sink into your spirit, as to the miraculous, miracle way, that is available to you.

Acknowledgements

To God be the Glory!

This book, *'No, We Don't Do Miracles, But God STILL Does!'* would never have become a reality if the Word of God was not true. He has proved that over and over again. However, without the input of our children and friends that have spent countless hours editing, checking dates and facts, changing names (*Names**), layout and design, this book would perhaps still be in the paper and pencil state.

To all that played a part in this work, many, many thanks, and God's richest blessings on all.

Table of Contents

Foreword

Lyle Carbert is on my "most unforgettable" list of people. I first heard of Lyle from his Father, a lumber dealer in a community at the end of the most northerly road in Canada. As I traveled north from Vermillion Bay on the Trans Canada to Red Lake, a huge wolf appeared out of the bush and ran beside the car for a while. A giant moose reared its huge antlers on the other side of the road. Finally, the Carbert home and warm hospitality for a week while my friend Maurice Fostrey and I conducted evangelistic meetings at the local Pentecostal Church. Lyle was not home but he made his appearance at Bible College in Peterborough, Ontario in September as a first year student while I completed my final year.

I could not possibly miss Lyle. He is larger than life in many ways. He seemed to fill whatever room he was in with his big physical presence, and also his outgoing personality. He had been a wrestler during his years as a student at Western University in London, Ontario, and now his zest for life, his irrepressible sense of humour, and his fervent desire to passionately serve God combined to impress me with the confidence that whatever Lyle did, and wherever he went, he would break the mould that was traditional Christian ministry. At a chapel service at the college I saw him with what seemed, because of his size, a very tiny violin. When he stood preparing to play, I wondered how he would ever get his huge hands and fingers to function on the slender neck of the instrument. But he did and tears came to my eyes as the sweetest tones emerged to fill the room. I was a Pastor at Brighton during my final year and as soon as possible I arranged for Lyle to come and minister in music and in God's Word at my church.

While at Brighton I helped to re-establish a congregation that had gone through hard times in Castleton, Ontario. Upon graduation and marriage to a very brave and godly young lady, Kay, this young couple came to serve the Lord in the village of Castleton.

Throughout the years we have been in touch from time to time. I'm not surprised that much of Lyle's and Kay's ministry has been like the Apostle Paul's "Tent making" years in establishing beachheads for God's work. I'm challenged by the sacrifices this couple has made for decades now. I'm inspired by the reports of "Signs and wonders" following their ministry as were evident in the ministry of the Apostles. I would also say that while we do not use the term "Apostle" to describe a 21st century minister of the gospel, I would say that they have exercised an apostolic ministry.

This book will bless, encourage, inspire and challenge every reader to dig down into the richness of God's provision for His people and to reach higher than ever for the fulfilment of God's purposes for us all.

David Mainse

Introduction

Isaiah 12:4 *". . . declare His doings among the people . . ."*

The first reason for putting something into print that hundreds, yea, maybe thousands, could have done, is that I perceive a dearth in testimonies of the miraculous in the average church and among multitudes of believers.

In our travels we meet many believers who have never personally seen or experienced a truly miraculous event. There is a tendency to relate all miracles to TV Evangelism or Mass Evangelism. Our strong conviction is that the percentage of miracles that take place in the spirit filled churches, should be much higher than in Mass Evangelism.

We are definitely in favor of Mass Evangelism and we support and pray for such. However, when we find the majority of churches, even the preachers, have never experienced a genuine miracle, we suspect the tendency to relegate the miraculous to Mass Evangelism, has impoverished the church of the expectation that, ". . . signs shall follow them that believe . . . " and ". . . the Lord working with them, and confirming the word with signs following" (Mark 16:15-20).

Be encouraged, *"No we don't do miracles, but God STILL does!"*

The second reason, for the story format, is to emphasize that life experiences, combined with environmental influences, and social and family expectations and examples, form character. Character determines leadership gifts. The five-fold ministries of Ephesians 4:11, that is, THE APOSTLE, THE PROPHET, THE EVANGELIST, THE PASTOR AND THE TEACHER are the manifestation of different characters revealed by the anointing and calling into leadership.

No seminary can make someone an Apostle or a Prophet, etc. etc.! No amount of laying on of hands or prophesying can turn someone into something they are not by character. Ordination by men should be the recognition of such a manifest gift of character formed by life, and revealed by the obedient response to the call and anointing of God.

Hopefully in the telling of this story of my wife and I, you might find the patient courage to be your sanctified self, walk in obedience to God's will and watch how God's leading will reveal to you and others, who and what you really are and how you fit, happily, peacefully and powerfully into God's Kingdom!

The third reason would be that you might enjoy the story for one of two reasons. You may enjoy, if you're old enough, the nostalgic memories of days with which you can identify. Or, you may enjoy the weird seeming, almost unbelievable stories that tell 'the way it used to be', if you're of the younger set. No, we didn't walk five miles to school in minus fifty degrees Fahrenheit, uphill both ways. But the stories in this book are as true and accurate as our memories! Be Blessed!

All our yesterdays prepared us for today! Each day we live, prepares us for tomorrow!

His Story

1

Birth and New Birth

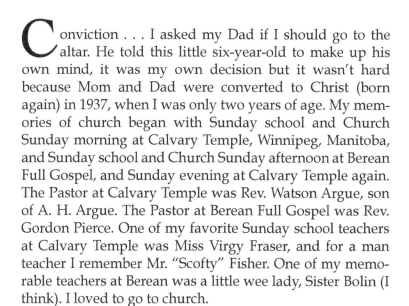

Conviction . . . I asked my Dad if I should go to the altar. He told this little six-year-old to make up his own mind, it was my own decision but it wasn't hard because Mom and Dad were converted to Christ (born again) in 1937, when I was only two years of age. My memories of church began with Sunday school and Church Sunday morning at Calvary Temple, Winnipeg, Manitoba, and Sunday school and Church Sunday afternoon at Berean Full Gospel, and Sunday evening at Calvary Temple again. The Pastor at Calvary Temple was Rev. Watson Argue, son of A. H. Argue. The Pastor at Berean Full Gospel was Rev. Gordon Pierce. One of my favorite Sunday school teachers at Calvary Temple was Miss Virgy Fraser, and for a man teacher I remember Mr. "Scofty" Fisher. One of my memorable teachers at Berean was a little wee lady, Sister Bolin (I think). I loved to go to church.

At age six . . . Sunday morning . . . Pastor Watson Argue was preaching . . . altar call . . . because of how guilty I felt (I won't go into details here but I was doing bad things at the age of six), I ran to the altar feeling like I had a heavy load on my shoulders. There, an older lady sat beside where I knelt and explained that my sins were all washed away. I cried profusely and accepted this fact with child-like faith and invited Jesus into my life. I remember the front pew at which I knelt. Calvary Temple in 1941, had a triangle of pews near the front on each side of the auditorium. I knelt at the front pew on the right side of the church when facing the platform.

I had an experience with God that started a hunger that found me in the prayer room after every service seeking God. I remember clearly how light I felt as I rose from my knees that Sunday morning and I felt like I floated back to the pew where Mom and Dad were waiting. The heavy load of guilt was lifted and I understood that all my sins were gone.

I would like to take time here to tell you my memories of the prayer room experiences. At the time of this writing, I have the distinct feeling that there are not many prayer rooms left where the hungering and thirsting believers thronged after every Sunday night service and some Sunday morning services to seek the face of God. While the zealous believers were heading for the prayer room, sinners were streaming to the altar to get saved, filled, healed and encouraged.

The prayer room was a fairly noisy place. Some people were weeping, some were praising, some were laughing, some were clapping, some were singing and some were talking in tongues (God given language experiences). Often people were healed, baptized with the Holy Spirit and delivered from bondage. At this time I cannot confirm with anyone I know, but in a little boy's mind in the early 1940's, my memory holds one story with some detail. I remember Lawrence Siemens was one of the men praying for a particular man. The man had an epileptic seizure in the prayer room and fell out the door into the hallway. There someone put a bone handled knife between his teeth and about three men, Lawrence Siemens being one of them, were down on the floor praying up a storm. As a little boy I stood there with my eyes wide open watching up close, a real heavy prayer time for a man to be healed of epilepsy (which I was seeing for the first time in my life). Well, God healed this brother! Fourteen years later he reported that he never had another seizure. An interesting note concerning this man, I believe his name was, Brother Fitz.

I was baptized in water and had such a deep desire for baptism in the Holy Spirit (I saw others having this experience, and it sure made a difference in them). I faithfully prayed long hours in the prayer room and at the altar, but it didn't happen to me.

2

Growing up in Winnipeg

A lthough I had given my heart to Jesus, I was still a little boy. Some of the stories of my growing up around Winnipeg may suggest I was normal and others maybe suggest some abnormality. Bill Brand's B.A. (British American) service station on Portage Avenue, freshly painted white walls, somehow seemed to be the suitable place to wipe my hands off after I had dipped them in some tar on the roadside. NOT GOOD! Fortunately, Bill Brand attended Calvary Temple and knew who I was, so he didn't skin me alive, but let my father know. Dad gave me some 'discipline' and a lesson on how to remove tar from a wall.

I had those childhood experiences of wearing my rubber boots after a good rainstorm, and finding the deepest mud hole to test them in. At least once . . . maybe more . . . I came home with only one boot, because I wasn't strong enough to retrieve my other boot out of the mud hole where I had stood and jiggled it in until the mud had sucked my boot off.

I think I had a secret desire to join the circus and do stunts on my two-wheeled bike. I tried balancing on tee-ter-totters, taking jumps off homemade ramps, and, I hope I'm not embellishing the memory, but I believe I got up to twelve people on my bike at one time and rode it for a ˉw feet.

I never started a fight in my life, because I was taught that was wrong. If I came home with a few marks and a little blood from fighting, I didn't get sympathy but was disciplined. I won't begin to relate all the fights I got in, two or three a week, but I had that flare-up point early in life, and would react fearlessly when provoked and just lash out. For instance, I punched my first schoolteacher when I was in Grade Two. Of course I'm not proud of that, but I reacted to her abrupt discipline, which I likely deserved. I was standing in line at the school door, and probably not paying attention, when she grabbed me and started to shake me. The problem was that she grabbed me by the fur on the hood of my brand new parka, and I just typically lost it. I lashed out with both fists as hard and as fast as I could. "I'm sorry, Teacher," I said. Fortunately, I was too small to hurt her too much, and the discipline was a story to be told. She gave me the strap and sent me to the vice-principal, who also gave me the strap and sent me to the principal, who gave me the strap again and sent me home with a note for my parents. I threw the note away, and lied to my mother about that and told her I was sent home because I was sick. Well, the details piled up by the truth coming out, and my mother gave me the strap. When my dad got home, he gave me another licking for lying. I think it cured the lying, but not the crazy anger.

When my older brother, Barry, would get into fights, I automatically lost control and would tie-in to his opponents. Barry was a little anemic and no fighter, and I was crazy enough not to hesitate to play the hero.

Our slight built neighbor boys, red-headed Barry and Teddy, about ten years old, were being picked on by a seventeen year-old bully, when my ten year old hero mentality kicked in again and I jumped on the bully's back and grabbed him by the hair with both hands. He let my friends go and tried to get at me. It was too late to change my mind, so I just started pulling hair out by the handfuls and threatening to pull more out if he dared to hit me. Looking back almost sixty years later, I realized he probably could have killed me except he was bleeding and crying and in such pain that he just gave up and went home.

In grade five, I 'fell in love' with my red-headed school teacher, Miss O'Neil. I realize now that the probable reason she had me sit in the front desk by the window, and stood beside me while she was teaching, stroking my hair and the back of my neck, was to keep me from misbehaving. She broke my heart anyway, when she left me for an older man that she married.

Approx. 1943 Carbert family at 429 Rosedale Ave.

I might have lost my temper when guys challenged me, but I didn't let my pride spoil the relationship with the girls. One time they ganged up on me and I let them drag me `appy for their attention). The problem was that I was too ud to let on that as they dragged me across the wooden 's of the platform outside the Lord Robert's School, my belly was collecting giant slivers. I just laughed and headed home where my mother and I worked with pliers, fingers, and iodine to pull these bits of lumber from my belly. The T-shirt was discarded for rags.

One of our jobs as a boy in Winnipeg was to help with the garden. At 429 Rosedale Avenue we had the one side of the yard all in garden, with lots of hoeing and digging. My industrious mother also planted a garden on a vacant lot a few blocks away where she always grew asparagus. It was strange how far it seemed to be to walk over there to hoe the garden in the warm weather, but it was no distance or difficulty to walk just down the street from the garden plot in the cold winter to play hockey on the outdoor rink, catalogues for shin pads and all.

At 429 Rosedale Avenue, Christmas morning was a challenge. We all slept on the third floor, the boys in the bedroom on the one side of the steep stairway, Mom, Dad and Barbara on the other side. There was a trap door over the stairway with railings on each side and a railing around the access hole for ventilation or air circulation.

Five o'clock in the morning we would be up, tip-toeing around, trying to lower the first kid down the access hole to the bottom of the stairs and then one by one sneaking down to see what Santa had left for us under the tree. The one memory that was special was when we found a new steel runner sleigh under the tree. We got dressed, it was still dark, and headed for the banks of the Red River just past Jubilee Avenue.

Well, that was a blast, but the thought of the high wooden slide standing at Polo Park was just too tempting, so, we hiked over there with our new sled and hauled it up to the top of this giant slide. Now, I can't remember what the slide was designed for, bobsled, toboggan or what, but it was not designed for some little kids on a steel runner sleigh. It seems in my memory that it might have been 40 or 50 feet high with a long slide run with about 1½" sides on it. Too dumb to know the danger we went ahead and enjoyed the thrill, until my father came looking for us. For some reason he seemed a little more aware of the danger than the thrill and was a little distraught with us.

429 Rosedale Avenue was where most of my Winnipeg memories stem from, probably because of my age.

Before I had a two-wheeled bike of my own, I decided to take the bigger tricycle and attempt to keep up to the bigger kids on their two-wheelers. To complicate matters my left arm was in a cast. I broke it when I tripped coming in to home plate which just happened to be a big Maple tree (you remember what it was like, don't you? A maple tree by the curb was home base, a fence post on the other side of the sidewalk was first base, another maple tree was second base, and the manhole cover in the middle of the street was third base). Anyway, riding a tricycle as fast as I could peddle, with a broken left arm in a sling, zig-zag, zig-zag, oops — out of control, nosed into the concrete curb. I landed with my chin on the curb, bit my tongue almost off, teeth went right through my tongue, bleeding profusely. Barrie ran to the house across the street, they packed my mouth with ice and put me in a little wagon and pulled me about three blocks to home. They wouldn't stitch the tongue but I had to keep it in ice as much as possible until the bleeding completely stopped and then I could only eat liquids for a while. While in this condition, I did something to warrant my father's discipline. The problem was it happened at the top of the steep attic stairs. Father was applying the 'board of education to the seat of learning' when I lost my balance and slid all the way down the attic stairs. The door was closed at the bottom but I hit it feet first, burst the door open and sprained my ankle. Well, when Dr. Tisdale, our family physician, came to the house for the third time in about a week, I heard him tell my mother to put me in a glass case until I was healed, before anything else happened to me.

One of the things I loved to do was ride the horse drawn bread wagon, with the Bryce's Bakery man. I would help him deliver the bread, and he would drop me off about a block away on his way back. The one time he gave me a 16 oz. loaf of fresh bread for helping him. It was all eaten before I got home. Well, that fresh bread was not digesting too well. I rolled on the floor with cramps as my mother's quaint sense of humor cut in. She laughed at me in between enemas and groanings. Thankfully, it was just like the Bible says, "It came to pass" and it did. From that day to this, I am very careful not to eat too much fresh bread too fast.

In the winter time we had a habit frowned on by all but us, of going over to Rathgar Avenue where the bus ran on a regular schedule. At night we would wait near the bus stop until the people were loading, sneak out quickly and grab on to the bumper at the back of the bus and slide around the block on our shoes. Usually those residential streets would have packed snow on them but every once in a while there were bare spots. How's your imagination? This stunt was done by us, 'professional stupids', not to be tried at home.

While living at 429 Rosedale Avenue, our cousins, Verda, Thelma and Evelyn, came to live with us (because their mother, my Dad's sister, Ethel had died). They stayed with us until they got married.

Other boarders were Arnold and Jessie Hamilton, and son, Harold, Ina Munroe and Miss Gordon, Goldie Walters, Charles Joyce, Miriam Goodwin's brother, etc..

My parents were given to hospitality (Romans 12:13). Besides opening their home to family and friends, we always had guests for Sunday dinner.

One such visitor was a man who had shared his life story at Calvary Temple, Sunday morning and came home with us for Sunday dinner. This was in the early 1940's. He had been imprisoned for using and peddling illegal drugs. I was sitting across the table from him, quite awed at this ex-con, when I heard a conversation that stuck with me to this day. My mother offered him some coffee and he graciously refused so Mom offered tea instead. His words were few but to the point. He said, "Sister, when God delivered me from drugs He delivered me from all drugs." Think about that will you. I have for almost sixty years.

We lived in rented houses all the time we were in Winnipeg; an Apartment on Fawcett Avenue where Barrie was born, 223 Thompson Drive where Barbara and I were born, 210 Banning Street where Keith was born, 647 Ashburn Street and finally 429 Rosedale Avenue.

When I was about eight years old, about 1943, I had an experience that I will never forget. The Carberts never owned a car until about 1954. In Winnipeg the street cars were still running and that's how we traveled back and forth for church. One Sunday night after church at Calvary Temple, we walked as usual up to Portage Avenue to catch the streetcar. The streetcar (an electric trolley car on rail tracks) stop was an elevated cement platform out by the tracks. We would have to stand there and wait for the right streetcar that would turn at Osborne Street to go home to Rosedale Avenue.

With all the bustling of the crowd, I got on the wrong streetcar. I ran to the back where I always liked to sit and the streetcar pulled away. When it didn't turn at Osborne Street but kept going along Portage Avenue, I looked up quickly to find the rest of the family but they weren't there. Panic was on the verge of conquering this little eight-year old. I sat there wondering and worrying about what to do. One stop went by before I decided to get off and try to find my way home. Home meant one half mile back east to Osborne Street and then a few miles south to 429 Rosedale Avenue. I was one scared kid trying not to show my fear.

I ran, and ran, and ran, my winter coat was open, there was snow and slush on the sidewalk, my scarf was flying out behind me and my mind was racing. It's after ten o'clock. What if they go to bed and lock the door before I get home? I'll have to sleep outside.

My folks didn't miss me until they went to get off the streetcar. My cousin, Arnold Hamilton, caught the next streetcar north and was looking for me in all the passing streetcars and along the road. He got back as far as Corydon when he spotted me running down the sidewalk. He got off as soon as he could and ran across Osborne Street to chase me down. I, 'Mister Cool', tried to pretend there was no problem, but Cousin Arnold got us on the next streetcar south and got me home safely.

3

The Carbert Family Move to Red Lake

———⌒⌒———

My older brother Barrie, gave his heart to Jesus when I was about ten and he was about fourteen. He became involved with the "Christ's Ambassadors" youth group. However, he spent most of his time with the wrong crowd and fell away from serving the Lord.

A year or so later, when my father Earl and my mother Mamie, felt led to leave the stability of a civil servant's job and life in the city and move to a hard-rock gold mining town, Red Lake, Ontario, our lives had an abrupt change. Mom and Dad's main concern was what might happen to their young family in this rough environment but felt certain, after fasting and praying, that it was the will of God. The year of the move was 1946, late June.

Barrie was fifteen years old that August. My sister Barbara would be coming to her thirteenth birthday in December and I was seventeen months younger, at the ripe old age of eleven, as of May 1946. My younger brother Keith had just turned seven in March. That was quite a challenge for Mom and Dad to launch out into a different lifestyle at their age thirty-nine and forty-five respectively, and a young brood like we were.

Red Lake, Ont. Probably early to mid 1950's

There was no evangelical-type church up there, three hundred and some miles northeast of Winnipeg and no road in. We had to fly in a float plane. The airport was Howey Bay of Red Lake. The town was literally built on the shore of the lake.

The only other option was a two week trip with seven portages on a tug boat and scow train. That was how most of the freight traveled to Red Lake, including our furniture, which included Mom's upright piano. I wanted to ride the tug boat but Mom and Dad thought I was too young.

1946, Red Lake winter on the lake with dog sleigh team

There was a liberal Protestant Church which must have had a hard time getting ministers. I wouldn't dare mention the name of the preacher who was there when we arrived. The Carberts made this their church home for about five years. I was only eleven and I knew the Bible better than the preacher (forgive me if it sounds like I'm boasting . . . I'm not . . . I didn't know the Bible very well either . . . the difference being I believed it and he didn't). The preacher seemed to pick the book he most recently read and gave a book report for a sermon. Pitiful! I mean . . . the nice man was pitifully ignorant of the truths of the Bible because, even back then, the seminaries of that particular church, had backslidden so far that they taught modern liberal criticism instead of faith in the Bible as the WORD OF GOD! The poor young man was doing his very best to try pastoring this strange mixture of people with no preparation of a walk of faith himself.

The next ministers, Johnny and Marg Freeman, were a definite improvement and became an influence on my life and close friends of our family. It's no wonder that the only churches of that type in Canada, that see the power of God in their churches, are those that happen to have a Pastor who has had a genuine encounter with God!

The alternatives were either the very dead liturgical church or another liturgical church, which rented the first one, once a month. A sincere bunch of people, some of them became close friends over the years, but church-wise, living in spiritual death.

Our family was musical. We had a little orchestra around the piano in the living room as we were growing up. Mom on the piano, Dad on the flat top Hawaiian guitar with a mouth organ (harmonica) on a bracket around his neck, Barrie played the trumpet, Barb played the accordion, I played the violin, and Keith just sang along (later he became an accomplished pianist, sang in the choir, and played a few other instruments). So, when we started attending the protestant church in Red Lake . . . Mom played the piano, Audrey

Dunn played the organ and I played my violin. Barrie quit going to church shortly after we moved . . . quit school in Grade nine and went to work in the gold mine where he developed a pretty good mechanical gift. He hit the work-world early and left home to make money out there in the big world. Barb drifted away from the Lord within a few years and I backslid, but kept going to church. Keith went to church because he had no choice, but never became a born again Christian until he was forty-three years old, in the city of Toronto, Ontario.

**429 Rosedale Ave., early 1940's,
Carbert kids and their mother**

While still in Winnipeg, I developed a real love for the violin. At the age of nine I was given a choice. My parents couldn't afford to buy me a Boy Scout-Cub uniform and a violin. So I had to decide which one I wanted. I chose the Cub uniform because it was immediate if I was to keep up to the other boys . . . but, I really wanted a violin. Well, my cousin Garth Carbert, gave me his three-quarter sized violin and I was able to have both of my wishes.

My violin teacher was the music minister at Calvary Temple, in Winnipeg. His name was Robert Sistig. He had been in vaudeville before he became a Christian. He used to inspire me to practice by doing tricks while playing his violin. I don't remember them all, but one of them was to balance a chair with one leg on his nose while he played his violin. I think another was to play his violin behind his back, etc., you get the picture. However, I needed very little pressure to get me to practice. I used to play into the late night hour just because I enjoyed it so much. I believe I went through seven books in a year and a half.

Within two or three months I was put into the large Calvary Temple orchestra. What an experience! I couldn't even hear myself at first. I had to learn to watch the music and the violinists beside me so I could tell where we were in the music. Good training! It probably helped me press on more than I can properly evaluate. So you see, that was my introduction to playing violin in church, and I did it every Sunday in Red Lake, until I went off to university in 1956. I wasn't serving God, until an experience in 1954, but every Sunday my mother would be on the piano and I would be there with my violin. Sometimes other instruments would show up for a short time, but Mom Carbert and I would always be there. What a training experience!

4

A Dramatic Change

W e were quite involved in the church, but my spiritual life ebbed out until I was running with a gang of boys . . . my older brother Barrie, being one of them. We did a lot of bad stuff, that I hesitate to say much about, partly for shame and partly so as not to inspire anybody to think it sounds exciting and want to emulate our lifestyle.

To complicate my life I had developed a demoniacal anger. I don't know how long it was a problem. My earliest memories of recognizing it was even pre-school. I was always a fun-loving, kick-up-your-heels kind of guy, but at the slightest interruption I would get caught off guard and go insanely mad. Every time I can remember I would just snap and my intention was to kill someone! Now, thank God, by His grace I never did commit murder . . . sometimes because I wasn't big enough . . . sometimes because there was someone there . . . or would come along just in time to either pull me off or bring me back to my senses. I can think of half a dozen times, as I grew older and could hurt someone really badly, that I would've killed someone if some interruption hadn't prevented it. Thank you Jesus!

I was in and out of school for attacking teachers from as early as Grade two. I am not proud of this, but I am happy for what God did in my heart in 1954 to set me free.

I went to Youth Camp at Manhattan Beach Pentecostal Camp, Ninette, Manitoba, for the usual reasons . . . fun, girls, fun, girls . . . etc., besides I got some breaks for being the lifeguard! The rules were, that all registered campers had to be in all the church meetings. On the closing meeting Friday night, the Tabernacle was full, hundreds of people. I was enduring the meeting. I don't think I heard a word that the preacher said that night. I know I hadn't shed a tear for more than five years. Suddenly, I became conscious that practically everyone in the Tabernacle was going to tears. I was puzzled because, although I had been soft as a child and sensitive to the moving of the Holy Spirit, I hadn't felt anything this time. I had a flashing thought that burst into my numbness, unannounced! Perhaps God was real! Perhaps it wasn't just some emotion that had affected my childhood! Maybe this was really God that affected everyone else, but not me!

Following hard on the heels of these puzzling thoughts came the revelation that it could be possible God was trying to talk to me, that I might have committed the unpardonable sin and hardened my heart. Well, without a recognized invitation, somehow this proud nineteen year old bolted to his feet and started to bawl and sob and headed for the tabernacle altar. I don't know everything that others saw, and I didn't care. I will try to describe what I was experiencing, while on my knees at the altar. I was sobbing as if a dam had burst. My stored-up tears, it would seem, could have filled a bucket. Between my eyes and a good sized nose, I put out enough liquid that we used up all available handkerchiefs and tissues and had a teen-age young lady, Ruth Ella, running for more. She and her Mom and Dad, Rev. and Mrs. Robert Donnelly, were the only ones left with me when I opened my eyes some two or three hours later. The main lights had been turned off in the tabernacle and just the light for the altar was still on. I really am not sure of the time elapsed, but I would estimate two or three hours.

I had spent that time alone with God in an encounter that kept speaking God's love, grace and forgiveness into my spirit. I laughed and I cried! I tried to respond to the revelation with a reciprocal love and a genuine thanksgiving, but I discovered that I couldn't talk English. In my mind, I was clearly stating my heart's condition, but it was coming out in a language I had never heard before. That experience, that the Pentecostal's call the Baptism of the Holy Ghost, was the beginning of the most phenomenal change in my life. I have never been angry like that, since 1954. The closest thing to anger anyone ever saw was impatience and not dangerous. I couldn't intentionally do hurt to anyone, more than absolutely necessary and only for their protection and good.

Let me add one more interesting detail to this story. My 'BAPTISM' took place in the summer of 1954 in Ninette, Manitoba. In Christmas 1989, our church joined all the churches in our town in Alberta to celebrate with a carol sing from church to church and in the streets. We ended up for lunch and fellowship in the United Church Fellowship Hall. A lady came to me and said, "You don't remember me, do you Lyle?" Well, I honestly confessed that I didn't. She said, "I'm Ruth Ella!" Well, you could have knocked me over with a feather! Sure enough, the teenager had grown up to be this attractive middle-aged lady and was living in this town. She could not possibly know the impact what that God encounter of 1954 had in my life, but somehow recognized the nineteen year old, who was now fifty-four and a half years mature.

Let me interject some interesting memories of our arrival in Red Lake!

My Dad and Barrie actually flew into Red Lake in the summer of 1945. Dad had been offered a job as manager of the yet-to-be built Ford garage, Handford Motors. Lorne Handford and his wife Gladys, had been school-time chums of my mother. Lorne had been left to discharge the property etc. of Howey Mines, now defunct. He had inside information on the location of the soon-to-be built highway and developed the land, right at the proposed junction of Highway #105 and the Main Street of Red Lake, for the location of his Ford Garage.

He hired my Dad and Barrie to come up in 1945 to tear down the cook shack and bunk houses and de-nail all the boards for material for his new garage.

The rest of the family, as was the custom, spent the whole summer on Mom's home farm near Kenton, Manitoba, LAKEVIEW FARMS, the home of Isaac and Jenny Cormack, my grandparents.

"Vanguard", one of Grandpa Isaac Cormack's clydesdales. To ride on one of these big horses was like sitting in a Cadillac.

5

Summers at the Farm

Farm days, every summer, were eagerly looked forward to by the Carbert kids, at least by yours truly. Maybe Barbara didn't enjoy it so much. She could be standing at the back door of the farm house and yell with fright because a cow turned its head and looked her way. The cow would be in the barn yard, which would be close to 75 yards away, in a fenced-in area.

However, I loved the adventure of the summer on the farm. It helped teach a good work ethic which my Dad always taught and practiced. Grandpa and Uncle Hughie had a lot of courage and would put us on the equipment, with little advice, and send us out into the fields. In the earlier years everything was horse-drawn by Grandpa's prize Clydesdales.

It's hard to describe the challenge of a little kid hanging on for dear life to the reins of a team of Clydesdales while balancing on the little, elevated metal seat and operating a hay mower. Those mower blades slicing back and forth at such a speed, and the levers had to be managed to lift the blades etc.. Of course, just for an additional adrenalin shot, we had one big mare, named Maud, who was a little spooky and unpredictable. It might have been somewhat of a little boy's imagination but Maud seemed to have big staring blue eyes that looked like she was ready to take off on a dead run at the least surprise. She never did, but I was sure she wanted to.

We would get the hay all mowed, my mouth full of dust (it felt like a real man-thing to carry a bottle of water and your lunch), then we would run the mower back to the farm yard. We had to learn to harness the horses and un-harness them and feed and water them as well.

The next chore was to hitch up the old trip-rake which also had one of those precarious seats with nothing to hang on to except the horses' reins. This had an added bit of excitement as you would rake until the hay was piling in pretty tight and then step on a foot-pedal that would trip the rake up . . . BANG (it gave such a jerk, almost knocking me off of the precarious seat) . . . leaving behind and dropping the hay in a pile. If the horses didn't jump too much, and you were still on the seat, then you dropped the rake again . . . ad infinitum. It was exhilarating, fearful, but with the feeling that you were doing a man's work . . . and that would please Grandpa and Uncle Hughie.

The next big job was to hook the team up to a hay rack and Barrie and I, or whoever was available, would go to the hay-field and fork by hand a giant load of hay onto the rack. There was a real knack to placing the hay on the wagon rack so that it didn't fall off before you got it into the barn. One would fork it on and the other one would move it around, if necessary, to fill all the holes evenly, and the one on the rack would continually tramp the hay tight. With a long-handled fork, I could just throw a medium forkful of hay up on the top of a full load, then the fulfilling part of the day was to be able to sit on the top of that high load of hay and ride . . . sometimes a spooky ride, sometimes a fast ride, trying to beat the rain storm . . . back to the barn.

"The largest barn I've ever seen". Grandpa's barn

Now my Grandpa's barn was one of the largest barns I've ever seen, even to this day. We would drive up the ramp at the side of the barn, open the big barn doors into the loft and drive the team and load up into the loft. We would turn it around and back it into the one end of the hayloft and unload by forkfuls. The opposite became the same. One would be on top of the load pitching the hay off and the other would be on the hay stack in the barn, placing and tramping. The hay was always stacked at one end of the loft and the straw was always threshed and blown into the other end. The loft had small granaries in it, I think three, for the different feed grains which went down a chute to the barn below to feed the stock.

When the haying was all done we quite often hitched up to the disc or the cultivator, or the rod-weeder or the harrows, etc., and worked the summer fallow ground. Later years, Uncle Hughie obtained some tractors which had their own set of challenges. The first in my memory was an old Cockshutt which wasn't equipped with power steering for sure. Grandpa wouldn't have much to do with the tractors. He stuck with his Clydesdales as long as he farmed. He did drive the farm half-ton, but that had its trying times as well. He ran into the side of the local train at the crossing . . . I think a total of three times and lived to tell about it. He had a tendency to try to stop the truck by pulling on the steering wheel and yelling "whoa"!

After Grandpa died, Uncle Hughie did most of the farming by tractor and had the courage to turn us loose on the machines.

I remember Uncle Hughie sending me out to the field with the old Cockshutt tractor pulling the cultivator. He demonstrated how he wanted it done and then left me out there to figure out how to accomplish this mammoth task. The instructions went something like this . . .! Do the headlands first! (This just means to go back and forth a couple of times at each end of the field so you would have room to turn without missing a chunk each time you turned). When you make your turns each time, come as close to the fence as possible without hitting it. Use the wheel brake to help you get a sharp turn, but keep your eye on the equipment behind you so that you don't turn so sharp that the equipment catches on the big tires and climbs right on top of you. Apparently people had been killed like that. Well, all that was frightening enough, because I wanted to do a good job for Uncle and prove that I was a reliable man. There was another factor. I was pretty small in the seat of that ancient Cockshutt tractor. There definitely was no power steering and it took both hands on the steering wheel with my feet braced against the fender . . . every once in a while pushing the wheel brake down . . . to get that tough old green machine to turn before I hit the fence and not tight enough to flip the equipment over my head. I also heard stories of farmers being killed by tipping the tractor over on the side hills (of which Uncle's fields were full). I would be traveling along, trying to make nice straight lines, and with the tractor moving along the side hills, which I'm sure were not as steep and dangerous as my fears made them to be, I would run over a little rock that would put my heart right in my mouth! . . . Well folks . . . I lived through it . . . and I learned to enjoy the solitude of the tractor away out . . . maybe a mile from the house. So I would sing at the top of my lungs so I could hear myself over the tractor and 'lo and behold' they could hear me back at the farm house.

Carbert kids on the old cockshutt tractor

6

Harvest Time

H arvest was an exciting time! Before I was big enough
to work in the fields I would spend my mornings
snaring gophers for five cents per tail and then at meal
times the ladies would put the lunch in the truck and then
put the truck in first gear . . . I would have to stand up to
steer it and touch the pedals . . . and send me off to the field
with the lunch. I believe, I was just six or seven, but I would
let my foot off of the clutch and inch my way out to the field
. . . hanging on with a death grip to steer that truck over the
approaches and between the posts (more than twenty feet
apart), and put my foot on the clutch again when I got to
the field. Wow!

Later on, of course, I had to stay out in the field or 'in the
granary' to shovel the grain away from the spouts as they
threshed, in between wagon loads, right into the granaries.
There are lots of stories of threshing! We used to catch mice
in the field and take them up into the granaries. As the grain
rose, it would come close to the cross boards that braced the
walls at the level of the eaves. They crossed in the middle,
the one over the other! We would start our mice at one side
of the bottom 2" x 6" and let them race across to the other
side by holding the bottom 2" x 6" down. Sometimes the
board would slip just as the mouse was running under the

middle and we would have to replace our mouse. One time, at lunch time I had a mischievous notion that taught me how fast my Uncle could run. He wasn't a very big man and had a limp, from the effects of infantile paralysis. I was sure, that if I put a mouse down the back of his shirt he could never catch me . . . HE DID!

Before threshing time, of course, the grain all had to be cut with the binder and made into sheaves. The sheaves all had to be *stooked* for drying and pick up. Then the hay racks were always pulled by horses, as long as I can remember, to pick up the sheaves and pull up to the threshing machine without hitting the chute or gear and chains on the sides yet close enough to skillfully pitch the sheaves . . . head first . . . into the feeder (without losing your pitch fork into the machine). Every stage of the harvest has strong memories for me.

The binder was quite a machine. The mower blade that cut the grain had to be operated at just the right level to cut the grain without picking up dirt or stones onto the apron. The paddle wheel that pulled the tops of the grain onto the apron had to be at the right height for the grain. The binder twine had to be threaded just right so that it would feed at the right tension. The tier had to be watched so that the sheaves would be tied right and kicked out properly behind the binder. Besides all that, you had to keep your eyes peeled for wildlife or pets lying down in the grain . . . and you were driving a team of four Clydesdales, sometimes with a team of four and sometimes six Clydesdales. Exciting or what! A great education for kids!

Before I was big enough to drive the binder, I had the job of exchanging the teams of horses at noon hour. I look back now and remember the adrenaline rush, as I would plan my day around this event. I would have to break in to my busy schedule of gopher snaring, or pigeon hunting, or horseback riding or egg gathering, where you had to watch out for that one old rooster that would fly at you in attack mode. Oh, let me tell you, while I think of it, of the time that rooster flew at my Grandpa Isaac who always carried a stock prod or cane. KLUNK! — and the old rooster was out cold . . . only to stagger back to its equilibrium in a few minutes . . . and never attacked Grandpa again. Whatever I was doing, I had to be close enough to hear the holler from the back door of the farmhouse just before noon to tell me to harness the team of four Clydesdales and take them out to the fields for the noon exchange.

See if you can imagine this little runt of a kid grabbing the horse collars off the post where they were kept . . . climbing up on the manger so I could reach these big horses (fortunately, well broke and somewhat quiet) . . . place the collar over the neck and set it in the right place in front of the shoulders . . . grab the hames and harness and throw them over the back of these big hunks of horseflesh . . . set them on the horse collar just right and hook the leather straps all together just tight enough . . . take one horse at a time out the door and hook them all together so that when you pulled on the reins they all turned, or stopped, or whatever . . . it was a daunting task to say the least. However, as complicated as that was, the real scary part was yet to come.

This little boy had to somehow guide these four behemoths out the farm driveway and sometimes more than a mile down the road to the field where they were cutting the grain. I remember, the two methods which competed with each other for scariness. The one method was, for this little lad to hang on to the reins and walk, run or drag along the road behind this big team (which could take off any time they pleased, without worrying about this little hindrance dragging along behind them).

The second method was to climb up on one of the middle horses and try to steer and control the whole team from this vantage point (without getting your feet squeezed between them). Either method was scary enough to make you feel totally at the mercy of three or more tons of horseflesh, especially when it came time to wheel them through the twenty-foot gate into the field without the inside horse being crowded into the near post or the outside horse being forced into the far post. Then unhitch the team from the binder (with Grandpa's help of course) and help hitch the fresh team up. Then . . . a fresh challenge . . . holding on to the team that got more and more anxious to get home to the barn with every passing inch of road . . . and getting them stopped outside the barn door and reverse the process, plus feeding and watering. I was taught, by word or implication, not to let on how scared I was and just act confident that I could do the job!

7

Mink, Gophers & Pigeons

L et me tell you a story of an unusual happening!
Grandpa Isaac was driving the binder one harvest,
when a spunky mink jumped at the horses and spooked
them. Grandpa was able to stop them and then grabbed
the whip, which was standard equipment on the binders.
The whip was approximately an eight to ten foot bamboo
pole with a leather thong on the end, only used to keep the
horses pulling evenly. So he grabbed the whip and jumped
off the binder to drive this cranky mink away. He swung
the whip and snapped it at the mink. The mink grabbed the
leather thong with his teeth and hung on as Grandpa lifted
it high over his head and slammed it to the ground, several
times, until the mink was almost dead and let go. Now, that
was a rare sight that I'll never forget.

At harvest time Grandpa would go to Rivers or Brandon,
Manitoba and pick up some hired help. If I remember right,
he paid them something like $40.00 a month with room
and board (that would be around the early 1940's). Some of
the good men could almost keep up to the binder, *stooking*
behind it. I never achieved anything close to that, even
when I got older and bigger. *Stooking* was hot, dry, hard
work. You were to grab two sheaves and stand them solidly
in the stubble, leaning together, and then stand another four

or more around them. That enabled the grain to dry. Then of course, when it was time to thresh, you drove your racks between them and loaded from both sides to be hauled to the threshing machine.

They hauled some of the grain by wagon about three miles to the elevators and stored the rest in the granaries.

Farming was not all work and no play. Besides snaring gophers or shooting or snaring pigeons, we always had a couple of riding horses, which we at times rode to the neighbors for a visit, or hitched to the buggy.

Especially at harvest, we went hard all day, but at the end of the hot summer days we used to go swimming in what we called a lake. I don't think it was over our head anywhere, but we would never know because the bottom was mud with lizards in it, so we never put our feet down any more than we had to. The experience of having a lizard squeeze out from under your foot had a tendency to make you swim in – not wade!

One of the harvest time experiences that would definitely encourage a lake experience was when they threshed directly into the barn. The old steel wheeled engine (at one time steam) would be parked out by the fence, with a long drive belt to the threshing machine parked by the barn. The grain was placed by elevator into the granaries in the barn loft and the straw was blown directly into the one end of the loft. My job, the one most hated and causing the greatest feeling of need for the lake, was to ride Tracey, the big blood riding horse, without a saddle, all over the straw to tramp it and pack it. Well, the rider just had to hang on and steer the best he could while this horse lunged and threshed around in this straw. I was in tears constantly, partly from fear of the horse throwing me and trampling me, and partly from the straw, dirt and chaff all over my body, in my face (mouth, eyes and ears), down in my pants and socks . . . YUK! — But again . . . you had to be tough. Farming is a great life if you don't weaken, but then who wants to be strong? The truth is, I loved the farm life, a great place to raise a family.

One of the highlights of the week on the farm, was the Saturday night trip into town. Quite often friends and relatives would meet at the Cormack farm, dressed to the 'T', ready for the dance or theatre or both, some would be planning on hitting the stores for a shopping spree, etc. They would all pile into the old cars and trucks and head for town. Saturday night was the one night of the week when you could get to bed late. Normally, during the week, there was an early morning call, approximately five o'clock in the morning, to round up the milk cows from the pasture beside the barn, to bring them in for milking before breakfast. During the week, nine or nine-thirty was bedtime.

Speaking of breakfast, we always ate well at the farm. We would have oatmeal porridge and bacon and eggs, with toast and jam and good farm milk every morning, soup and sandwiches for noon, and often a roast beef, or pork, with potatoes, gravy and vegetables for supper.

Some of you folks who have worked with sheep might identify with this anecdote. Grandpa Isaac had a pretty good sized flock of sheep. More than once, I remember the sheep getting out of the pasture three quarters to a mile away, and having Grandpa Isaac step out on the front veranda and bellow "Hyuh . . . Waggles . . . fetch 'em up Waggles!!!" and the old ram would wheel around and head back for the pasture with all the sheep in typical synchronism following. You see, 'Waggles' was the name of the mongrel collie dog that the sheep were used to having round them up. 'Waggles' would be sitting at Grandpa's feet barking, but the sheep responded anyway.

8

Life in a Gold Mining Town

Of course, once we moved to Red Lake, in 1946, our visits to the farm became a bit less frequent because the three older kids obtained jobs in Red Lake. The first job Barrie and I had was at McDougall's sawmill. Barrie was paid fifty cents per hour because he was four years older than me. I was only paid forty cents per hour, but probably was hired, because I could handle the old horse that pulled the slab cart and the sawdust cart out to the dump and back.

Shortly after, Barrie and I went to work for Lakeview Bakery. Barrie rode the delivery truck with Jimmie Towns until he was old enough to drive by himself. I worked in the bakeshop with John Paciga. I manually kneaded the bread dough in the big tubs, carried supplies down from the ware-house and whatever other jobs needed doing around the bakeshop or restaurant. We worked in the bakeshop at night, when it wasn't so hot, and tried to have fresh baking ready for delivery first thing in the morning. Most of the summer months we would be out of the bakeshop by four or five o'clock in the morning and I would walk across the street more or less and get into our boat, tied up at the back dock, and shove off on the lake fishing or sleeping until breakfast.

During school, Barb and I both had paper routes. Barb delivered the Winnipeg Free Press at the west end of the town and I delivered the Winnipeg Tribune at the east end of town. I remember when Barb wasn't able to do her route for some reason, that I did both and the customers, if my memory is true numbered approximately 300. Many times in the winter I would trudge through cold blizzards in my warm parka and cold rubber boots with a vivid imagination of being some great hero. Inevitably, I would have to stop at the Hayes Steel Shop to hang my wet socks up and dry my rubber boots (Hayes steel prepared drill bits etc. for the gold mines), they always had their hot furnaces ready for me. The next stop would be at the end of a narrow path along the face of the steep rock face on the shore of Howey Bay . . . McDougall's Store (Trading Post) . . . that's a story in itself . . . where I would buy a box of twelve ice cream Revels . . . eat half of them there and deliver papers to most of McDougallville and eat the rest on the way back through. I don't remember ever being bored in my life. Life to me was an adventure.

When Ken McDougall landed on the shore of early Red Lake to establish a trading post, I understand he wasn't allowed to start it in town so he moved down the shore to the end of the Bay close to the point of the big stretch of open water and started his trading post. When the Carberts arrived in Red Lake, some 15 or more years later (1946), this trading post was a log shack built into the earth bank about 100 feet up and back from the shore. Outside, you could walk up on the roof . . . inside you had to duck your head around the pots and pans and other sundry wares hanging from the beams. There wasn't much you couldn't buy in that store.

Ken McDougall, Bob Andersen and Fergus McDougall could all talk the native Indian language and were involved in the fur trade, so the trading post had the special aroma of furs and tanned deer hide etc.. This was always an intriguing adventure for me. The store was the entrance to what became affectionately called McDougallville . . . a collection of shacks and houses that were placed on the point of rock as if they had been dropped all at once by parachute.

As mentioned, by the time the Carberts arrived in Red Lake, Ken McDougall also had a busy sawmill established across the Bay from the downtown of Red Lake.

By the time I was fifteen years old I started working on construction during the summer and that meant we only got back to Lakeview Farm for short visits. Just for the record . . . one of those visits was forever remembered, as the summer I shot my young brother Keith. Well now, I had better tell you the whole story, so you'll see it in a little better light.

9

Tragedy on the Farm

M om, Dad, Keith and I . . ., I'm not sure who else .
. ., drove to the farm for our holidays. One of the
things we liked to do was take the little single shot .22 rifle
and shoot pigeons (sometimes Aunt Ann would cook them
for us). Uncle Hughie couldn't find the gun readily, because
no one had been using it for a while. When he did find it, it
was in pieces. He assembled it but couldn't find the special
bolt that held the barrel to the stock, so he improvised with
a bolt he thought would work. Out we went to refresh our
memories of pigeon shooting. I was carrying the gun and
Keith was instructed to walk behind me for safety. A flock of
pigeons swooped around from the far side of the barn and
Keith burst out in front yelling, "There they are, there they
are!" I . . . in my older brother self-importance and responsibility for safety, swung the gun abruptly and yelled for Keith
to stay behind. When I jerked the rifle the barrel separated
from the stock and fell, firing at approximately a 45° angle,
hitting Keith in the right upper arm, shattering the bone and
deflecting up into his chest area, where there is lead tracings
lodged beneath the skin to this day. I panicked, dropped the
stock of the gun and grabbed Keith by his good left arm and
ran, pulled, sometimes dragged, Keith towards the house,
some 75 or 80 yards away. Keith's right arm, of course, was

dangling like a wet rag and Keith kept crying and repeating periodically, "Why did you shoot me?"

About a third of the way to the house one of the three-strand barbed wire gates was closed but I was so hyped that I jumped over it. Keith, however, was already kind of going into shock and jerked his hand back and fell down on his knees. I reached under the gate, and grabbed his good arm again and yanked him under the gate and to his feet chirping all the time, "I'm sorry, I didn't mean to shoot you!" He was getting drowsy and I was getting more panicky! Aunt Ann heard us coming and met us at the door. She helped get Keith on the horse blanket on the divan. Fortunately she had a little background of nursing and did not panic, but knew what to do. My Mom and Dad were in Kenton, approximately three miles away. She phoned them.

The law of self-preservation took over, when I considered my guilt and my 6'3", 245 pound Dad heading to the farm. I headed for the barn loft! I climbed up on the first set of beams, which were 8" x 8" approximately 12'–15' off the loft floor. That didn't seem safe enough, so I climbed to the next set of beams which was 6"x 6" another level up. Then I decided to go to the top 4" x 4" beams from where I could climb over and look out the pigeon window at the peak of the barn. There I sat trembling with fear, guilt and awe as my Mom and Dad pulled into the house, put Keith in the car and pulled away to the hospital. I stayed up there a long time wondering what to do. I don't remember whether Aunt Ann called me or if I just came down, but she laughed at my obvious panic and calmed me down until we got word from the Hamiota Hospital, that things weren't life-threatening, but I had to go in and give a statement to the police.

The police were very understanding and helpful as they took my statement and gave me some advice. Keith's right arm was put into an elevated cast, I think they called it an airplane sling, where there was hope that the bone would heal, along with the circulation and the nerves. Keith was studying the piano and was also right handed. However, before many weeks passed he was doing fairly well with his left hand. Well, as soon as his arm was out of the cast, Mom started working on him, making him use his right hand. It was hard at first and if my memory serves me right, in order to make Keith play the piano with his right hand she tied his left hand and forced some right hand therapy. Thanks Mom! Keith regained almost all of the use of his right hand and arm and plays the piano very well to this day!

10

Early Pioneer Days

When we arrived in 1946 we lived in two tents, in the backyard of a log house, next to Dupont's grocery store. Mom, Dad, Barb and Keith slept in the main tent which was a 9' x 12' tent with a wooden floor and approximately 3' high slab walls for its base. Barrie and I slept in an eight foot diameter bell tent (along with Lorne and Gladys Handford's two dogs, Cocoa and Paddy, much to our delight). Our log house, just down the road, wasn't available yet. The folks that were living there didn't move out until late September.

We had a cook stove in the big tent on which Mom cooked our meals and heated water for our baths in a tub. These were taken in a square laundry tub. Total adventure for us kids, probably a little hardship for Mom and Dad. Also new for our adventuresome nature was the lake which was just across the road and down a steep rock cliff. We had never lived so close to so much water. Intriguing!

I once found an old row boat submerged down there. I bailed it out and used an old board for a paddle and proceeded to paddle across the bay. Well, a storm blew in and kept me pretty busy paddling, bailing, paddling, bailing . . . just to keep from being blown out of the bay. I finally reached the dock on the other side with a great sense of accomplishment and an adrenalin rush.

The tent Carberts lived in from June until October 1946, in Red Lake , Ont.

However, my Dad, the police and Mr. McLaren (who owned the dock) met me with a little more than a stern rebuke. The boat that I thought was abandoned actually belonged to somebody. I was seen out there in the wind and waves by someone who thought I was in danger, and I guess I was, but I was too ignorant to catch on to that, and my Dad was prepared to rescue me so he could discipline me . . . adventure for this city kid up in the sticks.

We started school in the fall which became more than an academic experience. Grades six, seven and eight were all in one room with *Mrs. Johnson** (the name has been changed). This meant that I, in grade six, was in the same room with Barb and Barrie. I'm sure, I wasn't the only problem in that class, but I seem to have lent some incentive to the problem areas. *Mrs. Johnson** had a tendency to hand out assignments of writing lines for discipline. I might have set the record for number of lines in one day by ending up with an order to write 5,000 lines. I don't remember even what the line was, but typically it would be something like, 'I will stop talking out loud in class unless asked to!'

**Mamie Carbert with the four Carbert kids
in front of log house, 1947**

Well, a lot of my memory of the details has faded over the years, but I will always be grateful for the gifted help of those who came to my aid. Two, who come to the top of the list, were Geraldine (who I was sweet on) and her close friend Joan. These girls had written so many lines that they had developed the ability to write more than one line at a time by putting more than one pencil between their fingers. The teacher only looked carefully at the first page or two, which I would write myself, and then just count the pages to make sure I had done my quota. We got them all done in one day!

When this teacher was really frustrated she would resort to the strap. You had to stand up in front of the class and hold your hands out front while she would swing this eighteen-inch long piece of leather down on your palms. Well we, and I say we, because I can't remember exactly how the inspiration came, told the teacher that it was illegal to raise the strap above her shoulder and if she did we would report her. Well, she believed us and that became a hysterical experience for us mean kids as we would laugh at her attempting to hit us hard enough to hurt with such a short stroke of the strap.

I tell you these things, to illustrate how impossible it was to discipline this unruly bunch of kids. *Mrs. Johnson* would maybe last two weeks in class and then be off for a week of medication for her nerves. George Campbell was the principal and we got to know what the problem was when we came into class and George Campbell was there to meet us.

Probably my favorite teacher in elementary school was Alex McQuaig, in grade eight. He was the only man teacher I had ever had. If I remember right, he had had a stint in the Navy, before teaching, which probably helped him be firm and fair.

11

My Formal Education

The next adventure in my education, was in grade nine, in what we called, the Continuation School. Probably it got that name because it was still in the process of qualifying as a High School. It was located just fifty yards to the west of the elementary school.

At Christmas time our regular teacher, had to take a maternity leave. The school board put out an appeal for a qualified teacher to take her place. They received a call from a teacher in Toronto, with an enviable résumé and credentials, who said she was available. They hired her by phone only to discover on her arrival why her résumé was so awesome, she was 81 years old. Well, that dear lady only lasted a couple of weeks. Let me tell you some of the drama!

My brother, Barrie, was night clerk at the Red Lake Inn where they accommodated this teacher with a room. However, on more than one occasion, she showed up at the Hotel desk because she had gone down the hall to bath . . . turned the tap on to run her tub full, got lost trying to find her room when she went back for soap or something, couldn't find her room or the bathroom, by the time she found her way down the stairs to the front desk the water was running down the hallway.

By this time, we lived above the North American Lumber store, downtown, Main Street. We were sitting at the breakfast table, with the windows facing the front street, when we noticed this teacher all bundled up walking east towards the Government dock, where the ramp lent access to the winter ice road across the lake to McKenzie Island. Now, you must understand that Red Lake in January is a cold place to be, dangerously cold for an 81 year-old lady to be trudging off across a lake. She obviously was lost. She must have gotten her directions turned around when she walked out of the hotel. So we put our coats on and ran after her, to get her turned around or we might never have seen her again.

She was teaching us French first class in the morning, but her memory was seriously impaired. Every morning, she would ask the class where we were in the text and we would always tell her the same page. Consequently, we never advanced past that page while she was there (I think it was page twenty-seven). I sat near the front of the room, but some of the kids realized, that she couldn't see what was going on at the back of the room and would wait until she was busy teaching and quietly slip out the back door. Now, it wouldn't have done me any good to play 'hooky' in a town the size of Red Lake, because I could never explain it to my parents who were sure to find out. Every day she would look up from her book and say, "What's going on back there?" All it would take to calm her fears would be for someone to say, "Nothing! There's nothing going on!" We used to toboggan on the hill between the elementary school and the continuation school. One time our 81-year old lady was walking from the elementary school to her class in the continuation school, when a toboggan just missed her, but spun her around, so that she was confused and started heading back to the elementary school. Again, she had to be rescued! Needless to say, her stay in Red Lake was fairly short.

12

Lots of Sports and Pranks

Because we spent most of our summers in Red Lake during the next few years, we became pretty much at home in the water, swimming, fishing, water-skiing, boating, canoeing, etc. When you live on the lake, with my love for the water, some skills were likely to develop along that line. We pursued the Red Cross Swimming Certificates and taught swimming for a while. We pretty well all the time had our own boat and motor or access to such.

In 1953, we decided to try this water skiing thing. I bought my first pair of water skis, 6' long, 6" wide, square back end with double keels on each, a rubber foot harness that lasted almost fifteen years (amazing). If not the first pair owned in Red Lake, they were one of the first. My old 9.8 Johnson motor wouldn't pull me so we depended on friends with bigger outboards. My friend, Andy McDougall, Ken's son, had a 25 horse Johnson on a 16' or 18' skiff. We decided to use his boat to learn how to ski. Well, I wish I had a video record of our escapades of ignorance. I could probably win $100,000.00 on the Funniest Home Video program. Nobody knew how to do it, so we worked at it by trial and error (mostly error), until we finally (probably by accident) succeeded!

**Lyle standing in the "skiff", with the
9.8 Johnson outboard motor, behind the
North American Lumber apartment**

We tried standing on a water level float plane dock, well how is your imagination? Splash! We tried sitting on this same dock. Well, I know what it is like, to be pulled through a growth of seaweed, as I hung on to the rope, but headed pretty much to the bottom. With much determination, after several tanks of gas and mouthfuls of water, we finally learned that the boat could pull us up out of the water, if we could hold our position properly. Voila!, we succeeded!

We became proficient enough that Murray McLeod and I put on a couple of Labor Day weekend clown acts on water. I won't bore you with all the details, but such as lady's dresses, 16" long 1 x 4 boards for skis, Murray climbing on my back as we clowned and dismounting in a somersault off my shoulders, etc. etc.. Fun! Once we learned how to ski, we passed on what little we knew and in all the years of helping others ski, we only had one failure, a girl who didn't have enough strength to stand up from a crouch on land, let alone on water. Fun! At the time of writing I am

75 years of age and water skiing would still be my favorite summer sport.

In Red Lake, the activity pretty well centered around baseball, football, basketball, volleyball, hockey, hunting and fishing, berry picking (how did that get in there? Oh, that was inspired by my Mom, Ann Liddle, or Greta Cassidy), and water sports in the summer. Of course, there were special occasion activities such as Halloween.

The city people may not understand this, but when we first moved to Red Lake running water was a rarity. Walking water was more common! You could not safely drink the lake water without boiling it! You had to find a decent well and walk to it, and at our place you had to take a little water with you to prime the pump (in the winter it had to be hot water to thaw the pump out), and then pump your pails of water and walk back with them.

Some of the grim details you'd like to learn of, would be the necessity of a small dosage of chlorine in each pail-full before drinking. Now, the disposal system, of course, had to be scientifically accomplished, so, everyone had to have a small building, preferably with ventilation (it seemed like the favorite ventilation was a crescent moon-shape, cut high in the walls or door), and a minimum of one hole in the bench big enough to sit on. (Some had lids and some didn't). Many were placed over an excavation about three or four foot deep. Some had a trap door in the back where a barrel with approximately 40 gallon capacity could be slid under the hole in the bench to receive any deposits. This type required the man, with the 'honey wagon' pulled by a horse, to exchange an empty one for the used one at least once a week. These houses were called 'outhouses'. Now the reason for this description was so you could more properly appreciate the activity on Halloween in Red Lake.

The objective of this activity was to see who could push over the most outhouses on Halloween. There would usually be a minimum of five or six guys to a group. Sometimes the boys from McKenzie Island would get all theirs dumped over so early that they would come across the lake into Red

Lake to challenge us. Does it sound exciting? You had to be in good shape to cover the whole town on the dead run! After you pushed it over, you sometimes had to run a little faster!

We were doing really well one year, and had a little head start. One of the boys wasn't very big, but he was fast. We had to approach the next outhouse through the bush behind the landowner's house. It was dark, but as usual, the little guy was out front in the race, when all of a sudden we heard SQUOOSH, and a disgusting upheaval. Mr. Handford had moved his outhouse ahead of the excavation and our comrade got sick and went home. Oh well, his sacrifice saved the rest of us.

I don't know if these exciting adventures have ever been told before, or even if they should be told. However, one person's fancy could well be another's disgust! Things such as taking a couple of the empty 'honey wagon' cans and hoisting them up the flagpole of the local constabulary of the Ontario Provincial Police; lifting small cars just off the ground and blocking them up; placing groups of three or four guys on each side of the road and pretend to be stretching an invisible rope across the road, the cars would hit the brakes and we would run away, etc., etc., . . . a special brand of fun in the Red Lake area when we were young.

I should at least tell of the ingenuity of one lady. We came to push over her outhouse and she came to the door and just stood there smiling. She wasn't being cranky, so we proceeded, thinking she must consider this part of the annual celebration. Well, we pushed, and grunted, and pushed, and pried, SHE WON! Inside the outhouse she had anchored four six inch thick fence posts, one in each corner.

Being raised through my teen years in Red Lake, not city, not country, but rock, bush, and lake, 100 miles north of the nearest railway and 300 miles north of the nearest sizeable city (Winnipeg, Manitoba) had a special influence in the forming of my character which in the telling of my story, you may discover is the forming of my ministry gift.

13

Not my plan, but God's

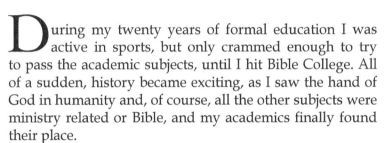

During my twenty years of formal education I was active in sports, but only crammed enough to try to pass the academic subjects, until I hit Bible College. All of a sudden, history became exciting, as I saw the hand of God in humanity and, of course, all the other subjects were ministry related or Bible, and my academics finally found their place.

By 1956 I was 'gung-ho' for Jesus, but I certainly didn't want to be a preacher! As a matter of fact, Rev. Walter Reinheimer reminded me that I had told him, I would never be a pioneer preacher like him.

Well guess what my ministry has been for fifty-plus years? I headed for University of Western Ontario to gain a Bachelor of Physical Health and Recreation honors degree, which (I told God) would net me enough income to live on a pastor's salary and build a church every year.

After a while, I caught on, that God was sometimes smiling at my ignorance and sometimes weeping for my pain, as He gently tapped me on the shoulder and whispered in my ear waiting for my surrender to His call to ministry.

By the summer of 1958, I set my course for Bible College. I drove spare milk wagon for Silverwood Dairy (four horse drawn and one truck), to fill in for the drivers going on holidays; I endeavored to sell memberships for the Peckham Bros. bowling alley; I sold Saladmaster Inc. cutlery, crystal, pots and pans, etc., and Gord and Phyllis Linton offered me free room and board just for helping with the chores, so that I could attend Central Bible Institute, a Baptist Bible College in downtown London. They also allowed me the use of their yellow station wagon, to get back and forth the 12 miles to London.

At the end of the summer, I still barely had enough money for books and tuition for one semester. I purposely didn't go back to Red Lake, as had been my habit, where I could work long hours on construction and make big money, because I felt I had to prove something and I was a little embarrassed at my two year struggle with the will of God. Besides, I had some special friends in London that I wanted to stay close to.

You know, the way I got to U.W.O. was because my principal at Red Lake District High School, phoned his old Alma Mater and spoke to his old friend, the head coach of the Western Mustangs football team (and I overheard the conversation). I heard T. A. say, "You have to get this kid in, because he can kick a ball 60 yards," etc., etc.. Well, some strings must have been pulled so that I was granted entrance into the main University in the BPHRE honors program, with the stipulation that I had to upgrade my grade thirteen physics and Chemistry.

I made the football team, but not as a kicker. At the kicking tryouts I slipped the first kick off the side of my foot, the second off the other side as I tried to compensate, the third kick went straight up in the air, a little up tight I guess! The coach put his arm on my shoulder and said, "That's alright, 'Red Dog', we'll make a lineman out of you." I tried fullback and tripped over the white line. I became left defensive tackle and loved it. When I told the coach my plans for Bible College, he coaxed me to come back for another year, because he was sure he could make a professional center out of me. Who knows, but I had my heart set to obey the call God had placed in my heart. I felt extremely honored twenty years later when the coach phoned Red Lake to ask my Dad how I was doing.

One other temptation was a letter from Indian Jack Jacobs, former quarterback for the Winnipeg Blue Bombers, at the time coaching the London Lords, a senior semi-professional league. Jack invited me to attend their camp. He offered me $35.00 for every game I dressed. I had to say no! I couldn't afford to lose my focus now.

While in London, I faithfully attended all the meetings I possibly could at London Gospel Temple. I walked everywhere pretty well, except when someone offered me a ride. I enjoyed the walk most of the time anyway, because I was always thinking natural conditioning. I pushed very few weights or as they would say 'pumped' very little 'iron'. I ran, did push-ups, sit ups, deep knee bends, star jumps, stretches and twists and walked a lot.

A nice couple, who owned the 4 x 4 Restaurant on Richmond Street near Oxford Avenue, befriended me. They offered me a ride to church one Sunday morning since their church was in the same direction. They gave me favors at the restaurant as well, which helped my meager budget. I often stopped in at the restaurant on the way by.

One Sunday morning, on my way to church, I stopped at the restaurant for some reason. There was a little man in there all upset, talking to my friend the proprietor. Apparently, he had been kicked out of a room at a house just up the tracks around the corner from the 4 x 4 Restaurant and was too scared to go back for his things. There seemed to be some complications that prevented him from going to the police and he was quite agitated over his dilemma. I listened for a few minutes, and then accepted the challenge, to help this little man and maybe talk to him about the Lord. I was dressed for church in my suit and long brown overcoat. I stood 6'2" and weighed 200+ pounds and didn't have enough sense to have any fear. It actually never entered my poor little naive mind. I walked around the corner and up the five or six steps to the porch with this little man. He knocked, the door opened and a big man opened the door who lifted a large knife toward the little man. The big man's eyes shifted to me, he put the knife down at his side and backed against the wall and didn't move a muscle as the little man walked into the back room and walked past us both, out the door. I bid the big man a "good day" and turned and walked out. After it was all over, I realized that God must have put a couple of big angels beside me. The little man said that the guy thought I was a cop.

During my time at University, I dated a couple of the young ladies from the church, but as I see it in hindsight, probably would have missed the will of God, if I had married either one of them as great as they were/are.

One young people's night at London Gospel, Marilyn, was home from Eastern Pentecostal Bible College and brought a friend with her to church (actually her roommate from Bible College). I remember the introduction in the downstairs of the church, just outside the meeting hall. The young lady had long hair, well kept, with an athletic gait to her walk, and a full pleated skirt. Who could have guessed this visitor to London and I were to meet again.

I registered at the Baptist College in the fall of 1958, after an examination of my qualifications and doctrines. They graciously asked me to sign a statement saying I would not cause any dissension in the classroom by propagating my Pentecostal doctrine. I agreed, with the understanding that I would never hold back on my testimony of Holy Ghost encounter with God. We started that week with, it seemed, everything in place to accomplish the call God had placed in my heart. On the Thursday of that week, a group of young people from London Gospel Temple wanted to go to Toronto to the World Pentecostal Conference and invited me along.

14

Final Surrender

When we arrived, one of the first people I met was my Red Lake pastor, Walter Reinheimer. Some of his first response to my explanation of my present activities was "What is a Pentecostal boy doing in a Baptist Bible College?" One thing led to another, I talked to my cousin, Arnold Hamilton who was a pastor, to several other relatives and acquaintances, and was introduced to Dr. Charles Ratz, the Dean of Eastern Pentecostal Bible College. He was insistent that we could surely work something out to get me to E.P.B.C. I had explained to him my financial disparity and he just asked me how long it would take me to raise the $600.00 for one year at E.P.B.C.

I estimated that with some strings pulled, I could probably get on at the Gold Mine and have that much in about six weeks. He asked if I could stay over at the Conference until the next day. I sent my friends from London home without me and stayed with Pastor Reinheimer at Rev. Bernard Parkinson's. In the middle of the night I had a vision or a dream that caused me to wake up and weep until approximately five o'clock in the morning.

In my dream (it was so vividly real that I felt it was a vision I was actively engaged in), I saw a large crowd of people casually walking by in front of me as I sat quietly against a tree. These people were getting increasingly dis-traught as they came closer to where I was sitting because they could hear the frightened screams of people ahead of them (as I could). Ahead, and to my left, was a steep cliff at the edge of a giant canyon, and people were just walking off the edge and falling to their death. My eyes water with tears, just to rehearse this memory. Like a flash of light, I understood the problem! These people were all blind. I felt so terrible that I, who had my sight, was sitting there doing nothing. I jumped up, in the dream, and ran frantically around in the crowd trying to stop them from plunging over to their death. It was hopeless! The few that tried to understand my plea almost got pushed off the cliff by the press of the crowd. God showed to me the solution was to open the eyes of the blind and they would multiply my wit-ness! I awoke in tears and sobbed until nearly five o'clock in the morning.

When I got up that morning, there was no turning back! All doubts were removed! Dr. Ratz met me and said E.P.B.C. would allow me to come late, if I wanted to go and raise the money. I had enough money to get back to London and go to the Baptist College to explain my situation. They were godly brethren and bent the rules enough to give me back half my tuition which was enough for my train fare back to Red Lake with Pastor Reinheimer. I sat through the rest of World Conference and then headed for Red Lake with Pastor Reinheimer.

We arrived unannounced at my home in Red Lake approximately seven in the morning, to the shock of my parents. After humbling myself, re: my independent effort to rectify my situation, I explained my plan to work hard for six weeks and then head for Peterborough.

Well, my Dad looked at Mom and started to weep. Dad, as manager for North American Lumber, had just received a building material bonus of $600.00 and they had just been discussing what to do with it. *It was a Miracle of Divine Intervention.* Normally, my parents would not have that kind of available money. They immediately wanted to give it to me with their blessings, but my pride was still pretty much in place and I talked them into loaning it to me, until the following summer when I would pay it back. I stayed for a week or so and headed back for E.P.B.C. on Thanksgiving weekend.

15

Apostolic Influence

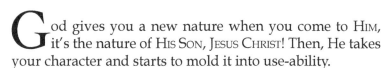

G od gives you a new nature when you come to HIM, it's the nature of HIS SON, JESUS CHRIST! Then, He takes your character and starts to mold it into use-ability.

However, your character is you! When the anointing of the Holy Spirit moves in you, it is your personal character that He wants to use. He will never make you into someone else's character because, He has molded you into the character you are! Be yourself, hopefully refined by the Holy Spirit and not just by social fads!

Allow me to insert here something for the 'Church' to ponder. Ephesians 4:11 says, "And <u>He gave</u> some, apostles; and some, prophets; and some, evangelists; and some, pastors and teachers" (KJV). I don't think you will find anywhere that God trained any of these gifts to become apostles, prophets, evangelists, pastors or teachers. He <u>gave</u> them to the church. An apostle is a character ministering in character! There may be different emphases or extenuating gifts, but his character is his gift. There may be different levels of maturity in the gift. There may be different levels of release in the anointing, but the gift is the character moving under the anointing!

May I humbly or otherwise, suggest that we have the gift of the apostle walking our streets, etc., (What is true of the apostle is true of all the gifts listed here), still un-reached, still un-anointed, still not available to the church because they are still unsaved! Well, that is an interesting thought! You may not agree, but give it full scriptural and prayerful consideration before you throw it out.

In 1951, approximately five years after we moved to Red Lake, a spirit-filled jeweler from Flin Flon, Manitoba, Cliff Cassidy felt led of the Lord to move to Red Lake, Ontario and open Cassidy's Jewelers. The Carberts and Cassidys started having prayer meetings together and suggested letting the Manitoba District of the P.A.O.C. (Pentecostal Assemblies of Canada) know, that they were up there in Red Lake, Ontario and in need of a Pentecostal Church. The announcement was made at the District Conference, where Walter and Louise Reinheimer were praying for the will of God in their ministry. Although they were not sitting together when the announcement was made they individually felt the call of God to Red Lake, Ontario to pioneer a Pentecostal church. The Reinheimer's, Carbert's and Cassidy's got their hearts together and agreed by faith for the Reinheimer's to move to Red Lake. We video-taped Walter, at age 80, in the summer of 2002, telling his story of the call and move to Red Lake. With his permission, we've transcribed and edited the video and have included it here.

**1959, Lyle with the founding families of
Glad Tidings Tabernacle in Red Lake, Ont.
(Lyle, Earl Carbert, Walter and Louise Reinheimer,
Greta and Cliff Cassidy and Mamie Carbert)**

16

My Pastor's Story

A fter Dauphin, Manitoba's experience, when the church burned to the ground in May 194?, we were getting $86.00 per month. We were paying the utilities of the manse and sometimes these took the entire salary. So here we had no church. We had lost everything and there was no money, and we didn't even have a building fund. It was just when the North Battleford group was going strong. Their Prophetess, Helen Fehr's mother was a faithful attendee of our church, her grandpa was on the board, so Helen would come and she would send North Battleford people to Dauphin and they would have meetings in the hall and I would have prayer meeting on Wednesday night and they would have it in the hall with my congregation on Thursday.

So then, we rented the Orange Hall for our services. In the summer we met with the board and decided with the congregation that we would build. We had $10,000 for the church, and insurance for $5000. Since the building burnt to the ground and they couldn't find out the cause, they thought it was the electrical fault of old wiring. So we got $10,000.

We hired two men to put in cement blocks, they don't do that anymore, and I wouldn't either, but it is still standing. A carpenter and I (I cancelled my salary), my twin sister, who was in children's work, came to work in the hospital, and preached for us on Sundays, free of charge. I said pay me $1.00 per hour and I will work 16 hours per day, and I will donate $8.00 per day to the building fund.

In three months we put up the brick, the floor, and the roof and got this building up.

The next spring, I was uncertain as to whether to stay or not to stay and I did a dumb thing, but I did it, I asked the congregation for a vote of confidence. And I said vote No or Yes.

After I resigned, I found that the congregation had voted Yes, which meant I should stay and I thought yes meant I should go.

So I resigned and we went to Winnipeg. We were threadbare. I only had one suit, and Arnold Hamilton came to Gilbert Plains for a Sunday and we went to visit where Ken Bunting was the Pastor at Gilbert Plains. As mentioned, I only had one suit, but I would wear them out, and Arnold said, "Do you want this button?" and I said, "Of course I want this button". So Arnold took a knife and gave me the button. I said, "I want it on my suit". I only had this one suit and I sometimes had to back out of the church because the back end had cracked open while I bent over . . . it was thread-bare.

So we came to Winnipeg and worked at the CNR graveyard shift as a coach-cleaner.

Old Mr. Bradford, was a Porter and he got this job for me. We rented a little suite, we just had one son, Lorne, and I worked graveyard shift. So I got some money for the winter time. When the spring time came I went to the Conference in Calvary Temple in Winnipeg, (of course, this was the only place that they had Conferences in those days).

Bill Gamble was at Flin Flon, Manitoba and Cliff Cassidy had just moved from Flin Flon to Red Lake, Ontario to open up a jewelry store there. Mr. Gamble was a Presbyter, so he gave his report of the North, (Louise and I weren't sitting together), and I had thought . . . I don't know what we are going to do.

Mr. Gamble said, "Somebody should go to the Red Lake area . . . the Carbert's are there and the Cassidy's have moved there and someone should go there and pioneer a work there."

Rev. Walter Reinheimer sharing his story concerning his calling to Red Lake, Ont.

Previous in 1921, J.C. Cook from Edmonton Bible School apparently had gone to Red Lake and found it too difficult. So in 1958, when I was going to World Conference, I met him because Mr. Cook was interested to meet this man who had gone to Red Lake. Anyway, when he went to Red Lake it was really rough times then.

However, Mr. Gamble said that someone should go to Red Lake because there are two Pentecostal families there and someone should open up a work there. Something like a bullet went through my heart and I met Louise to go for lunch at noon, downstairs in Calvary Temple, and Louise said, "Walter, we ought to go to Red Lake".

That's when the 40 hour work week came in on the Railway. So Friday night I did my shift and on Saturday morning I took the bus to Red Lake to meet the Carbert's and the Cassidy's. Mr. Earl Carbert knew the Fallonsbee's and they had an old suite, *and was it ever a 'sweet'*. He had spoken for it because in a month or two month we will have a pastor come in, and we want to rent that suite. So he spoke to Fallonsbee's. There were three suites in this log house: The Cassidy's on one side, we lived on one side and someone else (the manager of the Simpson's Store) lived in the front suite. After some time, the Cassidy's moved into the front suite, and then we got the church going.

So after the Conference we went back to Melville, Saskatchewan and got ready to move to this mining town. I had never seen a mine in my life, nor had I heard of a mine.

I was a farmer, with grade seven. During the Depression, when I was fourteen, because there were no crops for seven years and my Dad used to work in the winter time building elevators and us boys looked after the chores and went to school.

I said to Mom and Dad, I can get a job and earn a little money. In those days the government paid $5.00 a month, plus room and board and the farmer got $5.00 a month for keeping you and if you smoked, you got $5.00 more for tobacco. My great Uncle smoked and I didn't, so my Great Uncle took the $5.00. "The stinker could have given me the $5.00, but he didn't".

So then we went to visit a fellow that had MS, a farmer, Schindel was his name and we visited him and anyway this farmer had an old Model T in the hay fence, it had been sitting there for years, with 30 by 3½ inch tires, an old Model T which was a Bennett wagon. Because during the Depression they converted these old cars and put a pole on so horses could pull it and called it a Bennett wagon.

He said, "Walter you can have this old Bennett wagon to make yourself a trailer to move to Red Lake". So I got this old trailer, the tires were flat. Only God could have kept those tires. Anyway, so my Dad who had a blacksmith shop on the farm, helped me to make this trailer, why we didn't make it a two-wheel trailer for the stuff we had, we could have pulled it on two wheels.

I made a four-wheeler and you know that thing fish-tailed on the back of the car. And there was no pavement. We had a 1940 Chevy car which I had bought in Dauphin (a real Cadillac for its time).

1951, Reinheimer's "bennet wagon"

So we made this trailer and kissed our parents goodbye, with lots of tears, and we were on our way to visit Pastor Percy Munroe at Carberry, Manitoba. It was gravel road and #1 Highway was only oiled from Portage La Prairie to Winnipeg. The rest was gravel. The Trans Canada road wasn't built so you had to go through Rennie, Manitoba and Whitemouth, Manitoba.

We were only 12 miles from my dad's farm, when the first tire blew. We had to take it off, fix the tube, put it back in, put the tire back on the trailer, and pump up the tire with a hand pump. When we got to Red Lake, we had had thirteen flat tires. The thirteenth one was at Red Lake Road which was a 100 miles from Red Lake.

On our trip, we stopped at Carberry, Manitoba, then Winnipeg for a couple of days and I had gone to T. Eaton's

Company. I wanted to buy tires . . . *I was rich you know*. So when I got to Red Lake, I had $13.00 in my pocket.

So Eaton's said, we haven't sold a 30 by 3½" tire in years, but he said, just a minute and he went somewhere and he brought out three tubes, 30 x 3½" tubes, I bought the works. I had to put old mitts where the tire had a hole, and put this mitt in and then the tube so the gravel wouldn't hit the tube.

We were driving down the highway, Lorne was only three years old, and would look out the back and say, "Dad you have a flat tire." I would stop the car, and would you believe it, there would be a flat tire. Imagine, three years old!

When we got to Red Lake Road, we were actually four or five miles past Red Lake Road, towards Red Lake, when the last tire went into a 1,000 pieces. Now what? I couldn't fix that and it was in June and the flies and the mosquitoes were bad, and Louise was going to come with me. I said, "Stay in the car, lock it up, and don't let anyone in." Then I walked back to Red Lake Road where there was a little restaurant, and I mean, you couldn't find that in a million years. I said to the fellow there, "You wouldn't know of anyone who has an old Model T"? Well, he said, "This lad has one" . . . a kid of about 15 years old. "Yes", the lad said, "I have one and I'm going to fix it up some day". I said, "Can I see that car?"

So he took me into the bush, the trees had grown up around that car. I said, "My son, you will be 1,000 years old . . . you will never get parts for this car". It had one tire that was good, and I saw that. So I used all the salesmanship I had. And I preached to him, not the Gospel but with persuasion. I paid him $13.00 and the kid was happy and I took the tire off and put it on my shoulder and walked back to the car. That was the last flat and we went to Red Lake.

We stopped for the night and I went in to get a room for the night and there were some Americans there with their Oldsmobile's and big tummies (who carried the balance forward) who were opening up the Tourist camp (1951). I drove in with this car and this 'modern' trailer and there was one room left. We got it. Talk about God!

One guy said, "Oh my God, a sewing machine in the car". [It was probably Gold Arrow Tourist Camp.]

When we got to Red Lake, Mr. Jim Liddle was at the Carbert's and he said, "How did you make the 'sand hill'?" I said, "the sand hill, they were all sand hills." [The road (turkey trail) had been built in 1947. Therefore it was only four years old.]

So then, I sold that trailer to somebody in Red Lake for $25.00. I had gotten the trailer free from the farmer. We had thirteen flat tires, and arrived in Red Lake with $13.00.

The second day that we were in Red Lake, I was hired at the Campbell Red Lake Gold Mine as a warehouse clerk, remember I had only grade seven education. We had stopped at the Carbert's, they had left on holidays, and Mrs. Carbert had left a note on the table asking Louise to look after Barrie and you can stay here for two weeks, charge the groceries to our account as long as you cook for Barrie. So, in two weeks I got my first check. So I went and got a mattress from the Bay, because there was a bed and springs in the suite but no mattress. Not anything at all.

This suite was quite sweet. There was no water works . . . just running water from the well and the little house out back. It was this way for nine years. We had two more boys (1953 and 1955) while we were in Red Lake. Our son Lance used to get water with a pail and he felt that it was a LONG WAY, but it was actually just next door.

For the first month we held prayer meetings at the Carbert and Cassidy homes. Mrs. Laramie was our first Red Lake person to attend. Then we rented the Red Lake Theatre. We had put our tithes together and had purchased a piano for service. However, there were shows in the Theatre on Saturday nights, and the kids used to pour soft drinks on the keys and we would have to clean this up before service because Mrs. Carbert couldn't make it work. There would also be popcorn all over and it was a stinky place.

We were maybe there for a year or so. Then we bought an old warehouse, cheap. The District sent a small monetary gift to help purchase this building. But it had to be moved for two miles. So we cut it in half. Then I was able to hire the tractor and truck from the Mine to move this building. When I went to the manager to pay the bill he looked at the bill and took his pen and wrote on it . . . Paid in Full. Actually we skidded the building into town. When we had to go around the corner, a telephone pole which had not been cut off close enough to the ground, caught on the joists and ripped them into slivers

Anyway, we got it there, and when we looked at that building, my goodness . . . what a job. We put the back half in place and then the front half, and pulled them together. Tie rods had to be put at the level of the eaves to hold the walls in place. Then they were painted and these rods remained until the day the building was torn down.

Sometime in 1953, we had this building fixed up for services.

In all, this building was remodeled five times in nine years. We built a suite on the back for the Pastor to live in and then we jacked it up and put a basement under it, while this was being done, the parsonage part shook so badly, you would think that it was going to fall off of the blocks. A new front with a foyer was also added.

When the building was in place, there were Reinheimer's, Carbert's, Cassidy's, Laramie's, and Mimi Koeffert. Slowly, in time, there was a fairly large Sunday school with children attending from the town. We also rented a bus to pick up the children for Sunday school.

For the Sunday School Christmas programs, the parents would attend and we rented the Rainbow Lanes Bowling Alley/Dance Hall, and treats were handed out.

I worked for nine years at the mine and took no salary from the church. Gradually other people came, who moved to Red Lake to work in the mines and several families were reached for Christ from Red Lake.

Lyle's comment:
It would seem that this might help us understand some of the characteristics of the calling of Apostle! In retrospect,

even though I made the statement to Walter Reinheimer, that if I was ever called to the ministry, I would probably not do what he did. His influence was probably the Apostle-father relationship which helped to set the direction for my future.

Note of interest —

The Walter Reinheimer's left in 1960 and pioneered in Thompson, Manitoba. Then the Jack Duncalfe's came as Pastors.

So, from age eleven to twenty-one, Red Lake was the strong formative influence on my (Lyle's) life.

17

Steps of a Good Man

I walked in the door of the Bible College, and who should I see coming down the stairs, but the 'long-well-kept-hair-with-the-full-pleated-skirt' roommate of Marilyn. Her name was Kathleen Fairs, or Kay for short. It may have been the following weekend, I'm not sure, when Marilyn and her boyfriend, wanted to know if we could make their date a foursome, by me taking Kay to church with them. It was a walk date because neither of us had a vehicle. I thought that would be an interesting adventure with this obviously athletic young lady.

Well, we talked all the way to the Dublin Street Pentecostal Church and we talked all the way back to the Bible College. When we left the church, our friends went their way and Lyle and Kay went theirs. We walked to a little corner store that served milkshakes where we shared one because, that was all I could afford at the time. Then we proceeded to walk through the park towards the College, talking and joking. Kay seemed interested in the fact that I had played football, because her younger brother, Glen, had played in high school. She was telling me, how tough he was, but assured me that she could handle him (in her own girl-style way). So I started to brag how tough I was and that she wouldn't be able to handle me, then I'd slip a half nelson or some controlling wrestling hold on her as we walked and we laughed and joked until we stopped under a street light at the end of the park and started to talk about our callings from the Lord. As I remember it, I interrupted our friendly banter by saying something like this, "Kay, If we decide to seriously date, there is something you should know. I feel God's call very clearly, so as strong as our relationship could be, you would always be playing second fiddle to the will of God in my life. It will always be God first and then you!" Well, Kay was quick to respond with the fact that no man was going to come between her and God's call on her life. So, that was settled on our first date!

It seemed to be right, as we were married a year later and moved into one room in the married residence, and have now celebrated our 50th Anniversary on September 12, 2009. Was it all easy, oh no, but there were some powerful years of watching God prove Himself to us and through us, as He developed His ministry in us and our work for Him.

Her Story

18

Kay's Birth and Early Life

Life for Kathleen, began one afternoon in April 1937 on Potter's Road, Tillsonburg, Ontario. The beginnings of my life included Fred and Alice Fairs, my parents; older sister, Alice Elizabeth (Betty); Malcolm, my oldest brother; and Frederick, my next brother. At the time of my birth, my parents and siblings were God-fearing, Bible-believing Christians. Thank God for a wonderful Godly heritage. From that very first breath, I would be taught the truths of God's word, how to pray, the importance of attending church, but most of all, the way of Salvation unto Eternal life.

Three years later on March 12th, a younger brother, Glen was born. We were buddies in good and bad. When my mother wasn't certain who had committed 'the crime', she would automatically spank both of us. It seemed like we had an un-written commitment that we would never 'squeal' on each other, even if it meant that we received punishment, even when we had done no wrong.

Kay's parents, Fred and Alice Fairs

We were such good friends, that we would wait for each other at school and walk home together. On one occasion, Glen was asked who his girlfriend was. He very quickly replied that I wasn't his girlfriend but his sister.

My Mom used to tell me that I was a 'flood baby'. History verifies that the day I was born, was the day of the flood in Tillsonburg. The 'White Bridge' on Simcoe Street was washed out. My Dad had to walk to work in the rain, by crossing the very high train trestle bridge. The family doctor, Doctor Rankin was not able to attend my worldly entrance, so our neighbor, Mrs. Weeks, a midwife, attended my arrival. I was a bouncing ten-pounds plus baby. Apparently, so my mother said, I was so fat that I was ugly. Oh well, I have never let that statement influence me. You see, I knew that beyond any doubt, my mother and father loved me and all of us very much.

Kathleen and her brother, Glen Fairs

My recollections of the first four years of my life are 'sketchy', to say the least. The one memory that I have of living on Potter's Road is of a Saturday night routine.

This was bath time, in the wash tub with water that had been heated on a wood/coal burning cook stove. After a thorough scrubbing, and being snuggled in a big towel and then dressed into clean pajamas, I was given the delightful 'drink' of castor oil and orange juice. Delightful, is really a lie . . . it was totally gross! I still have very vivid recollections of that oily substance as I endeavored to choke it down. Mother made certain that there would be no way of missing this Saturday night event. After all, it was a common belief that this was a strong preventative medicine which kept us healthy and free from colds and the flu. I can't verify whether it is true or not, but to the best of my recollection we were all healthy and active.

Another memory is another Saturday night ritual, when Mom would clean all of our shoes and line them up beside the wash stand on the opposite side of the kitchen. There would be Dad's, Mom's, Betty's, Malcolm's, Frederick's, and of course, mine. Today, I can still see in my mind's eye that line of shoes with a shine that would almost blind your eyes.

This shine was important because we only had one pair of shoes each. Remember the year . . . 1937. The depression had been hard, but the economy was just beginning to have an upward turn.

The house on Potter's Road still stands today and is home to someone else.

I spoke of my Godly heritage. Even so, this did not mean that I had a sure 'ticket' to heaven and eternal life.

I do not have a first-hand remembrance of this event, but I have had it verified by my parents, pastor, and members of our church. It was hard times and money was scarce for everyone. If you had a job, you were one of the fortunate ones. My father worked at the foundry factory. We were blessed. Well, one day my father came home and said to my mother that he felt that he should take the last remaining dollar in his pocket to take some potatoes, bread and eggs to Pastor and Mrs. Swanton. My parents agreed, that Dad should go to the corner store and purchase these items and walk to the Pastor's house to deliver them. When our Pastor's wife answered the door, she broke out in tears, which was rather unnerving for my Dad, because she and her husband had been praying for these items. God had used my parents, to answer the prayers of His servants. As I am told, and experienced, we didn't miss a meal or payments. God is still faithful!

Dad, Fred Fairs, on the sleigh with horses "Bill" and "Max"

19

The Fairs Family
Move to the Farm

In 1941, the Second World War was in full swing, but my
Dad and Grandad heard that there was a farm for sale
just west of Tillsonburg, on the Quarter Town Line. The
house had been vacant for some time. Again my memory is
sketchy, but I can still see the dirt and cobwebs, and smell
the musty smell and damage in the house. However, the
opportunity of adventure was more inviting and before
long I was outside exploring our new surroundings.

Some of our neighbors and fellow church members,
namely, Hugh and Alta MacDonald, and Alex and Hazel
Reynolds came to help with the clean-up, repairs and preparation for the planting of crops. Of course, machinery (such
as it was) needed some BIG help to get it functional. But my
Grandad used to say, there's nothing that some hay wire
and binder twine can't fix. I grew up believing that, and this
small philosophy has been the means of many repairs over
my lifetime. (Maybe not hay wire and binder twine, but the
more modern items, such as duct tape.)

While the adults and my older siblings worked to get
the farm in order, my girlfriend and I played. I remember
Mr. MacDonald's utility trailer standing idle to the side of
the driveway. We soon found out that it was fun to walk

up the steep floor and have the trailer fall to the ground. Then we would reverse the pleasure. Of course, there was a bang as the trailer hit the ground. My Dad was not pleased with our pleasure, so we had to stop. Oh well, on to the next adventure.

There were some 76 acres to explore along with the barn, chicken coup and milk house. Sufficient to say, I have not got the time to relate all of my antics. My siblings didn't have to work all the time, so we managed to create some excitement together. I am sure, that on some days, our parents wished that we would remain in one place. But adventure called us on to new and more exciting things.

I remember the job of looking after my baby brother, Glen, who was born when I was three. I will always have the picture in my mind, of his wicker cradle in front of the kitchen window. When he would cry, it was my job to be there to entertain him. So, that was my 'job' during the renovations and move.

Entertainment for us on the farm was pure and self-made. There was no television, well, NO ELECTRICITY, and NO RUNNING WATER and NO TELEPHONE. The running water bit was done by pump or on wash days Dad would take the stone-boat and 'Queenie', the horse, down to the stream with a barrel and milk cans which we filled by using a pail. This was really cold spring water, with no pollutants. As we all grew older this would become the offspring's job. Thank God for brothers, because this was man's work. I usually went along, because man's work was more fun!

In those days, we used coal oil lamps or candles for lights. Our heat was a cook stove in the kitchen, and a pot-bellied stove in the living room. The children's bedrooms were upstairs. The heat to the upstairs was provided by the two stove pipes, one at the west end of the home and the other at the east end of the home. So, I would change into my pajamas by the stove pipe and then run to duck under the many quilts on the bed. On colder winter nights we had a 'hot-water' bottle. It was really a comfort! However, at times the lid wasn't screwed on tightly and it would leak. Horrible! But again we were always aware of God's provision.

I have very vivid recollections of doing my homework by the coal oil lamp. Of course, when it was time to go to bed, Mother used to accompany us up stairs until we were tucked in. Sometimes, we used the flashlight, but batteries cost money, so this was usually used by the older siblings.

I remember nights when the whole family would gather around the kitchen table for a night of fun by the light of the coal oil lamp. We would play board games . . . Chinese checkers, checkers, snakes and ladders, crokinole, and even Bingo which was a home board game.

Speaking of bingo (these were the days before Bingo Halls) we would use kernels of corn for the 'markers'. These were inexpensive and available – we grew the corn. Our Dad was the caller. My, oh my, such good memories.

Then on Saturday night we tuned in to the battery operated radio for 'Hockey Night in Canada', it was easy to remember the teams, because there were only six teams. There was always family rivalry when the Toronto Maple Leafs and the Montreal Canadiens played. For most of the family, their favorite team was the Maple Leafs but my brother, Fred's favorite team was the Canadiens.

We also were blessed to have a hand cranked Victorola to play our 78 records. We really had a great time taking turns cranking, in order to play the records. Of course, we all had our favorites and it was a great time of sharing and enjoyment.

Life marched on and time went by. One day the large hydro truck drove into the yard and that night we turned on the electrical lights. Modern Progress! We were able to get this 'modern convenience' because Dad knew the foreman for our area and this hastened the date of installation. Even though each room only had a naked light bulb screwed into a white porcelain fixture in the middle of the ceiling.

The next modern convenience was the telephone. This was really exciting . . . I talked with my girlfriends every night, and most of the time my Mom would ask me to 'hang up and get off the phone'. It was amazing what things we found to talk about. O yes, there were also calls from boyfriends, but I at this point of time had not met the man who would be my husband.

Eventually, Dad and my brothers installed a coal burning furnace which was wonderful . . . even though we had to keep it stoked and bed it down at night, hoping that the coals would last until morning.

Then Dad was able to get a plumber to run a copper line from the well to the kitchen sink. Grant you, it was only a cold water tap . . . but oh, it was SO CONVENIENT!

After I was married, Lyle and I helped dig the tile field for a bathroom. Now this was the epitome of modernization and my mother was able to have her choice of color for the fixtures, that being, rose! Oh yes, a change in our entertainment took place in 1951 when my Granddad purchased a black and white television. The hours of viewing were limited, but we really had arrived. We didn't have to go to my Great Uncle Harry's and Aunt Belle's place to watch 'Hockey Night in Canada', followed by Don Messer and the Islanders. We were not even allowed to hint that we would miss church in order to watch a program on the television!

Our reception for programming was by means of a tall aerial. As I remember, we were really 'blessed' because the aerial was located at many 'intersections' of signals. However, when we wanted to watch another channel, we would have to go outside and to the north side of the house and manually turn the aerial, until someone inside said to stop. This wasn't so bad, except in the winter months when the wind was howling and it was cold. Then there was always a discussion as to whose turn it was to go and turn it.

20

Spiritual Conversion

Our life was centered around life and chores of the farm and Church. I am very grateful for the importance that the Church Family had on my life. At this time Rev. V. G. Brown was our Pastor.

In June 1944, I remember well the Saturday that I was in the garden picking strawberries. I had been taught from the Bible the doctrine of the Second Coming of the Lord. I can remember, looking up in the sky and praying that Jesus would not return until I could get to Church the next day; for I had determined to accept Christ as my Savior. Looking up into the sky I was being thankful that there were no clouds, for the Bible says that Jesus is coming again in the clouds.

Finally, Sunday came and off to Church we went, as was our practice. However, my Mother had to remain at home to care for my younger brother. It was this Sunday morning, during Children's church under the direction of Mrs. Hazel Robinson and Mrs. Hazel Reynolds, that I accepted Jesus as my Savior. I remember quite vividly, the illustrated story of a large magnet (representing Christ) and lots of nails, and pins (representing people). The magnet came to attract the nails and pins, and wow, only some were gathered up, while others were left behind. The message that one needed to accept Christ's death on Calvary as atonement for sin, and then believe that He died for ME, I quickly, accepted Jesus, and thank God I have never turned back.

As I mentioned, my mother was at home caring for my younger brother. I could hardly wait to get home and tell her what had happened. She was thrilled and encouraged me to write in my small New Testament, the day that this had happened.

My brother, Glen had been hit by a truck while he and I accompanied my Dad and Granddad into Town. So he was at home, with his leg in a sling which was held at a 90 degree angle for a few weeks. This was a rough time, but it also gave us many good things, such as, jello, candy, games, and toys, and some extra 'luxuries' that we never could have. This was 1944, and there was a War on and these items were rationed. We had extra sugar and flour, as the man who had hit my brother, was trying to compensate for his action (he was inebriated at the time of the accident). My brother and I had a great time setting up the games and toys, in his bed. You see, my morning job was to play with him, so my mother could get the cooking and house work done. In the afternoon, I was able to go out and 'farm' with my Dad, but I had to sneak out, or my brother would cry, because he wanted to go. I remember, having to crawl on my hands and knees until I was past the windows, then I could get up and run to be with my Dad in the field.

One of the 'games' we used to play was making a 'tent'. I would pin a blanket around the top of Glen's 'hanging' foot which would make a good 'teepee' style tent.

It was fun playing with his cars and the other toys that he received while his leg was in this 'sling'.

That Sunday night, I begged my mother to allow me to go to church with Dad. It was this night that I received the Infilling of the Holy Spirit and I felt the Call of God to Ministry. I was seven years of age. It was June of 1944. The one person, that I well remember as I was having an encounter with God, was my father, who was praying along side of me. What a memory! I will always remember it. My parents have been a valued influence in my walk with God.

I remember my Mother at the kitchen table with her Bible open in front of her and tears streaming down her face, as she read the Word and prayed for her family and many other needs as they were brought to her remembrance. What an impact! I also remember my Dad when he would advise me with 'one-liners'. Such as, IF IN DOUBT, DO WITHOUT. Or IF YOU CAN TAKE JESUS WITH YOU AND HE WOULD BE PLEASED WITH WHERE YOU ARE, THEN YOU CAN GO. Or, IF ANYTHING IS WORTH DOING, THEN IT IS WORTH DOING WELL. Believe me, I will never forget his advice, this same advice has also been passed on to my children and I hear them passing it on to their children.

Another important event in my Christian walk was Easter Sunday, 1945. There was a Water Baptismal service planned. (This was a special Easter, because it was also my birthday.) I talked with my parents about being baptized. They agreed that I understood what it meant, and gave their encouraging assent. Next came the instruction from my Pastor and I was so excited!

21

School Days

————⌒⌇⌒————

I remember my father taking me to the entrance of the Baptismal tank, and the Pastor's smile and words of encouragement and scripture. I was so excited . . . I gave my testimony, but excitement over-rode my memory of what I said. Then I was immersed and came up with a clean, wonderful sense of being obedient to God's word. As I left the tank, there was my mother, smiling, with tears in her eyes, holding a towel for me. Life with Christ and a godly family was wonderful.

We attended school at Rolph Street Public School. This was the same school that my father attended. We were allowed to attend there because my grandfather still owned a house in the Town of Tillsonburg. In fact, it was closer for us to attend school in the Town than it was for us to be driven to the country school. You see, the school bus didn't come down our road, and my father would have had to drive us. If it was necessary, we could walk to the Town school, which we did many times. We walked to and from school; in all types of weather. However, my mother always made certain that we were dressed appropriately (until I became a senior, (grade 8) and then it was not fashionable to wear snow pants).

I can remember some of these days. It would be very cold with lots of snow and penetrating chilling winds. However, I would put on the 'I don't need snow pants' attitude and would hurriedly leave for school. Well, there were times, when I would have to stop and squat down to allow my skirt and coat to shield my bare legs. After all, it was bad enough to have to wear snow boots (I might add here, that girls did NOT wear slacks to school), and as I would adamantly proclaim to my mother, I did NOT need to wear stockings, that were ugly brown and cotton. I never had nylons until I was older. Even then, these would be too expensive for us to use for school. Such stupid pride!

The shortest way to go to school was to walk down the CN Railway tracks. I can remember how 'smart' we were if we timed our walk correctly. You see, in those days the tracks would be examined by a 'trackman', who would ride on a 'jigger', which he would pump with a handle similar to the handle on a water pump. The trackman was a friend of our father's, so he would stop and give us a ride. Now, this was High Adventure (probably, it would be a 'federal case' if such an adventure took place today). Well, the ride was always exhilarating and of course, much faster. When we arrived at the crossing of the Railway and Rolph Street, he would let us off and we would only have to walk a couple of blocks. My, how we felt that life was good!

Another way to go to school, was to walk down the Twelfth Concession, past the Golf Course, and across the 'foot bridge' to the Baldwin Street and Rolph Street inter-section. This we did on my first day of school. I will always remember this day. We walked to school, my brother Fred, my mother and I. You see, she had to register me which was done on the first day of school. There was no Play School or Kindergarten, so I was seven years of age when I first started. I can remember, walking past the Golf Course, and my mother commented on how I had done such a good job of getting dressed, because the pattern on my socks was straight (now, how important is that statement?).

This school was the school that my father had attended and graduated from, completing grade eight. My sister Betty, my brothers Malcolm and Frederick, were also graduates of grade eight from this school. My brother Glen also attended and graduated from there.

Even though I was seven when I started, I made up for lost time because I was promoted to grade five from grade three, skipping grade four. This was exciting, but I missed having the grade four teacher, Mrs. Parrott. She was loved by all of the students. I don't remember that this progression was any huge challenge. I know that at the end of grade five, I was promoted to grade six.

During my elementary school years, a band master came to our town to teach band lessons. My brother Fred, was first to enroll. He started playing the drums. I can't remember that he stayed with it very long, but I was learning the saxophone and my brother Glen was learning the clarinet. Our poor parents and siblings! When we were learning these reed instruments, we had to learn to apply the proper lip pressure on the reed and if you got too little . . . then no sound was made except the gush of air. If you applied too much pressure, they would squeak. Well, one can imagine how much squeaking would echo from the living room as we would practice. Of course, the older siblings, would protest loudly and we would be sent to experiment in our rooms.

As we progressed, the Band Master was interested in selling us our respective instruments. Without hesitation, our Grandfather, who lived with us on the farm, offered to buy my brother a new clarinet (in my opinion, he was Grandpa's pet). So this is what happened . . . Glen was the proud owner of a brand new clarinet (which I might add, he still has).

Now, my carnal nature could hardly stand this. After all, enough is enough! It was bad enough that Glen was his pet, but I was the one who wanted an instrument. I can remember, having a rather elaborate pity party over this. I believe the party extended over several days (sorry about this).

Well, my Father and Mother could stand it no longer, so after their consulting and budgeting etc. it was decided that a pig would go to market, and I would have a saxophone. Wow! So it was, they purchased an E-flat Alto Selmer Saxophone. It was a beauty! It was not new, but it was mine! It was played in band, in the church orchestra and was a companion of mine to Bible College and eventually into ministry. I still have this instrument today. My Pastor at this time was Rev. J. H. Hazlett.

22

Band Concert:
'to squeak or not to squeak'

————— ✑ —————

I must inject this story about my first band concert. The Band Master had scheduled a concert at the local Town Hall. The members were all pumped, primed and practiced for this BIG event. After all, none of us had played our instruments before a 'live audience'. So, the excitement was high and the nerves were tense.

We three, had gotten all dressed up in our Sunday best, in fact, my parents had purchased a new navy taffeta dress for me (I can't remember what my brothers wore, but I am certain that they were handsomely attired). You see I was scheduled to play a solo . . . *'I Dream of Jeannie with the Light Brown Hair'*.

My Mother had finally herded us toward the door, as my father was waiting in the car, when my sister turned to me and said, "If you squeak that thing when you're playing your solo, I'll throw my wallet at you". (Such pressure!). Well, I was surprised and shocked, but I am sure she would have done it because a squeak from me would mean embarrassment for her. My sister was my hero and I remembered that I would not want to embarrass her for anything. Guess what? I played my solo with NO squeak. I too was very thankful that I was able to do so well.

I well remember my grade eight year. We had two teachers for this grade, Mrs. Cuthbertson in the morning and Mr. Fairburn in the afternoon. Mrs. Cuthbertson was also the school's music teacher and she taught music to the other grades in the afternoons. Mr. Fairburn, was also the school principal. He was a great teacher, but put up with no nonsense. I will also remember Friday afternoons in his class. He would announce sometime around three in the afternoon (school was dismissed at four), that the first one to answer this question correctly could go home. Well, I was competitive enough that I was determined to get the correct answer, and believe it or not, I went home early for the majority of the Friday afternoons.

My older sister and brother did not have the opportunity to attend High School, because it seemed necessary for them to go to work to help out with the lack of finances that everyone experienced during and immediately after the Depression. My sister worked in the Borden's Milk Factory, until she went to Bible School in Toronto, Ontario.

During her second year, she was in an accident with her bicycle when she was riding home from Bible School to her job as maid/nanny.

When the telephone rang at the farm, my mother was told by Betty's friend, Frieda Edwards (later Norcross), that Betty had been in an accident and that she had broken her back. I don't remember details, except to say that my Mother immediately went to Toronto. I can remember trying to 'cook' for my Dad and brothers, I'm sure it was meager fair. My mother was invited to stay with Frieda and she was able to go to the hospital daily. When Betty was discharged from the hospital, she and mother traveled by train from Toronto to Woodstock, Ontario, where my Father picked them up and drove them to the farm, some thirty-five miles.

Now, what a time this was! We were all very glad to see them. Especially to see, that Betty was able to walk, even with a complete body cast from chest to hips. We were especially happy to see mother, because we would all eat well again.

Once again, I had to share my room and bed with my sister. That wasn't so bad, except she had this HARD cast and it seemed like I came in contact with it many times in the night. It seemed like I managed to hit my elbow, my head or my knee sometime or many times during each night. Another nuisance, was the itching that she endured. I used to take her longest knitting needle and try to scratch underneath that cast. Praise God, she recovered one hundred percent and never had a problem except for some discomfort when she carried her unborn children.

After her graduation from Bible School, she returned back to Tillsonburg, where she worked and also held a boys and girls club called 'The Trail Blazers'. I used to help with this program. In 1951, she married Aaron H. (Tommie) Conger, from Tifton, Georgia. After spending a year in Georgia they moved to Mount Morris, Michigan, and later purchased a house in Clio, Michigan. One would not miss this house, because she had painted it PINK, bright pink at that. They later built a house in West Branch, Michigan where they were living until her death in 2003.

My older brother, Malcolm worked at George's Feed Mill, and he eventually was able to purchase his own farm about a mile west of our home farm. He and his wife Norma (nee Leach), lived on this farm until their deaths: Norma in 1999 and Malcolm in 2001.

**Kathleen with her brother Malcolm
Fairs, beside the Plymouth that
she learned to drive.**

My brother Frederick worked at a men's clothing store: Harris Men's Wear. He worked here very successfully. He married Eva (nee McWade) and they built a new home on the lot at the north end of the home farm. He passed away in 1979 and Eva passed away in 1986.

Since the older siblings did not have the opportunity to attend High School they were determined that the remaining two younger siblings would definitely attend. So after grade eight, I went to Tillsonburg District High School on Annondale Avenue. My brother Glen also attended this school. I played in the school band, was on the School's Volleyball team, played and refereed basketball, was involved in the drama club, was the Major of the majorettes, and competed in the Track and Field meets. Glen made the school's line-up for the football team. This created an interest in the sport that I had never had before.

At the time that we attended, there were five years of High School. So at the end of the fourth year, I had a choice of either taking the grade thirteen and preparing to enter University or College or instead of grade thirteen, I could take a Special Commercial Course, which was preparation for positions in the business sector, as secretaries, or executives.

What a dilemma! I fussed, stewed and prayed about this, because I knew that I would be attending Bible College. So, I talked this over with my parents and I will always remember my Dad's advice. He felt that I should take the Special Commercial Course, because this would give me a career. In event I may have to support myself, then I would have something to fall back on. Well, this made good sense and I registered into this course.

Now, many years later, I realize the wisdom that my Dad had and I am so thankful that I followed his advice because this training has been extremely beneficial in our ministry. Many times I would be called upon to set up church books when we started a work or to take notes for Lyle or type his letters etc.. Thank God again for parents who prayed and had such wisdom in giving me advice.

I graduated from High School in 1956 and was given a job to work for the law firm of Gibson and Gibson in Tillsonburg. When the senior partner passed away, just a few months after I had started, I then went to work for Heath's Department Store. I worked in the office until I went to Bible College. They also gave me employment between my first and second year of College.

**Kathleen Fairs by the tulip garden her Grandfather
planted in front yard (1952)**

23

Kay is Off to Bible College

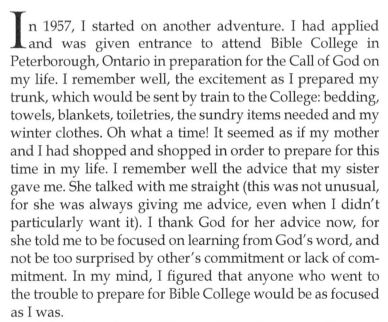

In 1957, I started on another adventure. I had applied and was given entrance to attend Bible College in Peterborough, Ontario in preparation for the Call of God on my life. I remember well, the excitement as I prepared my trunk, which would be sent by train to the College: bedding, towels, blankets, toiletries, the sundry items needed and my winter clothes. Oh what a time! It seemed as if my mother and I had shopped and shopped in order to prepare for this time in my life. I remember well the advice that my sister gave me. She talked with me straight (this was not unusual, for she was always giving me advice, even when I didn't particularly want it). I thank God for her advice now, for she told me to be focused on learning from God's word, and not be too surprised by other's commitment or lack of commitment. In my mind, I figured that anyone who went to the trouble to prepare for Bible College would be as focused as I was.

Otherwise, why would you go! Needless to say, I learned that everyone is human and that it is important to keep our focus on the Lord.

I look back on my years in College, and realize this was a 'boot camp' experience for me. I not only had to share a room with one or two roommates, which meant lots of fun and adventures and mischief. But, one had to learn discipline in order to study. To spare embarrassment to any, that may have been involved, I will not go into some of the 'mischief' that took place. It was just that, 'mischief'. My teaching from my upbringing, would not permit me to do things that were against God or man's law.

Thank God for faithful parents who knew how to administer the 'spanking' (especially my mother), or the pointing of a finger and the call of my name, "Kathleen" by my Dad. I was always aware of the authority that his BIG pointer finger held. That expression hurt me as much or more than the 'spanking'.

I was very aware of my parents' faithfulness in praying for their children. I would be out with a friend or friends and would come in at night to hear them praying for me. Sometimes, I had stretched the limits as to where I had been, and with whom, only to come home and realize that the power of their prayers were with me. I loved them for that and yet at times, I was bothered by that. I thank God for this, because I believe, that it was their prayers that sustained me through the years of youth and kept me from doing anything that would come between me and my walk with God.

I valued their example of reading the Word and how they practiced it, in every aspect of their lives. They not only read the Word, but they were doers of the Word.

The five Fairs siblings:
Fred, Malcolm Betty, Kathleen and Glen
(1976 at Dad Fairs' funeral)

We were never allowed to have 'roast pastor for Sunday dinner', because God's Word said to "touch not the Lord's anointed". We were taught tithing. God's Word said, "to bring all the tithes into the storehouse". We were taught faithfulness to the House of God. For God's Word said "to forsake not the assembling of your selves together" (and many more valuable principles). Thank God for this heritage!

I also thanked God for loving, caring and encouraging Pastors. At the time that I went to Bible School, my Pastor was Rev. J. A. Pearson.

Other opportunities came my way while I was in College. It was the requirement that the students would travel on weekends on assignments. I played the saxophone, so this lent to opportunities that may not have been available otherwise. I remember the one weekend that the school orchestra had been invited to play on a weekend assignment. It was always fun and a great experience and good fellowship, to be able to travel away from the College

115

and to be hosted in someone's home and to be able to share the Gospel in a church. I loved the traveling. However, I was in first year, so the actual preaching was done by a third year student or one of the Faculty. It didn't matter, because I enjoyed being involved in the work of the Lord, because this was my calling.

However, when I returned to the College, late Sunday night, there was a message in my mailbox for me to call home. So I went to the phone, even though it was late at night, and called my mother. She told me that my Grandfather had passed away. Needless to say, I didn't sleep much that night. My Grandfather had been a part of our family for quite a few years, and I would miss him, even though he was irritating at times. He also had a 'short fuse' and would lose his temper and cause tension in the home. It seemed like my parents were always the point of his displeasure. Besides this, my brother, Malcolm, was coming the next day to pick me up.

When I had previously received the call that my Granddad was very sick and that he was in the hospital, I was overcome with a heavy burden for him. I was not certain that he was prepared for eternity in heaven, and I was overwhelmed with the possibility of losing my Granddad and the fact that he needed to accept Christ as his personal Savior. So, I had spent some extended time in prayer over this and while I was in prayer, God had given me the scripture in Isaiah 59:1, "Behold, the Lord's hand is not shortened, that it cannot save; neither his ear heavy, that it cannot hear." This gave me peace, and within a day my Mother called and told me that she was able to pray with him as he repented and accepted Christ. Some of his final words to her to pass on to us were "Tell the kids to not stop going to church and believing." Thank God for His faithfulness! God honors His Word!

During my second year, when I returned to College from the Thanksgiving Weekend at home, I met this tall, blonde, muscular guy in the hallway to whom my roommate, Marilyn, introduced me. You see, this guy had attended Western University in London, Ontario, which was Marilyn's home town. They attended the same church, London Gospel Temple. His name was Lyle Carbert. (There are more details in the section of this book, 'Our Story').

Now here's the twist . . . when I was growing up in a small town, the young people from my home church, Bethel Temple in Tillsonburg, Ontario, had the misconception that we were not considered to be on the same level as the young people from the city church at London Gospel Temple. So, in my thought, he was just another one of those 'city kids', and I was not impressed by this fact.

So after the normal introductions, we went on our way. I didn't give him much thought or attention, but it would seem like he always appeared when least expected and was constantly 'in my way'.

In Bible College days, dates were not allowed, unless over the supper hour. You know, it was a big thing for a guy to carry your supper tray and to sit together at the meal. Then the guy and gal could go for a walk. Wow!!!

Anyway, this Lyle guy was insistent that he carry my tray and sit with me. Well, okay, but the next night too! No way, my independence kicked in. I sure didn't want to be classed as a 'couple'. But his persistence won out and we started asking the Dean for a 'pink slip' which allowed us to have a date. Imagine! Anyway, we double-dated with my room- mate and her boyfriend. One date led to another and pretty soon we were a 'couple'. So now, our individual stories become a story of a twosome.

With special permission from the Dean of Education, Mr. Charles Ratz, we were given permission to get married between my second and third year (which was permitted anyway), but for Lyle to marry between his first and second year . . . that took SPECIAL SANCTION. We received this, with the understanding that we would get married, and pay the tuition, room and board for both of us, and have no debt. God provided and thus we were married on September 12, 1959 in Bethel Temple, Tillsonburg, Ontario.

This was a huge miracle . . . Get permission to marry . . . get married . . . pay two tuitions for Bible College . . . and HAVE NO DEBT. Oh yes, there was sufficient money for 'toothpaste and shoelaces'. How big is God!

So now, our individual stories become OUR STORY.

Lyle and Kay on their Wedding Day

**Lyle and Kay, September 12, 1959, in
going away outfits after their wedding.**

Their Story

(As told by Lyle with Kay's help — so what's new)

24

Life and Ministry in Bible College

———————⟨⟨⟩⟩———————

In 1958, Kay was in her second year of Bible College and I was in my first year. We traveled together a little in my first year, as the Bible College would allow, but, of course in the second and third year we traveled as a married couple. In my three years of Bible College, we only missed about six weekends that we weren't on assignment to some church, and then we quite often were involved in some way in the local churches. Part of the reason for this extra opportunity was the fact that I played violin duets with my friend, Dave Moulden, whose folks lived in London and attended L.G.T. Violin duets were a rarity, and seems to still be pretty scarce in gospel circles, so it opened quite a few doors for ministry.

Kay was a year ahead of us in College and, especially in her third year when some of the churches requested a third year student to preach, she would get to preach and we as a group, would supply the music. We gradually developed quite a little music group: Dave and I on the violins, Dave also played guitar; Kay played the saxophone, we played duets or trios; Connie Elliot (now Donnan) played piano or accordion; Elda, Dave's wife, played marimba; and at times others would join us as we sang solos, duets, trios, quartets, etc.. I remember at my graduation banquet speech, suggesting that for all my professors' good teaching, Bible College had been more valuable to me in preparing me for ministry by exposure, rather than by academics.

Miracles, and the obvious intervention by the Divine seemed to be the pattern for ministry, so much so, that I think we took it for granted and considered it normal and to be expected.

The way God provided for my (Lyle) first year of Bible College had to be Divine intervention. During my first year, as the graduation exercises approached, where all the men were expected to dress in navy, or dark suits, I only possessed one suit, powder blue. I had no money to buy another one, so I was preparing to wear my powder blue suit, when a lady from Kingston, Ontario picked my name out of a list of students and felt God told her to send me, I think it was fifty-seven dollars and some cents. I went down town Peterborough and bought myself a dark suit to within pennies of the amount the lady sent me.

THANK YOU JESUS! We also received many 'Pentecostal Handshakes', as we used to call it, when someone would feel impressed to shake your hand and leave a deposit of money in your hand. God met all our needs.

I've often thought how gracious and patient the people were that we first preached to. For instance, I think I might have preached for almost an hour on Romans, chapter 6 at one church. Of course, I had probably been studying Romans 6 that week in College, so I was full of it. Fortunately, this town was in revival at the time, so they could probably handle it. At the end of the morning service a little nine-year old girl prophesied. Wow! I can feel it to this day.

After the night service, people were so full of the Holy Ghost, one sixteen-year old female teenager who did not know any French language, was so drunk in the Spirit that she could speak nothing but French as she staggered with help down to the back of the church. Her grandmother was waiting to get a ride home, but someone else had to volunteer to drive them, since the teenager was too 'drunk in the Spirit' to drive.

We were billeted in two different homes. I will never forget the impression it made on my life, when I was exposed to this godly family. The details may be off by a year or so, but there were two children in the home, I think about four and six years of age. They apparently had a disagreement in the backyard and promptly came in and placed two chairs facing each other and apologized for getting angry and then prayed together. I don't remember all of the prayer, of course, but some of the little four-year-olds prayer was, "Hallelujah, thank you Jesus for the green grass and fresh air, etc." There shouldn't be any problems in the churches if the homes all settled their differences like that.

One Sunday night, Dave was preaching. I've teased him since, that I have never heard a more mixed up version of John 3:16. Two young ladies were passing by, one was heading to commit suicide, but they felt they should turn in at the church. They sat in the back seat just inside the door so they could get out fast, but instead they were the first to the altar to meet Jesus as their Savior.

**Lyle Carbert and Dave Moulden,
violin duet (1958-1961)**

One other time, the group, I think it was made up of Dave and Elda, Kay and I, and Doreen Cowell singing, with Connie Elliott on the piano and Dave was playing his guitar. We were doing a song that we were fairly familiar with, "Give Me Strength, Oh Lord, to Stand". The problem was Dave's guitar strap let go and he was getting lower and lower as he tried to hold his slipping guitar. Well, if you knew Doreen, she just couldn't hold it and finally broke out laughing and we never quite finished the song. People were gracious to these Bible College students. Of course, we were somewhat embarrassed because we wanted to represent Christ first of all, and the Bible College secondly. These happenings had a way of getting back to the Teaching Staff at the College. Each Assignment Group was desirous to always do their best and leave a good impression. (So much for that!)

Bible College musical assignment group

During my first year, Kay's second year, the Bible School's choir was invited to sing at the Missionary Convention which was held in Kingston, Ontario and London, Ontario. We were both singing in the choir. Mrs. Smith was the choir director and we all had to 'toe the line' under her leadership. This was unique and special training for all of us. We dearly loved her and we have many special memories of choir practice, and of course, the trips.

However, for the London convention, Mrs. Smith was unable to go with the choir, but the plans were already in place. To this day, I am not certain why this happened, but she asked Kay to direct the choir in her absence. A surprised, nervous, but excited Kay received many instructions and directives from Mrs. Smith. So, the choir headed to London. Thank God, that the choir members all remembered their parts and were all very cooperative and God made us a blessing. After the service, Kay's pastor, Rev. J. A. Pearson, came up to Lyle and said, "I see she is already directing you." We were not married yet!

25

Money, Marriage and Ministry

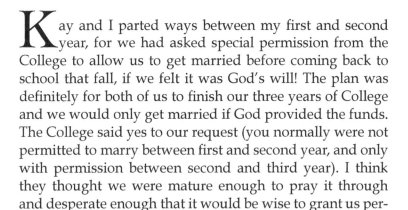

K ay and I parted ways between my first and second year, for we had asked special permission from the College to allow us to get married before coming back to school that fall, if we felt it was God's will! The plan was definitely for both of us to finish our three years of College and we would only get married if God provided the funds. The College said yes to our request (you normally were not permitted to marry between first and second year, and only with permission between second and third year). I think they thought we were mature enough to pray it through and desperate enough that it would be wise to grant us permission since we were already ministering together.

That summer, Kay had a job lined up at Glen-Muir's Drive-in, in the north end of Tillsonburg. I had a job on construction in Red Lake, Ontario, only about 1,500 miles apart. This was a wise decision, in that Kay could make more money working down East and it also allowed her to make the necessary plans for the wedding, and I could make more money up North on construction if I worked long hours. We both would live at home with our parents, which was also the cheapest arrangement. I arrived home on May 3, 1959.

I started work immediately for Stan Dell Construction. Within the first week Stan made me the labor foreman of the crew. At the start of the second week Stan suggested, I could sub-contract some of the work if I wanted. So I was labor foreman for eight hours and sub-contractor for the other eight to twelve hours that I worked. I picked the three best workers in my day crew and offered them shares in the sub-contracting. My crew, of four, was accomplishing more in the evening and night than I could get out of the crew of nine or ten during the day. I accepted this as a sign from the Lord, God's favor, and I phoned Kay to start planning for the wedding because the money was surely going to be there. I worked as much as twenty hours a day with God giving me the strength and Kay set the wedding date for September 12, 1959. By the end of the summer, Dad was paid back his $600.00 and we had enough money to pay for our tuition, room and board for the coming school year and still had a little left over for shoe laces and toothpaste. If not supernatural provision, it was certainly God's favor that provided opportunity and health. Praise the Lord!

We should have taken a movie of the registrar's face, as we stepped up to the registrar's desk and counted out the money in $20.00 bills, for both of our year's tuition, room and board and text books, etc.

I was involved with sports, such as Y.M.C.A. basketball, hockey and a few games of flag football. David Mainse, of 100 Huntley Street fame, was in his third year (the Witness Class), when I was in my first. David Mainse started a Bible College radio broadcast, 'Truth Aflame', while I was there. I had the privilege of being chosen as the announcer. The next year David Moulden took over the responsibility for producing the program and I carried on as the announcer. That was good preparation for a stint I did on radio. I'll share this experience with you later.

I had some spiritual challenges in Bible College. The first challenge was, to find out that everybody that goes to Bible College is not a mature saint, as a matter of fact the minority were! The second challenge was, to find out that when your guard is down your old nature is pretty close to the surface, and you tend to let your guard down when you enter Bible

College (at least I did). The third lesson, at least for me, was to realize that you are most vulnerable when encountering disappointment from the ones from whom you would least expect it.

Remember the compulsive demonic anger from which I was delivered? Well, a certain teacher had just the right attitude to catch me off guard. I almost lost it! It scared me so badly, that I ran all the way up the stairs to the third floor where the Bible College prayer room was. I would pray right through to confident victory and walk down the stairs, only to encounter this person again, turn around, all the way up, etc., three times.

Thank you Jesus! By graduation I was that teacher's fair-haired boy.

I had learned by one of my first meal lines that if you wanted to be at the front of the line, you had to show up about twenty minutes early. So I did! A certain third year student decided he could come five minutes before the door opened and just step into the front of the line as he had apparently been accustomed to doing. Well, thankfully, I had been delivered, but I wasn't quite sanctified enough to allow that arrogant attitude to take over. I didn't even get angry, but he did, and that never happened again.

One of the favorite tricks to play in Bible College was 'tubbing'. You filled the bathtub on the second floor men's dorm with COLD water. You and your buddies picked your unsuspecting victim (who either was a challenge or dutifully deserved it), grabbed him by the legs and arms and lowered him ever-so-slowly into the submerged position and ran.

One of the people who got 'tubbed' was the third year student who several felt could benefit from it. I didn't get directly involved, just in case he thought it was for personal reasons, but I watched from nearby! It actually had some funny highlights to that story that I would be happy to share privately.

I would like to take a fair amount of the responsibility for 'tubbing' the Dean of men, Norm Schlarbaum. He was well-loved and respected, but he went ahead and became engaged to Dorothy. So we felt that deserved a 'tubbing' celebration.

'Tubbing' by this time had been outlawed because the water always ran down and caused problems in the ceilings on the main floor. However, we organized who was going to be at which arm, leg, head or whatever, and proceeded one evening down the hall to his apartment. We stood outside his door and sang, "For He's A Jolly Good Fellow", etc.. I believe Bob had his saxophone, or something like that, and we sang and played with great volume.

Well, the Dean just cranked up the volume on his stereo, so we sang louder and knocked on his door. He was suspicious and delayed answering for some time. Finally from inside the door came this booming sergeant's voice, "What do you all want?" I shouted back, "We would like to honor you on the occasion of your engagement!" After many exchanges and delays, Norm Schlarbaum came out all dressed up in some old pants and a t-shirt, dressed for a 'tubbing' (You see, Norm had this seventh or eighth sense, that let him know when something unusual was up. It was almost impossible to get anything past him or surprise him). We picked him up, carried him up the stairs and plunked him in the cold water. Good success! Good sport!

There were experiences like dishes, pots and pans, night watchman, etc. that I'm sure everybody enjoyed.

26

God's Miraculous Deliverance

While I was in my second or third year, there was a guest speaker at our spiritual emphasis week in the Dublin Street Church. A lady came into the evening service that had a fixation for this man of God. He apparently reminded her of the doctor who had jilted her. My friend and I were assigned to protect him. We were told to walk in with her, sit one on either side, so we could grab her if she bolted for the platform. My friend got in the front pew before her, but she hugged tight to the end of the pew. Kay and I just slipped in the pew behind her.

Sure enough on cue she bolted for the platform with my friend hanging onto one arm. I stepped up quickly and grabbed her by the other arm and we picked her up so that her feet were off of the floor. Kay followed behind us. The lady was noisy and trying to tear her clothes off! Her feet were running full speed in mid-air! We just carried her through the side door and down the stairs to the lower auditorium where we put her on her knees at the front seats. She was writhing and hissing like a snake! (Now, I want you to understand, that this was the first time that we were directly involved in a demonic deliverance or exorcism.) I commanded the demon to come out in Jesus' name! The lady turned and growled at me in a bass voice, "This kind cometh not out but by prayer and fasting". I was caught kind of stunned, because I had felt the Lord had been talking to me about fasting. I had decided to start the next day. Now, I thought that maybe I had missed it and I was too late!

Suddenly, I woke up to the fact that the voice I had just heard was not the lady's voice. She could not possibly have spoken with that full bass voice. I commanded again for the demon to shut up and come out and he did. The lady got up, sat in the seat and started to sob and say, "Thank you, Jesus, thank you Jesus!" Then she went silent for a few moments. I was not aware what my friend was doing, but I suspect he was on the other side praying with me, probably ordering Satan to get out as well. Dean Schlarbaum had followed us down the stairs and was standing beside us against the wall, I suspect praying the same as we were, but I was so focused on this lady, I barely noticed him. All of a sudden the lady started to hiss and shake and writhe again and down she went to her knees. We commanded the demon to leave again. The same bass voice said, "Hit me right here and I'll come out!" (as the lady reached over her shoulder and patted her back), (Dean Schlarbaum's comment was that he thought that I might hit her and knock her through three rows of chairs).

Again we commanded the demon to shut up and leave, and he did! She sat up again and started to sob and thank Jesus again. She sat quiet for a few minutes and then started to hiss, jumped up and ran towards the front stairs yelling with her own voice, "I don't want to be set free, I don't want to be set free, I like it this way" and out the door she went never to come back.

I was bothered with that and considered that experience as a failure. As I prayed about it, here is the lesson I felt the Lord taught me, and it has stood the test of many years and experiences. We have authority over the demons but we do not have the authority over a person's will. God Himself won't force you against your will. If you are determined to go to hell, you break the heart of God and of those that love you, but, nobody can stop you! God actually has stopped me from on-going deliverance with a person who doesn't want it, because they get worse each time. "The house is swept and garnished", but empty, when the demons come back and move in "the last state is worse than the first" [Matthew 12:44, 45].

My friend and I took on another project one night in the wee hours. There was a knock on the door in our married residence which turned out to be a drunken man who was looking for a place to sleep and some money. Well the bed wasn't possible because our wives were in their respective beds, so we took (let's call him Roy) Roy down to the first year classroom in the basement of the married residence. My friend and I started to pray up a storm, and sometime later, Roy sat up turned and looked at us as if he had come out of a trance. He was sober, puzzled, and didn't recognize us or where he was and he didn't even understand what was going on inside of him. We shared salvation with him and he wept his way through to faith. We asked him if he had anymore alcohol with him and he reached inside his coat and pulled out a flask of whiskey. He asked what he should do with this now that he was a Christian. We suggested that he should dump it down the sink in the kitchen. He got up and followed us to the kitchen and stood there, glug, glug, glug, pouring this whiskey down the sink. He said, "I must be crazy! I sure never did anything like this before!" I wish we could tell you the good news of the rest of the story, however we never were able to follow up on the only drunk I ever saw sobered up as we prayed. Only God!

27

Automobile Miracles

One interesting miraculous provision, was an assignment to Renfrew, Ontario. We drove there in my friend's '51 Oldsmobile (which, by this time, was already a step of faith). When we went to leave on Sunday night, Dave knew we needed gasoline, but in the after meeting excitement forgot to fill up. The gauge was already on empty before we left and Dave knew he could not drive out of town that way, but didn't wake up to the reality until we were too far to expect the car to make it back to Renfrew. We kept going, praying and looking for some opportunity to fill up. We passed through several little towns, but at that hour of the night, nothing was open. So, we prayed some more and kept going. Most of the way was bush, as I remember it, with the odd little village popping up periodically. The car kept going as if pushed by the breath of God, for there could not possibly have been any gasoline left in the tank. Dave assured us that, when that tank said empty, it was empty. We finally pulled in to Kaladar, Ontario some 75-80 miles later and ran out of gas at the pumps. Thank you Jesus!

The next morning, the phone in the married residence rang, and it was for the Carberts. As we had begun to expect, it was Mom Fairs. Her question was, 'what happened late last night?' As we compared time, we learned that Mom had been awakened during the night, actually the exact time that we were traveling, to pray for us. She didn't know what was happening, but knew that she had to get out of bed and pray for us. She prayed until she felt that God had answered and we were all fine.

That would be an example of a prophetic dream or a word of knowledge [1 Cor. 12:8].

Mom Fairs had the gift of intercession and was available to the voice of the Lord at any time of day or night, without knowing the problem. She was obedient to answer the call to pray, and God used her in this gifting many times. We valued Mom Fairs as one of our prayer warriors, because she was sensitive to the voice of God. When she went to her heavenly resting place, we missed this ministry gift, but God called others to fulfill the need.

We had a Bible College assignment to Tillsonburg, Ontario, (Kay's home church) when the generator went out of the '51 Oldsmobile. My friend was sure that the brushes were shot. He found a screwdriver and removed the old brushes, sure enough they were worn out. We arrived Sunday morning, so there was no place open to get the car repaired. We finally found a garage in Tillsonburg that was open, where we could buy a set of brushes for that particular generator. We proceeded to put them in. All we had was the screwdriver that we screwed them out with. My friend would carefully line up the screw and the brush, I held my hand underneath to keep it from falling down under the car or into a crevice in the motor. We were dressed for church and feeling pressure for time. Well, the parts almost made it and then dropped . . . twenty-one times. Then my friend decided Jesus was a better mechanic than we were and laid hands on the car and started to pray. The brushes went in the first try, but upside down. So, he took them out and they went in again the first try. Jesus was not only a carpenter,

but handled the mechanics for a '51 Oldsmobile. We made
it on time!

The Oldsmobile was fast playing out, so we started
praying and looking for another vehicle. Downtown
Peterborough, we spotted a beautiful 1953 Cadillac nine passenger limousine on a car lot. Wow! That's what we needed
to haul our group plus the instruments and luggage. We
had looked at some old station wagons and we could get
more in this limousine. The asking price was somewhere
between $1,100.00 and $1,200.00. Well, we had no money
but felt we should pursue this. $1,200.00 back then was the
equivalent of two years in Bible College. Where could we
possibly get that kind of money? We dickered and prayed,
prayed and dickered, we offered them $800.00 cash (we still
didn't have any). They said absolutely not and then told
us the history of the car, probably to impress us. Canadian
General Electric bought a new limousine every two years as
their staff car. When they traded the old one in, the Roman
Catholic Convent bought it for the nuns travel car. The
emphasis was to impress how well the car was cared for.
This was the nuns' trade-in. Well, we stuck to our price and
used all the persuasions we could, including explaining
clearly what it was to be used for. They said no again.

One afternoon we received a phone call at the Bible
College from the car dealer. They said if we could come
up with the $800.00 cash, they had decided to sell us the
limo. Half the prayer was answered, but still no money. I
had never borrowed money from a bank before, and this
didn't seem the most opportune time, since I had no income
except by faith. Banks don't seem to understand that too
well, and I had no money in my pocket.

Kay suggested calling her brother, Malcolm to see if he
would back a loan of $800.00 from the bank. Now is the time,
when nobody but Kay and I would understand the strange-
ness of this suggestion. Malcolm wasn't stingy but he was

careful with his money. Kay seemed to get special favors from Malcolm, without even asking, but Lyle was new to the family. An $800.00 loan at the bank seemed pretty far out except we felt we were to go that route. Malcolm made the trip to Peterborough from Tillsonburg, looked the car over, went with us to the bank and co-signed the loan. However, God provided and we never missed a payment!

My third year in Bible College was an experience of faith. God met us in a variety of ways! Kay had gone to the Unemployment Insurance to apply for a job, specifically clerical work, on a four-day week, because our ministry required our availability to travel on the weekends, starting on Friday. The person at the U.I. office, assured her that they had to find her a job with these specifics or she was eligible for unemployment insurance. So, she was given a check every two weeks. Kay was now doing her P.H.T. degree (Putting Hubby Through). She did some babysitting. She was also contacted by the local Public School system to do some volleyball and basketball refereeing. Her cousin, Lucille (who was one of our bridesmaids), suggested Kay to her father, who was principal in Whitby Elementary School. When the need for referees was known, there was a shortage of lady referees for the girls' teams, Lucille suggested Kay to him. Thus, she was busy refereeing in the area schools. They paid the traveling costs plus fees.

Weekends we were out traveling in ministry and even some during the week but when payments were due the money was there. The tires on this Cadillac were expensive so the tire shop advised me to use recaps, after all, they carried a mileage warranty. I don't know how many tires we peeled but the tire shop kept replacing them right to the end of the school year. The mileage on the highway was great! The big boat rode so smoothly that Kay would put the bucket seat down in the back and type our notes as we traveled. One trip to Lethbridge, Alberta, we averaged 25 miles per gallon. God supplied the right vehicle, because we could put the instruments inside the car, between the front seat and the back seat, plus seven or eight people and put all luggage in the trunk.

God's Magnificent Provision

We were approaching graduation when I was given the honor, and honor it was, to be the class preacher at our graduation in Massey Hall in Toronto. The rules were that I had to have my message prepared, typed and memorized a month ahead of graduation. My assigned subject was 'The Baptism of the Holy Ghost'. I got into that preparation with a passion and was blessed many times over, during the research just to see the power of God down through history. I don't know that my 'sermon' was so great, but I'll never forget the explosion in Massey Hall, as God honored His Word with signs following. The message was followed by tongues, interpretation, and prophecy and then the student body choir, led by Mrs. Beulah Smith, burst out in song as the whole audience of 2,000 people rose to their feet and sang, '*Until Then*'. What a sense of God's presence.

28

God's Calling to Serve in His Vineyard

W ell, one of the disconcerting lessons I learned at this time, was the beginning of my understanding of the politics that was creeping into the Church. Immediately following the graduation banquet I was approached by the District Superintendent to go to a church which had been chosen for me, with an enviable salary, etc., a well-established church that apparently wanted me to come as their pastor. I discovered that the District Executive had a tendency to do these favors for the graduation speakers or the valedictorian.

The first problem was, that some time prior to this, Rev. David Mainse, who was pastoring a little church nearby, had a concern for an old work that had been closed down for over three years, about seventeen miles from David's church, and had asked us to pray about it. Kay and I prayed, and without ever having seen the place, felt a definite call to go to this troubled area after graduation. I tried to explain the situation to the District Superintendent, but he seemed really red-faced, angry, and upset with me, as if I was going against the District Executive decision.

Now, I hope you can understand my reaction, because, I was, in my ignorance not sure how to handle this unexpected reaction. The Superintendent stated quite adamantly that "the District won't support you in there". I responded, "It never entered my mind to ask for support from the District. I believe that if God gives me a horse, He will also give me the oats to feed it". The Superintendent then informed me that the District had already decided to close that place down for good. Well, I didn't think that would make any difference to what God had told Kay and I to do, so I stated that to the Superintendent who just shook his head and walked off. I quickly said, "Brother, please don't be upset with us. We'll pray about your suggestion and let you know".

Well we did pray as openly and bare-heartedly as we could, but nothing changed unless it was more excitement to do the will of God in that place. I informed the Superintendent who didn't seem very pleased with this twenty-six year old upstart. The Presbyter for that section was Rev. Don Ellis, who prepared the people in that place for our coming. Don Ellis pastored in a church just twenty miles away and knew some of the people that had formerly attended this church. Kay and I went home to Red Lake and worked for a couple of months as we prepared to start in our first church, July 1st, 1961.

Red Lake was a shocking experience for Kay the first time she visited there, because she had been raised on a farm in Tillsonburg, Ontario. She was somewhat protected from exposure to the elements of a hard rock northern town in Ontario. The alcoholics were a constant on the streets of downtown Red Lake. The native Indians that were alcoholics hung around town to feed their habit. Most of the native people on the Reserves were a beautiful, self-sufficient, live by their own culture people. But the Reserves were mostly reached by long boat rides or plane rides and not nearly so readily accessible to the booze in town.
The first Saturday night that Kay was in Red Lake, we

witnessed this rather stout native lady dragging another lady by the hair and kicking her. Both ladies were obviously inebriated beyond sensibility. What a shock for my sheltered bride! Often, she noticed some of these drunken women would be walking along and just stop and spread their feet and relieve themselves. As disgusting as this seems, it really was preparation for some of our future ministry to a variety of addicts.

When we were scheduled to leave for our new church, Red Lake was isolated by one of those giant Northern Ontario forest fires. The highway was cut off by the fire, the town had been notified to be ready, at the sounding of the siren, to take fresh water, etc. and head for the lake, where as many boats as they could round up would transport us up the lake out of the way of the raging fire, which was heading, from the west, straight towards the town. The people who knew how to pray, prayed! Probably some who didn't know how to pray, learned in a hurry! One of the concerns was, with a fire of this magnitude, that the oxygen would even be scarce for these thousands of people gathered on the lake. Well, as forest fires do create their own winds, and as people prayed, the fire turned, almost at a right angle, and headed south southeast, which meant it was going to miss the town but cross highway #105, the only road out of town. It looked like delay! But God!

We were able to leave Red Lake by July 3rd, 1961 and head out in our Cadillac. As we passed over the bridge at Bug River, I think about eight miles south of town, we could see where the fire had crossed the highway and had burned down an old log cabin of a pioneer, W. John Franks, who had prospected and trapped in there for years. We later learned that he was safe. As the fire approached, he grabbed a blanket and jumped in the river with this wet blanket over his head until the fire had passed over. That had been his home for thirty-three years.

Before we leave the Red Lake story, please indulge me to tell you another prospector's story.

142

Jacques St. Paul was a friend to the teenagers. He was an old prospector who roughed it in a log cabin at the entrance to Skookum Bay. He was a small man, although his brother Clem was about 5'11" and broad shouldered with a barrel-chest and huge arms from working as a bona fide lumberjack.

I saw a drunk man challenge Clem to a fight in front of the Lakeview Bakery, but Clem wouldn't fight. After a lot of aggravation, Clem just reached out with one hand and picked that man up and pushed him against the wall, warning him to back off. The antagonist was kicking and flailing the air until Clem just dropped him and walked away. No fight!!!

Jacques was a small retiring man who could be missed in a crowd, but the young people used to frequent his log cabin for the hospitality and indulgence. Jacques would let them smoke, etc., and feed them some of his homemade stew. The food wasn't to my liking, but I used to love borrowing his canoe. The food often consisted of coffee boiled on top of the old wood stove which he just kept adding solids and liquids, as desired. Sometimes he had a roast, which was boiled and left in the open pot on top of the stove. He would just take it out, cut off a slice, and throw it back into the pot.

We used to especially like to borrow his canoe at night and three or four of us would paddle around Skookum or along the lakeshore in the big stretch. One memorable event, which we repeated more than once, was to paddle up quietly and watch the native Pow Wow. I don't know if half the stories told were true, but because of them this experience held us in a great deal of suspense. We were told all kinds of weird stories of what they would do to us white kids if they caught us. Well, who knows, we never got caught!!!

29

Bible Camp Experiences

———————⌒⌒⌒———————

O ur schedule was to arrive at the Lakeshore Pentecostal Camp, just outside of Cobourg, Ontario for the annual camp meeting. Kay was going to help Orville and Dorothy White in the kitchen and I was to be in charge of the Booth, duties that were ours for the summers of '61, '62 and '63. We were housed in a little room next to the railway tracks. Every time a train went by you felt like pulling your feet up, until the train was passed, so they wouldn't get run over.

Lakeshore Pentecostal Camp where Kay and Lyle worked for the summers of 1961 through 1963

Camp meeting was a time for meeting a lot of new people and enjoying great experiences. One of the summers we served there, Pastor Orville White asked me to preach at the Friday night service in his church at Port Hope, Ontario. Sometime during that Friday morning, I went to put a pop bottle in the cooler and went right to my knees in pain. The pain just seemed to take my legs out from under me. I had never experienced such a problem in all my quarter century of living. I discovered, that I could stand carefully, if I didn't turn my body or move my hand more than about eighteen inches from my side. We called the camp nurse and she could not tell for sure what it was. She instructed me to not aggravate the problem and if it persisted or got worse I would have to go in to Cobourg to see the Doctor. So, I hobbled around carefully the rest of the day trying not to aggravate the problem. I put pop in and took it out of the cooler by sidling up close to the cooler and bending my knees to lower my hand into the cooler. I felt silly, because every once in a while I would over extend my capabilities and end up on the floor in pain. I wondered how I would be able to preach that night, and kept praying for the Lord to touch me.

It came time for us to leave for Port Hope, so I carefully edged myself into the car and someone else drove. We arrived at the church and I moved up the stairs and onto the platform with great care, so as not to be embarrassed by an attack of pain.

The service went along fairly well and I tried to slowly stand when everyone else stood and sit very carefully when everyone else sat. Just before I was to preach, Pastor White called on Brother MacDonald to pray. Brother MacDonald, with his Scottish brogue, began to pray. In the middle of his prayer he shouted out, "and heal Brrrro. Carrrrberrrt", and I raised both my arms with no pain. Hallelujah!!! I proceeded to do all the calisthenics I could think of to check it out. I was completely and instantly healed. Praise the Lord! I never did find out what caused the problem, so I suppose all the doubters would find some excuse to not give God the credit for the healing. I don't particularly care what the problem was or the explanation of the method. I just was extremely thankful to God that when we prayed I was healed.

In the summer of 1962, when Candace our daughter was just a month old, Kay again went to help in the kitchen at camp as usual. We were thankful for a 'gramma' who took on the babysitting job in a little cabin on the grounds. Ralph and Evelyn Rutledge were expecting their first child and were attending the camp. Because of what happened next, Kay gets remembered every July by Evelyn.

Ralph and Evelyn were not familiar with the Eastern Ontario area, and therefore they had no one who could suggest a doctor for the very pregnant Evelyn. As babies have a way of doing, they come into this world pretty much on their own schedule. This is precisely what baby Rutledge was about to do.

A frantic, soon-to-be-a-Daddy, Ralph, knocked on our cabin door and with a flurry of words told of their predicament. Kay got in touch with her doctor, who had delivered our Candace a month before. He told Kay to have Evelyn come to the Cobourg Hospital and he would meet us there.

Thank God for available medical help and a Doctor who took his medical status seriously. That's how Ruth arrived into this world.

There was a family named Brown, who were from Kingston, attending camp. They invited me to stop in and visit them in Kingston some time, because they had some special footage of me water-skiing at the camp. In Red Lake, Ontario in the '50's, I often dressed up like a clown or a fat lady and put on a little comical water ski act as previously mentioned. We teamed up with Murray McLeod on a couple of occasions. I got inspired to carry on the act every once in a while over the years, at such places as Lakeshore Pentecostal Camp in Cobourg, Sylvan Lake Sunnyside Pentecostal Camp, etc.. Apparently, the Brown's got some enviable footage of my stint at Cobourg with a big lady's hat and dress. I never saw it, but maybe by some unusual providence I may yet.

In the three summers that we were involved there, there were some memorable speakers, such as Tommy Barnett, Brother Barham from Texas, H. H. Barber from Winnipeg, etc. We, at our small church, all thirteen of us, were honored to have H. H. Barber consent to preach the Sunday morning service for us since he wasn't involved in the morning service at Camp. He encouraged the people by sharing how he had started his ministry in a little church in Elmira, Ontario.

I took on the task of helping police the grounds at night, since I was a late-nighter by nature. I used my Cadillac limo for my cruise car around the campground. It had started to burn oil pretty badly, so I had purchased another Cadillac for its motor. The body had been damaged badly, but the motor was in good shape, so my ambition, which ran ahead of my knowledge, was to just take the old motor out and put in the newer motor. That sounds simple, but for me it wasn't. I wouldn't bore you with the tedious method of this non-mechanic as he laboriously took each nut etc. and placed it in a pattern on a piece of cardboard, so he would know precisely where it went when it came time to put it together again. Job done! It ran!

However, I didn't know enough to check the motor mounts. Driving this big boat of a car around the campgrounds, chasing teenagers, etc., I cracked the motor mounts. During camp we drove back and forth to our little church, to preach on the weekends. After camp we drove to Tillsonburg to pick up our meager belongings for our historic move to the living quarters on the back of our first church.

The Cadillac was loaded to the hilt, with a cardboard wardrobe and some other sundry belongings fastened on top. My brother, Keith, and his girlfriend, came to help us and were traveling with us in the limousine, towards our new place of ministry, when the car started to boil even to the spraying up on the windshield. I hadn't been able to connect the sensor to the dashboard successfully with the motor change and didn't even know the car was getting hot until it started to spray out. We were approaching Markham Road on the #401 Highway. The traffic was very heavy. I was in the inside lane and decided to try and make it to Markham Road.

Well, we made it over to the turnoff lane and wheeled down the off ramp to a B.A. or Gulf service station. I pulled in, shut the motor off, lifted the hood carefully, and was met with a cloud of steam. The mechanic came and looked at it and said to just sit down until it cooled, but he thought it was pretty serious. So, we sat down and waited and prayed. When it cooled down the mechanic took a look at it and determined that we had blown the head gasket and warped the head. The cause was simple. The motor mounts broke and let the motor settle. The fan just cut my hose at the bottom of my radiator. They agreed to look for another motor for me etc. which added up to more money than I could imagine coming up with. Or else, the mechanic said he would give me $75.00 for the car as is, and loan me a half-ton truck to finish my move.

**Two cadillacs, two fathers, two brothers and Kay
(the one wife)**

If I had known better, I probably could have asked a
lot more because the mechanic's father was an automotive
engineer who completely rebuilt the motor and restored the
car to almost its original condition. Oh well, I felt the Lord
said to let it go. When I think about it, it might not have
been the best thing for this preacher to drive into this little
village of 289 people with a car, as I've jokingly suggested,
would still have the back-end coming into town as I nosed
the front end into the garage.

I'll help you understand how much room our Cadillac
had, when I tell you that we could barely get all the stuff
from the car into the half-ton truck, and even then Keith and
his girlfriend had to snuggle down in a corner in the back
of the half-ton (I don't know that they minded the snuggle).
We made the trip.

30

Our Firsts: First Place of Ministry and Our First Daughter

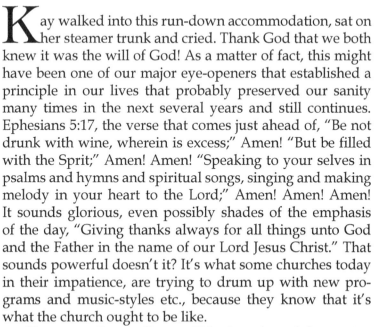

Kay walked into this run-down accommodation, sat on her steamer trunk and cried. Thank God that we both knew it was the will of God! As a matter of fact, this might have been one of our major eye-openers that established a principle in our lives that probably preserved our sanity many times in the next several years and still continues. Ephesians 5:17, the verse that comes just ahead of, "Be not drunk with wine, wherein is excess;" Amen! "But be filled with the Sprit;" Amen! Amen! "Speaking to your selves in psalms and hymns and spiritual songs, singing and making melody in your heart to the Lord;" Amen! Amen! Amen! It sounds glorious, even possibly shades of the emphasis of the day, "Giving thanks always for all things unto God and the Father in the name of our Lord Jesus Christ." That sounds powerful doesn't it? It's what some churches today in their impatience, are trying to drum up with new programs and music-styles etc., because they know that it's what the church ought to be like.

However, all our efforts will be in vain and frustrating if we don't learn this one lesson that God somehow was able to establish as a pattern in our lives. "<u>Wherefore be ye not unwise, but understanding what the will of the Lord is.</u>" Allow me to put it in my colloquial way as, "Don't be an idiot, before you do anything, find out what God's will is and do it!" In later years, I've formulated this statement; "After you are born again, there is absolutely, unequivocally, nothing, I mean nothing, more important than to learn to know the voice of God and obey it!" Everything else, and I mean everything else (your personal ambition, your private agenda, your personal goals, your wife, your husband, your family, what the rest of society thinks, what the church thinks, or even what you might imagine to be normal as successful or failure), everything else is just stuff that happens! There is absolutely, nothing, more important or more successful than obedience to God's perfect will! Amen!

Be encouraged my Christian friend, God isn't into confusion and you can pray after the pattern of James 1:4-8, "But let patience have her perfect work, that ye may be perfect and entire, wanting nothing. If any of you lack wisdom let him ask of God, that giveth to all men liberally, and upbraideth not; and it shall be given him. But let him ask in faith, nothing wavering. For he that wavereth is like a wave of the sea, driven with the wind and tossed. For let not that man think that he shall receive any thing of the Lord. A double-minded man is unstable in all his ways."

You can know the will of God if you dare to ask God and be ready to believe and act on what He speaks into your spirit. The results are none of your business, for fear that you might feel pride at seeming success or depression at seeming failure. The results are not your-doing, but that of God Almighty. All He asks of us is obedience, so that He can get His eternal work done, and He deserves all the credit. God knows what He is doing! Amazing! We keep thinking we can improve on God's plan! JUST OBEY! The last time I checked God's dictionary, I couldn't find the word 'whoops' in there. God is never caught by surprise, nor does He make any mistakes!

31

First Impression

S̶o we walk in the back door of the parsonage of our first place of ministry. The kitchen had been freshly painted, white with cherry red trim. The rats had taken over the basement and bats had taken over the attic; the roof leaked and had soaked the piano in the church auditorium; the sheet of ceiling panel was hanging down in the master bedroom upstairs; the windows had been boarded up for about three years; the cement steps out front were flaking and cracking; the outhouse (our plumbing system) was attached to the garage (which means it couldn't be moved) and was so full that a man couldn't sit on it without touching; the well hadn't been used for so long that it was polluted; the cistern in the basement was floating with dead rats that fell in and couldn't get out; the basement floor was dirt, riddled with rat holes; the people in town wouldn't talk to us; clover in the yard was four or five feet high with stalks like young trees; out the back door they had developed the habit of dumping their garbage into the little valley and dumping sawdust on top of it (rats' haven), etc..

The first job to be done, was the shingling of the roof. Pastor Don Ellis our Presbyter, helped us purchase some shingles and organized a work bee to repair the roof. Our neighbor, an older gentleman, was impressed when he saw the crew on the roof including Kay, as she joined the men shingling.

Our neighbor was probably one of the first people in town outside the church to be friendly. As a matter of fact, when he died, his wife became friendly with a Baptist friend, six miles down the road. They asked me to marry them and I agreed. She was United Church and he was Baptist. This was my first wedding, his second for he was a widower, and her third, for she had outlived her first two husbands. I might add that she outlived this one as well.

**Lyle's first wedding,
his second, her third**

We started into the task of cleaning up! My wife is especially good at this with her administrative organizing ability. We started immediately cutting clover with a scythe. The clover was so tough that it was gradually bending the scythe back. The side yard seemed quite sandy, so I started digging trenches for a septic field and a hole for a hand-poured septic tank. Kay was pregnant, but she was out there tamping cement with a hand-tamper for the septic tank late into the night. I was not going to touch that outhouse. I picked up a used tub and toilet and sink and, with the help of a plumber whom we were trying to bring to Jesus, we got the bathroom all working!

We had a little rat terrier that we had trained to do tricks. One of his tricks was to jump as high as five feet in the air to take cookies or whatever out of my mouth. We had told the plumber that he could not smoke in the house. I can tell your imagination is working already. This man, out of habit, took a cigarette out of his pocket and stuck it between his lips, when, zip, Boots jumped up and took the cigarette right out of his mouth. The man was startled, and said, "Okay, I get the message!"

Of course, we removed the boards from the windows in this old church and fixed up the yard to the best of our ability. We eventually installed an old furnace in the basement, so that we could take out the old space heaters.

When the first cold snap came in the fall of 1961, you could pretty well tell how long you had preached by how many times during the service you stepped off the platform, while singing or preaching and stoked the fire in the middle of the aisle, about two-thirds of the way towards the back.

By mid-winter, it was obvious that the walls weren't insulated (actually later we discovered that wet sawdust had settled in the walls). Even with the two foot log stove in the living room and the cook stove in the kitchen, both stoked with wood and coal for the night, until the back of the stove was red-hot, were not sufficient to keep a dipper of water sitting on the counter in the far corner of the kitchen from freezing.

With this extreme cold weather, the bedroom upstairs was about the same temperature as the outside. We piled all of our blankets on the bed and slept in long johns and sweaters. Even at that, I would jump out of bed, dress as fast as I could, run down stairs and stir up the fires. When they were 'roaring' hot, Kay would get out of bed, dress quickly and go down to make breakfast. Hopefully, the water in the pail was thawed out by this time. Sometimes, I would have to place the pail of frozen water on the stove to thaw out.

Our daughter wasn't born yet. However, there were days after she was born, that we would place her playpen on the kitchen table in order for her to play. The floors were very drafty. Such were some of the experiences of our first years as Pastors.

32

The Joy of the Lord

Whenen we arrived, our congregation was made up of five senior pensioners: with a mother of ten, four of whom came to Sunday school and Church. Her husband who had an alcoholic problem, wouldn't give her money for the church, so she faithfully tithed her groceries. Praise the Lord!

I was young and healthy, but I felt the Lord had been quite explicit that I should give myself full time to ministry and not work for pay. I helped eighty-three year-old Mr. Sommers drill some water wells around the country, but I wouldn't take any remuneration. The maximum offering in that church, I had been informed, was about $5.00 per week. The church, prior to finally being closed, had been in existence for over thirty years, with some great preachers, seemingly alternating with some disasters. Five dollars a week was still impossible to live on and run the church in 1961. But God . . . !

My first trip to the little general store went something like this: I walked the quarter of a mile (because you remember I had no car, after the demise of the Cadillac) to buy some bread and milk. I went into this friendly country store, but nobody would even make eye contact with me, including the old farmers sitting there chewing and spitting in the spittoon. I took my milk and bread to the counter to pay for them. Two young fellows were there on my right hand. I said, "Nice day", to the closest fellow, but he didn't answer me. Instead he put his open hand up between me and him and looked at his buddy and pointed towards me and then twirled his finger in a circle towards his right temple, signifying "He's crazy", meaning me of course. I left the store with a friendly "Be seeing you!" and walked home.

For the first year it was customary to walk down the sidewalk and meet someone who would summarily cross over to the other side of the street until we passed, and then come back over to the same side. Nobody would talk to us so we had lots of time to pray, read and study and to fix up the building and property.

This attitude seemed to change rather suddenly after the arrival of our daughter, Candace Arlene on June 21, 1962, weighing in at eight pounds nine and a half ounces. This was apparent, as gifts started to arrive at our door, such as sweater sets, blankets, etc. It would seem that her birth brought a 'break-through' in that little village.

Imagine the concern I (Kay) had, as I was in the hospital after Candace's birth and her Daddy came to visit us. He had some 'not-so-good' news. We had rats in the basement and that very morning the local newspaper had an article concerning a baby who had its nose bitten off by a rat. What had we gotten ourselves into? A new baby and a basement which was home to many rats.

Well, my fears were set at rest when Lyle arrived the next day, to tell me that our dog, Boots the First, a rat terrier, had almost dug himself under the wall digging for the rats. Now, no fear . . . Boots was on the job!!! Every night, and when Candace took a nap in her crib, Boots would take his post under her crib. How dare the rats to come close to that crib. It never happened! Praise the Lord!

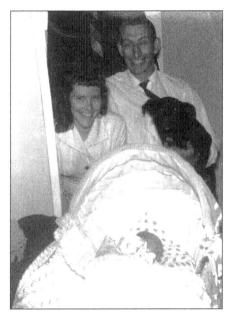

**Lyle, Kay and ten day old, Candace,
whose birth God used to break down the
resistance in the town.**

Within the first year we had pretty well rid ourselves of most of the rats, with the help of our rat terrier and some rat poison. After we started to poison the rats we had to keep Boots, from going down the basement and burying himself under the walls as he dug the rats out including some rat-chewed potatoes that the rats had buried. Instead, we would descend the stairs with a poker in our hands. The rats, sometimes dying from the poison, would run along the cistern wall and meet you at eye-level and stare. Klunk! One more, dead rat. We finally got rid of the bats by plugging the access holes up so that they couldn't get in. But before we did, I would like to tell you two bat stories.

One was when I caught a young bat and put it in a cardboard box. There was a little blond boy (I 'm sorry I've forgotten his name) that had made a habit of short-cutting through the garage while the building was unoccupied and we befriended him and chatted with him every day and encouraged him to feel free to pass through the garage if he pleased. When I caught this bat I decided to show it to him. He had never seen a bat before and was quite intrigued. I suggested he could have it as a pet, if he wanted it. He did, so I sent box and all home with him. I don't suppose that was the best way to 'win friends and influence people', since he came back the next day to tell me his mother was not too pleased and wouldn't let him bring it in to the house. She made him leave it in the box outside, lo and behold, it was gone in the morning.

33

Unusual Experiences

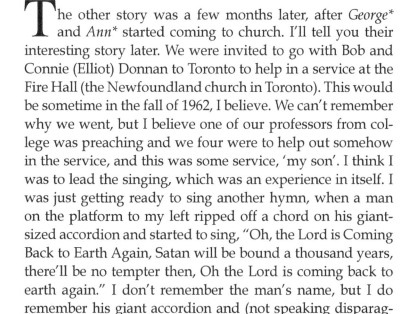

T he other story was a few months later, after *George** and *Ann** started coming to church. I'll tell you their interesting story later. We were invited to go with Bob and Connie (Elliot) Donnan to Toronto to help in a service at the Fire Hall (the Newfoundland church in Toronto). This would be sometime in the fall of 1962, I believe. We can't remember why we went, but I believe one of our professors from college was preaching and we four were to help out somehow in the service, and this was some service, 'my son'. I think I was to lead the singing, which was an experience in itself. I was just getting ready to sing another hymn, when a man on the platform to my left ripped off a chord on his giant-sized accordion and started to sing, "Oh, the Lord is Coming Back to Earth Again, Satan will be bound a thousand years, there'll be no tempter then, Oh the Lord is coming back to earth again." I don't remember the man's name, but I do remember his giant accordion and (not speaking disparagingly) I remember him having what is commonly known as a hair lip. It sure didn't hinder his volume as he belted out this hymn.

He repeated the chorus a couple of times, when a little man near the front on the right-hand side started to testify louder and louder until he broke in to a bona fide altar call, and the man on the accordion, took off on the next verse.

Up popped another man on the left side, testifying and preaching right into another altar call. Then the man on the accordion took off flying again and a third man about half-way back jumped into the aisle, and I mean jumped, and started to preach up a storm on the Second Coming of Christ, another stream of souls ran to the altar. We'll never forget this third testifier. He jumped up and down as high as the pew and preached with a powerful anointing. They didn't need me to be in charge of the singing, the Holy Spirit took over and we just tried not to get in the way. After a while the college professor preached and another stream of people came to the altar. The church was packed to the doors with standing-room only! As people came to the altar more people came in the door. Glory! We enjoyed all the Divine interruptions. Now back to the story that came out of this trip.

When Candace was about two or three months old, we were invited to go to Toronto. Kay had never had to leave her baby girl before and was hesitant. However, *Ann**, bless her heart, persuaded us to go and she would come and sleep in the spare bedroom and look after Candace.

Boots (our rat Terrier) was trained to not go into the spare bedroom. He would lay right under Candace's crib in our bedroom. *Ann** had gone to bed reading 'Rivers of Blessing' by G. F. Atter. It had spoken of the Holy Spirit like a dove, and *Ann** fell asleep lying on her back, thinking about this presence of the Holy Spirit being like a dove, when swish, she felt this rough brush of wings going by her face. She said that her first thoughts were, that she thought that was pretty rough for the Holy Spirit. She jumped out of bed in the dark, and reached for the light switch by the door. The light came on and there she found herself face to face with a person. She said, that she pretty nearly died of a heart attack until she realized that the other person was her reflection in the vanity mirror right beside the light switch. When she finally got her breath, she realized that object in flight was a bat, which had come down from the attic. It flew under her bed and she didn't know what to do, so she tried to coax Boots into her bedroom but he wouldn't come. She finally calmed down and went downstairs to get a broom to sweep the bat out from under the bed.

When we arrived home the next day she was still bug-eyed and her eyes got bigger as she told of her experience. I think that was the last of the bats that we encountered. Part of the solution was to replace the ceiling panel that was hanging down.

34

Growth in the Church

One by one, people started to show up for church, some fairly regularly and others just once in a long while. There was a bachelor, I suspected in his thirties, a couple with their red-haired teenaged daughter, another man who lived in a small house on the next road straight back of the church, and a local barber. I have a story to tell that I was asked to include for Hester (Rowbottom) Borsheim, who has done Kay's hair for years and periodically cuts mine.

I went into the barber's place with ulterior motives, of course, because I needed my hair cut and he needed to hear about walking with the Lord. He had pretty well finished cutting my hair and trimming around my ears when we kind of came to a high point in our discussion about the things of the Lord. He had his scissors nervously snipping away when he started to excuse his illicit relationship. I, in my youthful, usual brashness said with much passion, "If you don't get honest with yourself and with God and straighten your life out you'll go to hell!" The barber just kept snipping those scissors even more nervously and went right across my eyebrows. I've had bushy eyebrows from that day to this and have to constantly pull the long hairs out that curl into my eyes. The moral of this story is not to preach hell-fire and brimstone to your barber while he still has any tools in his hand. Thank the Lord he wasn't shaving my throat with a straight razor! However, the barber used to come to church fairly often after that.

David Mainse had resigned his church and moved on to another pastorate. The young man who followed him in that pastorate, was my classmate and good friend Bill. Under David Mainse's ministry in that church, *George** and *Ann** got saved. *Ann** could drink or cuss any man under the table. *George** had been raised Anglican, but never knew the Lord. When these two became Christians, it was town news, and the turn-around in their lives had an impact on this little church. *George** and *Ann** used to drive around town in their big '58 Dodge and make at least two trips per Sunday morning, picking up people for church. They never held any official position or desired such. They were spiritually humble and appreciative of their salvation. *George** sometimes ushered but then, either of these folks would do anything to help in the church including the cleaning.

One board meeting, under the Pastor's leadership, one of the board members, who was *George** and *Ann's** neighbor, brought a letter signed by all the board members and requested the Pastor to sign it. The gist of it was, that they had discovered *George** and *Ann** were not married and presumed to be living in sin. The request of the letter was to remove their church membership and let them know, that they were not welcome to attend that church until their testimony was clear.

Some of our first congregation

Pastor Bill phoned me to ask me what I thought. I was righteously indignant, to put it mildly, but God enabled me to hold my peace. I didn't know the whole story, but I knew *George** and *Ann**. Apparently, they had decided to try and serve Jesus at home and not attend any church, if it was going to cause that much trouble. They lived approximately half-way between the two churches. I asked the Pastor if he would mind, if they worshipped with our church, until they could get this straightened out. We both agreed that that was the thing to do.

I called on *George** and *Ann**, and explained that they should go somewhere for their own spiritual health and that they would be welcome to attend in our church, until this could be cleared up. They were adamant, that they wouldn't dare come to our church, because they knew one of the ladies there to be a real trouble maker, and they didn't want to cause a problem in the church. I asked *George** to tell me the whole story.

George* had been married before, but was advised by his doctor to leave his wife because *George** was regularly ending up in the hospital with arsenic poisoning. They discovered that his wife was lacing his lunch sandwiches with arsenic. So, *George** left his wife and through a variety of circumstances ended up living with *Ann**. Twenty years later they got saved and went through strong convictions, concerning their living as husband and wife. *George** had a bad heart and the doctor told *Ann** that if she left him, he would have to have a housekeeper or go to a home.

George* was praying in the house and *Ann** went out to the barn. In the yard between the house and the barn, *Ann** said the Holy Spirit said for her to continue on as *George's** housekeeper, but to move her bedroom upstairs while his bedroom, because of his heart condition was to remain on the main floor. When she surrendered to the Holy Spirit's suggestion, she said that she felt the blood of Jesus washed her all clean from her sin and guilt.

From then on, they never lived as husband and wife. The neighbors didn't know that there was a problem, since they had lived as married in that same house for twenty years. The dear legalistic brother, a little dull on the discerning of spirits and a little hasty to find a chance to lay down judgment, had almost destroyed two valuable servants of God.

I asked *George** where his wife was. He said the last he knew she had been working the streets of Toronto seven years earlier. I suggested he check with the Bureau of Vital Statistics. He wrote them a letter, and found out that she died about the same time that he and *Ann** got saved. They were attending our church when the news finally came.

We stayed in this town two and a half years and had just left, when they were married legally on the Saturday and the former trouble maker asked the new Pastor if they were married, because she had heard they weren't. He could say, without the need for an explanation that he knew for sure that they were. So she could put that ugly rumor to rest.

While we were ministering at this church, we held Sunday school and Sunday morning services in town, and started Sunday night services in a neighboring town hall on the Main Street. There was already a spirit-filled church with whom we had good fellowship called The Oasis. However, I felt strongly to do some evangelism in this town. This town had a population of about 1,200, whereas our town had a population of about 289. We did street meetings in both places and showed some Gospel films.

As a matter of fact we were told by the local police to shut down our outdoor meeting in the park. I had just talked with a senior Pastor friend that week, and he informed me of the advice he had received from a lawyer friend. The law cannot stop you from free speech in a public place unless you are impeding traffic or breaking some law. So, I said to the policeman that he had better check the law before he made a martyr out of me, because I was not going to stop. He informed me that he had been sent by the town council to enforce a local by-law. I said, "Sir, I don't mean to be disrespectful, but you go back to your town council and inform them that they have an illegal by-law, that you can't legally enforce. I will carry on with my public meeting in this park and give you time to check the law that protects my rights to do so." So the police left us alone and we continued to hold public meetings and rented the Town Hall for Sunday evenings.

The Town Hall was on the Main Street on the second floor. At first, we didn't have very many coming out, but I stood up on that high stage and opened the windows so they could hear and see me from the street level. Then I waved my arms and sang as loudly as I could with Kay on the piano, which reminds me of another gift from God.

35

Miracle at Seventy-five

W hen we arrived in our first church, I played a violin
and Kay played a saxophone. You can't lead singing
with a violin and a sax, so I tried some ukulele chords on
an old triangle, home-made guitar that Dave Moulden had
loaned me, and they turned out to be in the key of G. So we
sang lots of our first songs in the key of G, and Kay took
what she knew, and with the help of my brother Keith and
the Lord, she learned to apply it to the piano. We gradually
learned to play in any key on the guitar and Kay became
fairly proficient at reading music and eventually playing
some by ear and some by memory.

Folks came in to that old Town Hall and got saved. The
hall was heated with a stinky old oil burner, not too efficient. But I'm going to tell you the miracle that I consider
one of the greatest in all my experiences, and it happened
on Sunday night in that stinky old hall.

There were about 35 people in attendance and we hadn't
been singing very long, when I felt I couldn't contain myself
any longer. The anointing was so powerful, such a sense
of God's powerful presence, that people started weeping
all over the hall. I wanted to speak the message that was
bursting in my spirit, when it seemed that God sealed my

lips together and I was sobbing along with everyone else but couldn't speak.

After some time, and I really don't remember how long, or if I was actually conscious of how long, suddenly a seventy-five year old lady in the front row jumped to her feet sobbing and blubbering and shouted, "God has been showing me that I've been nothing but a trouble maker all my life."

She repented in tears on the spot and her seventy-seven year old sister, who had the sweetest spirit, had been sitting beside her and shouted out loudly, "Praise the Lord! Amen! Amen! Praise the Lord!"

Monday about noon hour, this repentant seventy-five year old came in tears to visit us. She had gone all over town asking forgiveness and confessing her faults and apologizing, but some people who knew her for most of her life, couldn't believe it was true and rejected her appeal for forgiveness. Well, it was real!

Let me tell you some of the past. When I arrived in this little church and moved our stuff into the parsonage, I helped Kay rearrange what furniture and appliances were there, to suit her. Well this lady just walked in and had a hissy fit, because we moved things and told us to put it back the way it always had been. I think God gave me a special dose of firm sweetness as I told the lady that this was now our home, and we would organize it to suit us, and furthermore, we wanted a new standard of privacy and she should knock at the door, not just walk in. We both assured her, that we would be glad to have her come to visit, but from now on, please knock and wait for us to decide if it were a good time to invite someone in to our privacy. Well, she left and knocked every time thereafter.

However, we learned from our Presbyter that she had run preachers in and out of that church for over thirty years. She controlled the money. The truth, we discovered, was the little bit of money that had come in was kept by her in a fishing tackle box and recorded by her in a small scribbler. Of course, she was one of the major causes that many of the town's people had left the church over the years, and many others would never come.

Now, she wasn't the only reason, but carried her fair share of the blame. She legalistically tithed her fruit and vegetables. She would pick ten boxes of strawberries and make sure she gave the first one to the preacher. She would count out every ten potatoes and give the first one to the preacher. She grew some real tasty small tomatoes and the preacher always got the first one of every ten, etc. My Presbyter explained it this way: "that lady is like a good Holstein cow, she will give a brim full pail of milk, and then she'll put her foot in it."

Her husband was a little older than her, but rarely if ever would go to the church. But, she knew the Lord as her Savior and could pray and work as hard as any saint, she just needed some stuff healed by an attitude adjustment and God did it! There was such a change in her, that her husband got saved and filled with the Holy Spirit in his old age. She turned all the money and books over to us and we put them in order. She was a giver over and above her tithe, and you should know, that their son spent most of his life as a missionary, as well as his daughter for the next generation.

When God can change the character of a seventy-five year old lady, with the kind of turn-around she experienced, that has to be one of the greatest miracles we ever experienced, and you'll see there are more to come.

We left this church shortly after this miracle, but the Pastor that followed, told me that this elderly, but renewed couple led the visitation all over that area and were really on fire for God.

36

A Widow – A Widower

We had no fixed income for the two and a half years we were in this church, but we never missed a meal or suffered any deprivation, because God miraculously supplied.

Our first gift that really humbled me was from a dear eighty-five year old, tiny little lady from about ten miles away. We needed some money (no surprise), and we were believing God to supply it, because we were being obedient in every way we knew.

God apparently woke this little lady up in the middle of the night and told her she was to give $5.00 to that Pentecostal preacher. She didn't know my name and she had no transportation, so she went to her neighbor, who had a car, and asked if he would drive her to town, because God had told her to do this. The neighbor was a Free Methodist, but liked us because we had those street meetings and Gospel films etc. So, he brought the dear lady to see us. She said to me that she wanted to give me this $5.00.

Well, if I blush, I think I might have blushed with embarrassment then. This little wee widow lady giving me, this strapping 200 pound man, $5.00, was too much for my pride and I turned it down as graciously as I could. She burst into tears and told me that God had awakened her in the middle of the night and told her to give it to me. Maybe I blushed again, but I felt humbled and apologized, as I explained to her that we had been praying for it and would be pleased to receive it from the Lord. Man alive, did she get blessed, and so did we! She and the neighbor then came in for a hot drink and discovered that Kay had to boil the water on a cook stove. She inquired whether we had an electric kettle and Kay told her no, but we didn't mind boiling water in a pan on the stove. The next day the neighbor showed up with her at our door. She brought us an electric kettle because she had two of them. I don't know the lady's name, but she'll not only get a reward for her faithfulness in giving, but for obedience, so the Lord could use her to teach me.

When we arrived at this church, you realize we were carless because of the demise of the Cadillac. The Superintendent that was so upset with me for coming to this church, drove about sixty miles in his Volkswagen Beetle (although he was quite a large man), just to apologize to me and make arrangements for me to buy a 1953 Bel-Air Chevrolet for about $300.00 from a friend, who picked good cars up in the auction. The Superintendent became a dear friend and revealed his true humility. The reason he drove a Beetle was so that he wouldn't put himself above the Home Missionaries in his District. The District sent me $50.00 a month for six months to pay for this car. It lasted pretty well for a year or two. It got to the point, when we were driving at highway speed that I would have to tie one of my wife's belts under my knee and over the gear shift lever, just to keep it from jumping out of gear.

Many a Sunday in that church, there would be very little money in the offering plate, but there would be enough food on the altar, that we ate well all week. So, when Christmas was coming up and we were supposed to drive to Tillsonburg for the family Christmas at Kay's parents' home, we would figure how much it would cost to drive there and back and focus on that much to meet our need. However, my tires were so worn that the threads were ready to let go and I needed enough money to replace them. I found a deal at Canadian Tire, but I needed $60.00, which seemed like quite a bit to believe for at the time.

One morning my good brother *James** called and told me to come out to his house. *James** was a little gruff but real. He had fought in the First World War in the Cavalry. He had never driven a car. He walked about a quarter of a mile to town and then up to the church every service. He shook so badly that when he stood up to testify, the whole row ahead of him got shook up as he hung on to those old theater seats. His background was in the Salvation Army, and he was a loyal, faithful, dependable brother in the Lord.

Well, we headed out there all ready to pray with him or listen to some of his First World War stories or whatever. We sat down on his couch and he walked over to his china cabinet, reached in to his sugar bowl and took out a roll of money. In his usual gruff manner he said that while he was praying, God had told him to give me this much money for me to put tires on my car. Well, I hadn't said anything to anybody but Kay, and how would *James** know I needed tires anyway, he never owned a car.

We thanked him and we prayed together and visited. While we were visiting we opened the roll of money to count it. *James** wasn't rich. He lived on his pension and ate a diet of home-canned meat from his wife's cache in the basement and what vegetables he could grow. When I noticed that there was more money there than I needed I explained to *James** that I had already priced some tires and I wouldn't need that much. *James** became a little more than gruff and let me know, in no uncertain terms, that that was exactly what God had told him to give. I think maybe I'm a slow learner!

I apologized, and took the money with real appreciation and awe. I went straight to Canadian Tire to get the tires put on and found out that I had missed the sale. Well, the additional money that God told *James** to give me was within pennies of the new price.

37

Prayer Meeting Dilemma

W e did have one week of a different diet, since all that came in was potatoes, bread and eggs. You would be amazed at the ingenuity that God gave Kay. I don't think we had the same looking meal twice: eggs fried, eggs-in-a-hole, bird's nest, omelet, scrambled, boiled, etc. Amazing!

Our mid-week prayer meetings were held in different homes. A dear elderly sister invited us to hold one in her place, since she lived just a few doors down the street from the church.

This sister, as was the custom with several of the older folks who lived alone, closed most of the rooms off for the winter and just heated and lived in one or two rooms during the winter. Before she closed up her dining and living room, she decided to re-varnish the furniture so that it would have all winter to dry. Well, she opened up these two rooms for prayer meeting and put the heat on.

Our prayer meeting was progressing well. I had led in a song and exhorted from the Word. The congregation had all been able to sit on the couches and soft chairs, but I pulled one of the dining room chairs out in front of everybody, so I could play my guitar and face everybody. We took note of all the prayer requests and everyone turned to kneel in prayer. Fortunately, our dear sister was on her knees and leading out in prayer before most of the others were even kneeling. I went to stand up and heard a sound like my pants ripping. I settled back and started inching my pants off the varnished chair that hadn't cured before the heat was turned off.

Kay and another sister just caught sight of my dilemma before they turned to kneel at the couch, so they were enjoying a muffled chuckle, as prayer carried on.

When I finally got my pants free, I unthinkingly, turned and knelt at my chair. Since I was the last one to lead in prayer, I also was the last one to leave the kneeling position. Besides Kay and this sister, I have no idea who else might have noticed the white patch on the seat of my charcoal pants.

We stopped by this town in the summer of 2002. They have turned the old church into a two story house with a two car garage and moved the congregation into an old renovated apple warehouse in the next town. I wonder what they did with the two 4'x 8' sheets of plywood that Kay painted to make a sign, which I slid into a triangle of posts grooved out just to fit them, facing on an angle, to be read coming from either way. I'll have to ask, I guess!

One comical note, before I tell the vision that God gave me as to when to leave.

I was waxing eloquently, with great zeal and gusto, on a portion of scripture found in 1 Timothy 2:8-15. When I got to verse 15, I got my "s's"& "sh's" mixed up and quoted with loud expressive tones, "Notwithstanding she shall be shaved, uh . . . Uh, in childbearing (I wisely continued instead of trying to correct it), if they continue in faith and charity and holiness with sobriety."

Before, I even finished the verse, my wife and the lady sitting next to her caught it and started to laugh. Strangely enough, no one else seemed to have heard it, but those two ladies couldn't stop laughing and we pretty well lost the rest of that service. Then *Ann** came to the ladies and wanted to know what was so funny.

One late night in prayer I had a vision. I saw a threshing crew hauling sheaves of grain to the threshing machine. They were driving teams and hayracks, which made me think I was just getting a flashback to my younger days. The thing that finally caught my attention, after I had watched several teams come and go, was the plow that was sitting just inside the gate. There was grain growing up through it that would never be harvested. It wasn't completely stopping the teams from getting around it. The harvest was still going on, maybe just a little slower. I pondered that vision for about three days before I finally heard the Lord speak strongly into my spirit, "You are the plough!"

I phoned the Superintendent, and told him I had to leave, because God told me to, but he asked me if I could please stay until September 1, 1963, so he could get someone to come in to pastor. So I did and then promptly left.

I heard great reports of things happening for the glory of God! Harvest went on unimpeded! God was calling us to a new field of ministry.

38

Three of Us in a Trailer

A fter I had resigned and turned the church over to
Pastor Richard Thomas, I hung around for two
months or so, until he could come. During those months
I received a call from Ron Hall in London, Ontario. He
had been holding prayer meetings and youth meetings in
homes and some Sunday services in a town nearby. This
town, was nicknamed 'stone town', because the downtown
buildings were made out of limestone from the rock quarry,
and because some felt the religious spirit that controlled this
town was as hard as rock.

Ron asked if we would pray about coming to this town
to pastor this new work. We didn't have to pray long! We
both felt that was what we were to do, to be in the center of
God's will. The Western Ontario District apparently had a
28' x 8' mobile home that they were going to loan to us for a
place to live. The owner of the Fina Service Station at the east
end of town, had already offered the extra trailer spot at the
back of his parking lot, already set up for complete hookup.
I think the District had purchased this trailer to facilitate a
special evangelism outreach, which was on hold because of
complications. So, we felt blessed to obey the leading of the
Lord and moved to this town in the fall of 1963. There was a
living room, kitchen with a small table, a tiny but sufficient
bathroom and then a little bedroom in the back.

Candace was just about fourteen months old and still in the crib. We obtained some two-inch copper piping and cut it into four lengths that the legs of the crib could fit into and hold the crib high enough over the foot of our bed for our feet to slip under. We didn't have to reach far if she needed care in the night.

All the service stations along that highway were suffering from break-ins and robberies, except the Fina Station behind which we were parked. That sounds like a 'God-thing', and maybe we should give God the credit, but the crooks probably didn't think about that when they approached the Fina Station at night. The owner kept a large German shepherd watch dog inside at night. If you even got too close to the outside, the dog would go so wild that he would strip the trim off on the inside of the doors and windows. However, during the day it was a different story. Fourteen month-old Candace was toddling around at that time and the dog would just sidle up to her and keep her out of trouble, like a baby-sitter. They became buddies, wherever Candace was, so was the dog.

Mom, Keith, Lyle and Dad Carbert at the 28' x 8' District trailer at our second place of ministry

We had our Sunday services both morning and evening in the Odd Fellows Hall. Up on the end wall there was a large painting of the all-seeing eye of God. Within a short time the crowd gathered up to a group of about thirty-five or forty, several of whom were contacts of Ron Hall. Of course, each family was so uniquely different from every other one, that it brought many special giftings into the little church. We held our Bible Studies and Prayer Meetings in the different homes.

At that particular time there was an influx of prophets (not so well received by many at that time), that I traveled around with some of my flock to hear and assess. There were prophets from the States, from Africa, from South America and I don't remember where they all came from, but nurtured by the charismatic revival of the day. One name I remember coming to a little country hall was Gerald Derstine.

Another man from South Africa held a similar meeting. He was in his bare feet and as the meeting started he began to definitely act like a prophet. He pointed at a man near the back and shouted loudly, "You sir . . . God told me that you slapped your wife just before you left home, so you had better repent and apologize to your wife before this meeting goes any further." Well . . . the brother did exactly as the prophet said and the meeting continued with more similar strong revelations. To say the least, there seemed to be the fear of the Lord in those meetings.

Full Gospel Businessmen were seeing many ministers, of denominations formerly opposed to the supernatural gifts and baptism of the Holy Ghost, now coming into a dynamic experience in the Holy Spirit. The monthly magazine had someone new every issue from the Presbyterian, the Christian Reformed, the Roman Catholic churches and so on.

God was moving in 'Stone Town' as well.

By this time, Kay was at the piano and I had a little more freedom on the guitar. God gave me a simple method that worked and I ran with it. God, in His great wisdom, probably showed me the simple method, knowing that I might not live long enough to perfect the proper way. But it worked.

One brother had a testimony of deliverance which I'll never forget, but a demonic anger possessed him. He owned a fleet of trucks and periodically a truck would break down and send him into a rage. He would grab the nearest hammer, preferably a sledge hammer, and proceed to smash the truck into un-useable condition. Needless to say, the business suffered to the point of extinction. When he came to Jesus, the anger left. However, he was strongly influenced by an extreme 'holiness' group and brought some of the negative side with him into the church.

One Sunday service in the hall, my wife wore a single strand necklace of cultured pearls which had been given to her. This man came in with a whole row of his followers, sang a song or two, then he noticed the necklace on Kay's neck. He, and the whole row of followers stood up and walked out. When we went to talk to him, he let us know that the necklace was an offence to him, so Kay never wore any jewelry again while we were in this town. He kept coming periodically and, to our knowledge, was still our friend and brother in the Lord.

In this town, I felt the Lord still wanted me to depend on Him for our needs and not to become bound by a 'job' and a 'paycheck'. Kay helped out in Ostler's Meat Market at times, as they called for help. I sometimes helped Bob Ostler when he would go out to farms and butcher cattle, but never for pay. So we experienced many personal miracles.

We were in the 28' x 8' District trailer for about a year. The District apparently needed it for their program and we went shopping for a place to live. Mr. Burt, who lived at 324 Jones Street in a small house, had fixed up the upstairs with a suite and a private entrance.

You went up the long narrow staircase which turned to the right about two thirds of the way up. At the top of the stairs was the entrance to the 9' x 9' bedroom on the left; the 15' x 8' living room on the right, just past the bedroom door also on the left was the kitchen 9' x 6', and in between the kitchen and living room, at the end of the hallway was sandwiched a three-piece bathroom. We felt blessed! Pastor Don Emmons, of London Gospel Temple said that London Gospel Temple would pay the $35.00 per month rent on the suite. Remember, we felt this was again a place of God's provision where we were not to work for money, so every gift was appreciated as God's provision. Praise the Lord!

A man and his wife, (we'll call him *Sam**) came to the church and sometimes brought their daughter. *Sam** was very concerned for his wife although he wasn't yet a Christian himself. She was a Christian that got side-tracked by what I would call, a 'religious spirit', and began to act strangely. I don't know what opened the door to this trauma, whether her age, or her past, I don't know! Through this hard time, *Sam** asked me if I could help him. He gave his heart to the Lord and began to attend church quite regularly. Sometimes his wife would disappear and he would ask me if I would go with him to try and find her. These excursions gave us a lot of time together for fellowship, which he needed and for teaching. In the past he had hired detectives to track her down, but now I had the privilege of traveling with him, as he had learned some of her favorite hideouts.

324 Jones St. at our second place of ministry.

39

The Prayer of our Two-year Old

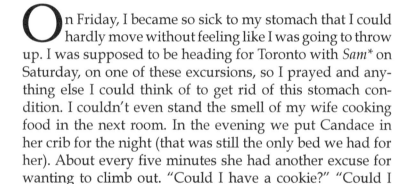

On Friday, I became so sick to my stomach that I could hardly move without feeling like I was going to throw up. I was supposed to be heading for Toronto with *Sam** on Saturday, on one of these excursions, so I prayed and anything else I could think of to get rid of this stomach condition. I couldn't even stand the smell of my wife cooking food in the next room. In the evening we put Candace in her crib for the night (that was still the only bed we had for her). About every five minutes she had another excuse for wanting to climb out. "Could I have a cookie?" "Could I have a glass of water?" "Could I go to the toilet?" etc.. I was lying in bed, trying to stay still so that I wouldn't throw up. I had a fever and ached all over and was hoping I wouldn't have to cancel my trip with *Sam**.

Candace finally ran out of excuses for climbing out of her crib, or maybe decided she had pushed our patience to the max and was lying quietly for a time and then piped up with a request, that there was no way I could refuse. She said, "Daddy, can I come and pray for you?" Well there was no way I could refuse, so I said, "Alright and then you climb right back in bed and go to sleep". Over the edge she climbed, knelt down beside my bed, laid her little hands on my feverish arm and prayed, "Jesus, make Daddy all better,

Amen!" She climbed back in her bed and I was asleep in less than five minutes. I woke up early Saturday morning, hungry, the fever had all gone. I decided not to cancel my trip, but try some porridge for breakfast. I ate a big breakfast (as usual) and at seven o'clock *Sam** picked me up to go to Toronto. I was completely healed as a little two year old had prayed. Praise the Lord!

At noon hour *Sam** took me to a real nice restaurant in Toronto and I settled for one of my favorite dishes, spaghetti.

One Friday morning I was praying for a specific amount of money to pay a bill on Monday. If I haven't explained this before, let me do it now. We never talked about our needs to anyone ahead of time. We, to this day never let anyone, but God, know our needs until after they are met. Then, of course, as we are doing now, we love to tell or 'declare His doings among the people.' (Isaiah 12:4).

When we moved to this town, my '53 Chevy died. My brother Keith from Toronto often came to visit us on the weekends, so he loaned us his Chevy II and rode the train back and forth. On January 31, 1964, as we attempted to drive out in the country for a youth meeting at another family's home, we were caught in an ice storm. The roads were virtually a sheet of ice, a skating rink, if you please. I wasn't too nervous, because I learned to drive on ice, in my Red Lake exposure. As we slowly approached the T intersection, I lightly touched the brakes, thinking I could lightly pump them to slow down (I wasn't traveling fast anyway). Something strange happened and the brakes seemed to lock up and not let go. I tried to steer this slowly sliding car to the right snow bank to help me drag around the corner. It just kept sliding, gradually turning sideways until it hit the gravel shoulder just through the intersection. Oops, it looked like it had just enough momentum to start to tip. As if in slow motion the car balanced precariously and then turned on its left side, hesitated and then very slowly rolled on its roof forcing the fence post through the windshield on the passenger side. When the car started to roll, Kay took Candace, who was all bundled up in her snowsuit and held her against the roof as the two of them slid against me.

However, *Sally's** mother had been killed in a car accident exactly a year earlier, and *Sally** panicked and hung on to the passenger door as she went up and over and the fence post came right through the windshield, broke her jaw and cut her knee open. The rest of us never even had our hair messed up, but just climbed out of the car. A passerby called the ambulance because *Sally** was hurt. The hospital checked us all out and she was the only casualty. I'm telling you this story, to explain, why we were car-less again for several months. Now I'll share the miracle with you.

Sunday morning *Sally** was prayed for and God miraculously healed her jaw and the cut knee gradually healed with no after effects.

40

Miracle Car

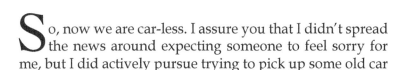

S o, now we are car-less. I assure you that I didn't spread
the news around expecting someone to feel sorry for
me, but I did actively pursue trying to pick up some old car
to get mobile again.

Meanwhile, the Pastor at the Mount Brydges Pentecostal
Church had to make a trip to Toronto and took a new
Christian with him for fellowship. The man was in the construction business and had a little money. He started telling
his Pastor that he had read in the District church news, how
someone had given a car to Pastor Spillenaar, a missionary
to the north and that he was thinking of giving a car to
some missionary and wondered if the Pastor knew where
he could give it. The Pastor had heard I needed a car, so he
mentioned my name. This man said that he would give it to
Lyle Carbert then.

Let me tell you I had been praying for months, "Lord,
I'll humble myself, I'll even drive a Volkswagen or ride on
roller skates, just get me something to get me mobile."

The man had his Pastor contact me to come over to
Mount Brydges to pick it up. The Pastor told me about some
tent meetings he was having in Mount Brydges, so it would
be a good time to come and get in on these meetings, while I

was picking up the car. Well, I was all excited, that God had supplied a car for me, but I had to drive sixty miles to get it.

Sam* was excited for me and volunteered to take me to the tent meeting and pick up the car. I had prayed on Friday for a specific amount of money to pay a bill and then not given it much thought. We decided to go over to Mount Brydges on the Saturday night.

The meeting was powerful. Franklin Walden from Georgia was the evangelist. He only had a grade four education, read his text very poorly and slowly, put his Bible down and started to minister. He didn't have much of what was called 'higher learning', but he knew how to hear from on High.

He moved freely and powerfully in the gifts of the Spirit as listed in 1 Corinthians 12. God gave him some very definite 'words of knowledge' concerning people attending that night. Many signs followed the preaching of the Word.

At offering time, Franklin challenged the people to believe for a miracle. He said that he needed a financial miracle and that the Lord had given him specific instructions as to what to do. He made it very clear, that he was not to take the money raised from the gifts of the people present, unless they would believe God for a specific amount and believe God to provide it supernaturally. He provided envelopes with his name and address on it and asked the people that were there, to pray that way, and to write the amount they would believe for on the inside of the flap. As soon as, and only if, God miraculously supplied that amount we should mail it to him. God said that was how he was to believe for his financial miracle. This sure registered with me so I took an envelope and wrote my SMALL FAITH amount on the flap.

The Pastor introduced me to the man with the car. He asked me a few questions about my income, Ha! Ha! It was pretty hard to explain to this relatively new Christian about living by faith and obedience. Well, he exploded! The reason that I'm not mentioning his name is because I don't want to embarrass him in any way. My assessment from what he said was that I wasn't very well known and he wouldn't get any recognition for his philanthropy. He was angry! He didn't want to give me this car, he said because I could never afford to drive it. I gave him the answer that God had taught me to say, "If God gives me a horse, He will certainly give me the oats to feed it!"

Then, I encouraged him that he didn't need to feel obligated to give me that car. He wasn't beholden to me. God would supply my need somehow, and not to give me the car, unless he was sure that God told him to. He stormed around, pacing and talking and finally said, "Come with me!" I followed him across the street, where we got in his brand new Buick, and he backed out of his garage, tires squealing and was peeling rubber forwards before we even got stopped rolling backwards and drove about two or three city blocks to an old garage and gave me the keys to a 1960, four-door sedan Mercury, fully loaded. It had the long sloping windows back and front, and looked like a big black boat. A beautiful car!

His Pastor told me the story afterwards. This man had sold the car to one of his employees and co-signed at the bank. The young fellow took off and left him with the car, which meant he had to pay the loan at the bank for a car he had already paid for. He chafed under that and didn't know what to do with the car, until he got this idea of giving it to a minister somewhere.

Well, I want you to know, that that car was a gift from the Lord and the man that gave it continued to serve the Lord, and I understand, grew strong in the Lord and prospered financially.

I had prayed on Friday, went to a tent meeting with *Sam**, and received a car on Saturday, had a pretty good Sunday morning service, did a street meeting on the street corner Sunday night and rose to a challenge for my bill to be paid on Monday.

Before noon on Monday, a knock came to our door. I ran down the stairs and opened the door to a stranger who awkwardly asked if he could come in for a moment. Of course, I welcomed him upstairs to the living room. We must have talked for half an hour or more. He seemed quite hesitant to explain why he had really come to see me, so I asked some questions concerning his spiritual condition. He told me, he had given his heart to the Lord several years earlier and that he attended an Anglican church in Toronto. His mother lived somewhere in the vicinity of this town and he decided to drive out to visit her.

Yes, yes, and why had this man come to my door? Finally, he began to embarrassedly share his story.

While he was praying Friday night, the Lord had impressed on his heart to look up the Pentecostal preacher while he was in our town and give him this specific amount of money. He didn't know any Pentecostals. He had never done anything like this in his life before, and wondered if we would think this was strange.

He drove to our town on Monday morning and asked around about the Pentecostals. Someone knew that Bob Ostler was a Pentecostal, so he went to the store and inquired from Bob how to find the Pentecostal preacher. That's how he came to my door. I assured him he had definitely heard from God and been obedient. He gave me the money, we prayed together and he left.

His name, I'm sure is recorded in heaven, but not in my memory. I got all excited and prepared to pay the bill. Then I saw the envelope of faith promise to send the money to Franklin Walden if it came in supernaturally. I only hesitated a moment, and then quickly put the money in the envelope addressed to Franklin Walden in Georgia and mailed it.

Before the day was through someone else, who knew us, drove several miles to give us twice that amount of money. I paid my bill and had my weekly allowance from my Father, God Almighty! Thank you Lord! Great is Thy faithfulness!

41

The Loss of Mom Fairs and a Need for a Christmas Miracle

Kay's Mom died June 4, 1964.

K ay tells the story!
We were still living in the trailer. I remember the phone call from my brother that my Mother had had a heart attack and was confined to bed. Because of an experience in her child hood, Mom didn't want to be hospitalized. Dad was understanding, and had promised her that he would do everything in his power to keep this from happening. So, arrangements were made for a hospital bed to be put in the living room. However, she would need 24-hour care.

When my brother called, we decided that I would go home to the farm and nurse my mother. On Sunday night after the evening service, we drove to Tillsonburg. I remained there to cook for Dad and Glen, and look after my mother. Lyle drove back home on Monday to attend to the needs of the congregation. This continued on for a few weeks.

During this time, my mother and I had many times of sharing, and God was gracious in giving strength. On a Wednesday afternoon, Dad and my brothers were installing stock water bowls in the barn. They came in for 'coffee' and at this time, Mom came into the kitchen. She paused behind Dad's chair and said, "When these are installed, I want to see them." Dad replied, "You will see them, even if we have to carry you to the barn." She chuckled, and proceeded to the bathroom.

Then, we heard the sound of Mom falling. I rushed into the bathroom, followed by Dad and brothers. However, Mom was gone. We administered CPR and called the doctor. He assured us that she had passed, even before she had fallen.

This was an assurance that we had done all we could for her physically. But I, who had been responsible to care for my Mom, internalized the guilt of her death. We are aware now that Satan was doing his usual 'dirty-work'. This was a dark time for me, but I kept up the daily routine, this was necessary because Candace would be two on June 21.

One Sunday morning while in church, I was playing the piano and the Spirit of God was present. I became aware that something was happening. I had a sense of huge scissors which began cutting at my ankles and proceeded upwards to the top of my head. I had a strong sense that I was free. I began to weep as God continued to renew and refresh my spirit.

In the afternoon, after lunch, we received a phone call from my sister Betty.

She asked what was going on and what happened. She said that she had a great burden during the church service for me, and had requested prayer for me. So she was asking if I was okay. I began to weep again, as she started to share what had taken place during the morning service. When we compared the time, it was the same time that I had the 'scissor' experience.

We became very aware that Satan had used this mental suggestion of guilt to cause bondage for me. Praise God, Betty was sensitive to the whisper of the Spirit, and had taken action on my behalf. Praise God! He is faithful!

42

Christmas Miracle

———— ❧ ————

As Christmas was approaching, Dad Fairs asked if Kay and Betty could do one more Christmas like Mom had always done. Kay and Betty talked it over and came to the conclusion that they would try! Betty realized that she no longer cooked like her mother had, because she had been cooking 'Georgia-style' for so long, so the cooking would likely fall on Kay's responsibility.

Kay set about making out a shopping list for the Christmas preparations. There were all those special Christmas ingredients like maraschino cherries, mincemeat, currants, raisins, chocolate chips, etc. beside the regular everyday ingredients, which we didn't have.

If I say our cupboards were like old Mother Hubbard's (bare), I would not be complaining or exaggerating. We just lived one day at a time and thanked God that sufficient, and most of the time more than sufficient was there.

Kay either had an unnoticed faith, or made the list out on a whim, because she added at the bottom of that list, that it would be special if we could give Candace a white blouse, with a pink pleated skirt, white leotards and black patent leather shoes, and if possible a little doll and a book for Christmas.

Well, yours truly, 'the great man of faith and power', took a look at the list and said, "Well, I have fifty cents in my pocket, so I'll walk down to Ostler's Meat Market and pick up a quart of milk and a loaf of bread".

I wouldn't have been gone twenty minutes all together. I walked in the door and took the turn in the stairs, there was Kay sitting on the floor in the living room in tears, with stuff spread out all over the floor as she continued to unpack the boxes.

Just after I left, the CN Express truck had pulled up to the house and delivered several boxes of goods and left. Kay had taken out her specialized Christmas list and ticked every item off, including the white blouse, pink pleated skirt, white leotards, black patent leather shoes and a doll and a book. Beside these specialized items, there were such things as juice, canned fruit and vegetables etc.

Weep with us here as you realize this obvious 'God-thing' and God's concern for the details of our desires! Praise the Lord!

We had many grocery showers even as far back as Bible College, but nothing as specific as this. It came from a group in the St. Thomas Pentecostal Church, which means it was packed and shipped before Kay even made out the list. Hallelujah!

We remained in this town just short of three years. The dependable congregation had reached about forty people plus new ones looking in. I had made some friends around town, one of whom lived just around the corner from Jones Street by the name of Gordon Hale. He had an extensive library and gave me some books. I'm not an accountant, but I always was a 'book keeper' (for those with a different sense of humor that's a kind of joke). I neglected to tell you of the books that *James**, from our first church, gave me. There were some real antiques amongst them that he gave me for my library.

Next door to Gordon Hale's place was an old house going up for sale that could easily accommodate a church, with a little renovation. We began to deal on that when an interruption came.

43

Word of Knowledge

———————— ❧ ————————

In October 1965, Kay's younger brother, Glen, made plans for his wedding in a small town in Saskatchewan. So, we planned a trip to Saskatchewan the first week in October or actually the last week of September. Dad Fairs had never traveled out west, although Mom Fairs and Kay had taken a trip west and a cruise to Alaska with her Uncle Percy Burn in 1956. We loaded the car with the three of us, and Dad Fairs, and headed west to Red Lake, Ontario. We left our car in Red Lake, and traveled in Dad Carbert's car.

After the wedding, Mom and Dad Carbert, Dad Fairs, Kay, Candace and I left together, for points west on a holiday trip to Victoria, B.C.

Pastor D. S. MacLean invited me to speak Sunday morning, October 5, 1965, at the Full Gospel Church in this town. If I remember correctly, my message was on Isaiah 53:1-6. Several came for prayer and Jesus met many needs, which blessed me greatly. My brother-in law, Glen, told me that one man, whose leg was healed in that meeting, reminded him of it for several years. Praise the Lord!

We hurriedly ate our noon meal and headed west. The plan was to get as far as a certain church in Alberta, in time for the Sunday evening service. I love to preach, but thought no one would know me there and we would just take in a good service and I had some business I wanted to talk over with the Pastor. He had been doing quite well with the early program of the Amway Corporation. I had attended one of his sales training meetings, while he was visiting in Ontario and signed up as a distributor. I thought he would never recognize me and I could take the opportunity to ask him some questions after church, or even Monday morning before we left.

We arrived in this town (unforgettable entrance, driving along the flat prairies and all of a sudden find yourself on a steep descent of about 400 feet to this town in the Red Deer River Valley, 'The Badlands'). We booked in at the motel and proceeded to look for the church. We arrived a few minutes early and felt we should go and get a sand-wich and come back. I think the restaurant was about two and a half blocks from the church. When we arrived back at the church, the song service was in progress, so we slipped into the third pew from the front, all six of us. The song leader, was leading the good singing of some old hymns so everyone was standing. The Pastor recognized me and came down from the platform during the singing to shake all of our hands. As he shook my hand, he said, "God didn't tell you not to preach tonight, did He?" I replied to the effect that I wasn't sure that He had told me to preach either. The Pastor just said, "Pray about it," and went along the row shaking hands. When it came time for the preaching of the Word, he stepped up to the pulpit and said, "I was just going to preach on the Kingdom of Heaven, which you've heard me preach before. I'm sure you'd rather hear Brother Lyle Carbert from Ontario who's visiting here tonight." I felt an unction and a message welling up within me, so I said yes.

The text was Isaiah 59:19b: "When the enemy shall come in like a flood, the Spirit of the Lord shall lift up a standard against him." The anointing of the Spirit was great and my message was clear in my heart. My wife agrees with that, but said my sermon was bad, and I went through about six different sermons to get to where I was going. I have no recollection of what I said, but the underlying message has stayed with me to this day.

God moved in a powerful way, but all the time I was preaching, the young people were acting up, to the point that I almost spoke out to correct them. I didn't, but the Lord seemed to have me focus on the one young lady who was sitting quietly on the outside aisle at the end of the pew. All through the preaching, I was hearing God speak a word of knowledge (1 Corinthians 12:8) into my spirit. I had two problems with what God was speaking into my spirit concerning some behavioral and attitude struggles with which this young lady was dealing. The first was that they didn't seem to fit this well behaved young lady. The second was the fear that was gripping me of being wrong and disturbing this church. I was a visitor who couldn't possibly know whether I was right or wrong concerning this young lady's heart, except it was a compelling call upon my heart to speak the words to her.

I finished preaching and the congregation went to weeping and praying, one or two messages in tongues (as in 1 Corinthians 12:10) with the gift of interpretation, and at least one prophecy. All the messages were focusing on some individual in the service that had to settle an issue with God that night, as it would be the last opportunity. I knew nobody but my family and the Pastor and couldn't imagine that this strong exhortation could be for this seemingly sweet young teenager, but God kept pressing my spirit to go down and tell her what He had revealed of her heart. I don't know how long this went on. Nobody was orchestrating it. People just kept weeping and praying. I finally stirred up enough courage to act on what I felt surely had to be God's instructions.

I stepped off the platform and headed down the center aisle so that I could go behind that section of pews and come up the outside aisle to the young lady. I arrived at the back of the church and was frozen with fear. I wheeled right around, and marched right up to the front corner of the church and faced the wall and cried out to God. I couldn't even talk in English, as the Spirit of God prayed through me. Romans 8:26, "Likewise the Spirit also helpeth our infirmities: for we know not what we should pray for as we ought; but the Spirit itself maketh intercession for us with groanings which cannot be uttered."

My courage returned and I "set my face as a flint" (Isaiah 50:7) to carry out this task. Back down the center aisle I charged, only to reach the back and freeze up again. This routine was repeated three times until finally I was able to make the turn at the back of the church and head towards where the young lady was sitting. I don't think anybody else noticed me, since everyone was in prayer, but I just made the turn at the back of the church when the young lady burst into tears.

It encouraged me that I was on time, and I slipped up the outside aisle and knelt beside the young lady. I started repeating what the Lord had spoken into my spirit, when the young lady jumped up and ran to the altar. She knelt at the front pew and I knelt beside her and kept unloading everything the Lord was telling me. The Pastor's wife, sat on the other side of her and kept saying periodically, "You know that's the Lord, *Susan**, don't you!?" "You know that's right *Susan**, don't you!?" and so on. Well, that was like saying 'sic him' to a dog and I continued on, until I had said everything that God had revealed to me. I really don't know all that happened to that sixteen year old that Sunday night in 1965. You would have to ask her. What I do know is that God cared enough to focus in on one young life and minister eternal verities by His grace.

I met *Susan** several years later and found out that she was a beautifully Spirit-filled lady, a wife and mother! Thank you Jesus for your faithfulness!.

44

Car Full of Glory

W e left this town Monday morning and headed west for the first look at the majestic Rockies by all, except Kay, who had traveled through them by train about nine years earlier.

Dad Carbert was driving his 1963 Pontiac with Mom at his side and Dad Fairs beside her in the front seat. Kay and I were in the back seat with Candace. I was playing my guitar and the carload was singing songs of praise. We started down the long hill on #1 Highway towards the lake at Exshaw and then we started to sing, "Then Sings My Soul, My Savior God to Thee, How Great Thou Art". Dad Fairs burst into praying in other tongues, Mom Carbert joined in the supernatural praise, Dad Carbert (a very conservative man) took both hands off the wheel and joined the tears of praise. The car stayed perfectly in its lane for quite a few hundred yards as we wept and sang and praised, down that long hill and around those curves. I'm telling you it was a 'God-thing'. You would really have to have been there to understand.

Our trip was glorious. We visited relatives that we hadn't seen for years and had opportunities to share the goodness of the Lord along the way. I won't mention all the stops, but we traveled to Victoria, to visit cousins, then south to Seattle, Washington, and then to Kennewick, Washington to attend service at cousin Verdun Delgatty's church. Then we swung north through Trail, B.C. to visit cousin Bob Delgatty who was the Pastor, and returned home through Kenton, Manitoba, my mother's home town and back through Winnipeg to Red Lake, Ontario. Then Dad Fairs, Kay, Candace and I headed back home to south western Ontario.

Probably six times in the following year we joked about maybe getting called to that town in Alberta, and then felt guilty about even thinking that way and joking about it. God often dealt with us ahead of time about His plans for us, but never revealed the plan too early, knowing my sudden shift of burden, as soon as the Lord showed the next step. Also, we were deeply focused on our town at the time and couldn't even think about someplace else. We were thinking about getting a place of our own for our church. Things seemed to be slowly, but strongly leading that way.

This town was really a good location for us as far as our own friends and relatives. Keith was in Toronto, maybe two hours away. Tillsonburg was only forty-five minutes from us, so we could visit Kay's Dad and brothers. Clio, Michigan, where Kay's sister lived was only about three hours away. London, the old University stomping grounds for myself, plus all my friends at London Gospel Temple, was only thirty minutes south and Gordon and Phyllis Linton's farm was about half way to London. We often took our breaks by visiting the Linton's, where the kids grew up calling me Uncle Lyle, and our kids eventually learned to swim in their pool years later.

So everything was coming along fine, with new people gradually being added and ministry opportunities nearby. One such ministry opportunity was another one of those times, when I didn't know what I was doing, but saw God come to church with us and cause a Divine interruption. A young Pastor in a small town in Ontario, approximately 60 miles from us, had just recently graduated from Bible

College. He asked me if I could come for a weekend of meetings.

The Sunday morning service was going along fairly well, when a lady half way back stood up and started to speak loudly and fluently in a prophetic-type voice. I was sitting on the platform, but had never been in this church before, so I knew no one but the Pastor, and knew nothing about the church history. I felt troubled at what I was hearing and was looking to the Pastor to correct the situation. When I perceived that it wasn't going to be dealt with, I stepped forward, and the Lord breathed a word of wisdom (1 Corinthians 12:9) through me that went something like this: (please understand, I couldn't possibly repeat it word for word, but here is the gist of it abbreviated). "Sister, I perceive that you could definitely be used of God to prophesy as you seem predisposed to that, however, I want you to stop right now because you've been tricked into speaking by a wrong spirit. What you are saying is definitely not from God."

Then God gave me wisdom far beyond my understanding and I learned, as I explained sentence by sentence why what she said was not from God. I then encouraged her to wait on the Lord and not hesitate to allow God to use her in the gifts of the Spirit when her spirit was right. Please recognize a truth that God has recently been re-enforcing in me. My greatest experiences in ministry have always been, when I didn't know what I was doing! This experience was like that! It was a 'God-thing'. Thank you Jesus!

What I didn't know, was that this lady had been manipulating this church for many years through this false prophecy, and nobody had tried to deal with her. The lady broke in repentance, wept before the Lord and the people, and according to the Pastor she became a real blessing in the church.

We had such a powerful service, with God manifesting His power and glory that a brother asked if I could come to his home to pray for his wife who had been plagued with sickness that kept her bedridden. The Pastor drove me over there and we walked into the bedroom with her husband who immediately went to the head of the bed by her side, while the Pastor and I stood at the foot of the bed.

I remember giving some strong words of exhortation towards faith for her instantaneous healing and then started to pray. The Lord stopped me in the middle of my 'great prayer of faith', and something like this poured out of my mouth: "The Lord says that there is un-forgiveness, bitterness and resentment in your relationship. No amount of praying will bring you healing. The Lord says to repent and forgive, and you will be healed." (Word of knowledge, 1 Corinthians 12:8). The Pastor and I walked out and went back to the church to get ready for the evening service. Just as the evening service began, in walked this couple, smiling through their tears. God is good!

Rev. George Johnstone, Pastor of the Pentecostal church in St. Thomas, Ontario invited us to preach there on a Sunday morning and report on the progress in our church. I remember, that I preached from Isaiah 53:1-6 and called for people to come for healing. If I remember correctly there were thirteen people who came for prayer, which was great, except I noticed a lady near the back that had a neck brace on, who didn't come. God was about to straighten out some of my theology. I automatically reasoned that the lady with the neck brace just missed her healing because she didn't come up for prayer with the rest.

Then I started going along the line, anointing with oil and praying 'the prayer of faith'. Each person I prayed for, I tried to figure out with my head whether or not they would get healed. Well, God did a great job of straightening out the truth of, "For my thoughts are not your thoughts, neither are your ways, my ways, saith the Lord. For as the heavens are higher than the earth, so are my ways higher than your ways, and my thoughts than your thoughts." (Isaiah 55:8, 9)

As it turned out, each one I was sure would be healed wasn't, and each one I was sure wouldn't be healed were healed. I came to the end of the line and there sat the lady with the neck brace. I figured she was shaky in her faith and wouldn't likely receive her healing. Well, she was healed and removed that collar brace that she had been wearing for years while taking regular chiropractic treatments.

Her brother happened to be the Pastor from the town in Alberta that I visited. I didn't know that until I visited that town. The Pastor told me that she was free from pain for the first time in years and never put the collar brace back on or returned to the chiropractor. Praise the Lord! Yes, He is faithful! I learned that my place was obedience, the results are His business, for His purpose, for His glory, by His power. Amen!

45

The Call to Alberta

I felt the need to spend some time alone with the Lord, fasting and praying. Our little apartment didn't allow room for such, so Kay decided to take the time to visit her sister Betty and brother-in-law, Tommie and their three girls, Peggy Ann, Betty Sue, and Merry Lynn in Michigan. If I have the dates right it was in June of 1966.

Kay and Candace had been gone a couple of days. I had spent the time reading, praying and endeavoring to listen to the voice of God. It was Tuesday night when I fell asleep fully clothed, spread-eagle on the bed. At two-thirty in the morning, the phone in the living room rang. I jumped up off the bed, to head for the living room, not really all that far. My brother, Keith, had purchased a small black and white television to watch when he came on the weekend to visit us. It was sitting on the end of the vanity and plugged in behind the foot of the bed. I ran around the foot of the bed, caught my foot on the cord, pulled the T.V. on the floor and fell across it and slid to the phone in the living room. I picked it up and said, "Lyle Carbert here". The Pastor from Alberta introduced himself. I knew! I knew! I knew, what the subject of this call would be and I didn't want to answer affirmatively.

The Pastor explained, that they had called a special prayer meeting to decide on a Pastor for that church, since he had resigned. What he failed to tell me, was the situation that preceded the call. I'll share with you a little later. He just said that they had taken a vote and decided by a 98% vote to invite me to come as their Pastor. I knew, oh did I know, that I was supposed to say yes, but I didn't want to. I responded with "I'll have to pray about it. How soon do you have to know?" The Pastor said, that they would kind of like to know before Sunday and that they actually had one other name from whom they were waiting a response. I was a little taken back by that suggestion, but said I would let them know by Saturday night.

I fussed for a few moments, with the confusion that always comes from second guessing God, and then I phoned Kay in Michigan. They got out of bed and went to prayer. Sometime just after seven in the morning, Kay phoned and reported the answer they all received was for us to say "yes" and go to that church in Alberta.

Well, as difficult as it may seem, from anybody else's point of view, I wrestled with responding for a few days. I talked it over with some of my respected peers, but I knew that the answer couldn't come from them. I had to hear God's voice and obey that, no matter what anybody's opinion was, including my own.

Some of the questions in the natural were: How could I afford to move to Alberta when the church couldn't afford to move me? It seemed to be bad timing for the Ontario church. We were just beginning to consolidate a nucleus of people and prepare for a building of some sort. I didn't feel the work was finished, and in the natural, Kay was going to Tillsonburg on Mondays to help her Dad, after her Mom had died. She would do the laundry, clean the house and prepare some meals for him to eat during the coming week. She felt like this would be 'running out' on her Dad, and her responsibility to him.

I phoned Rev. Don Emmons to inform him of our thoughts. He assured me that he and the District were very supportive of this church and that should not be one of my concerns. He assured me, that they would make certain, that someone would be there to carry on, and of course, to listen to the will of God and do it and they would be supportive. I realized, that I wasn't ready to let the baby work go, without some assurance, that it would be cared for, so Pastor Emmons assurance was probably the final step for me to do what God had prepared me for and say, "Yes". I didn't wait until exactly Saturday night to call the Pastor, but probably Friday to inform him I would come. He praised the Lord and sounded genuinely excited, as he gave me the name of one of the Board members, and how to contact him.

Kay's dilemma however, was her concern for her Dad. So on the next trip to the farm, she explained to him about the invitation to pastor in Alberta. He paused a moment, and then with tears in his eyes, he said" Your Mother and I dedicated you to the Lord when you were a baby, and I will not take you off the altar now and go back on that. You must do what God wants you to do, and my blessings go with you." When Kay told her brother Malcolm, and his wife Norma about this call to Alberta and how Kay was worrying about her Dad, Norma said, "I will look after Dad, you go and do what God has called you to do." Malcolm was all the time shaking his head in assent. They were very faithful in this commitment. God certainly looks after every detail when we obey Him.

Now, for the situation that preceded the call in the middle of the night. If I had known all this ahead of time, I could very easily have missed the voice of God by my head getting in the way.

By the time of this special prayer meeting, I was told that the church had already voted on twenty-three names. That was only the ones that the Board had sanctioned. The Board had ruled out twelve names that the congregation never got to vote on. That would have been disturbing to me. I don't even believe in preaching for a call or candidating as some call it. I believe in praying, getting the mind of God, and inviting the prospect to do the same. The will of God can never be determined by hair color, size of family, church income, salary offered, future prospects, or anything else in the natural! Those things just add confusion to the simple call to do God's will.

While we are on the subject let me share with you an anecdote that may help you to understand my conviction. While I was a Presbyter of a certain section of Alberta, I received a phone call from one of the executive members from another section. He said, "Hello, brother, I am thinking of moving and wondered if there was a good church for me up in your section?" My response was, "There is never a good church for someone who is looking for one. You had better pray and get the mind of God."

The reason the special prayer meeting was called, was because the Pastor said that it was obvious that they were not getting the will of God the way they were going. He called them to come together and pray until they heard from God.

After an extended time of prayer, the Pastor asked if anybody had heard from the Lord. Apparently, a long standing member, spoke up and said something about a young man from Ontario, that had come through about a year ago and had talked about playing football and wrestling in University, but she couldn't remember the name. That was the only man that God brought to her mind. The Pastor recognized the description and said, "Oh that would be Lyle Carbert from Ontario. Did anybody else think about Brother Carbert."

I was told that about six more people spoke up and said they felt the same way, but thought of the distance, etc.

and felt it wasn't reasonable to invite me for one reason or another. One man stood up and recounted the service, in October 1965, in detail. They discussed it, and called for a vote which turned out to be almost 100%. By this time it was pretty close to midnight. Of course, it was approximately 12:30 a.m. mountain time, two hours later in Ontario.

Well, we said yes, and true to form, I was ready to fly out there and start preaching before the next Sunday.

The Board had already made the decision that I was scheduled to start as of the first of September 1966. I tried to assure them, I wanted to come immediately. They informed me that they had already arranged for a young man to come for the summer and that he would be living in the parsonage.

I left Ontario and arranged for the moving van to take my furniture to Alberta by September the first. We had packed the books from my office into sturdy 'liquor' boxes and sent them on directly, as was arranged with the Board. Imagine the impression these boxes made on a church board. However, the books all arrived in excellent condition.

Kay and I drove our 1960 black Mercury up to Red Lake and I went to work to help pay for our moving expenses etc.

46

The Big Move from East to West

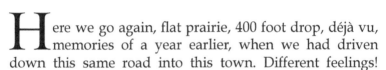

Here we go again, flat prairie, 400 foot drop, déjà vu, memories of a year earlier, when we had driven down this same road into this town. Different feelings! Different purpose! Different vision!

We found the Shell Service Station and picked up the key for the parsonage. I believe this was on a Thursday. As we remember, our boxes of books had already arrived and were piled down stairs in the bi-level house with a semi-circle driveway in front. Some change in housing from our first church, to our second church with a parsonage, with two bedrooms upstairs and two bedrooms downstairs, plus a fairly large family room with lots of cupboards and closets in this house. The kitchen wasn't large but practical with a dining room and living room in an L-shape. Lots of things would happen in this parsonage in the next five years.

To the best of our memory, it seems like the movers arrived later that day and we were able to get our beds set up for our first night in the parsonage (as the Parson) of this church in Alberta.

We showed up for Sunday school and church on that first Sunday of September 1966. As yet I had not met anyone in the church except the deacon with the key. The reason we met him, of course, was he gave us the keys to the parsonage and the church, and he and his boys helped us move our stuff into the house.

After our first Sunday morning service, we were at the door shaking hands of greetings and welcomes, when the Board member who seemed to be the spokesman, asked if I could meet with the Board in the lower auditorium as soon as it was convenient. I agreed! This was the first time I was to have a Board that had been put in place by someone else other than me. I was excited to meet them.

As soon as I arrived downstairs I was greeted and formally asked the question that the Board felt they needed an answer for and some direction for my vision. "Pastor", they said, "we have about twenty-five teenagers in this church that we are afraid we are losing. What programs do you plan to use to keep them?"

I answered with a question, "What programs have you used?" (I knew the former Pastor's ministry. He had ideas coming out of his proverbial ears. Any church he pastored, I was sure would be very busy with His God-given ingenuity.)

They gave me an enviable list of youth activities that the youth had been involved in. I thanked them and said, "I'm glad you've tried all those programs, because I have no new program. I believe that when the fire of God burns around the altar, your youth will be there. If the fire of God isn't found at the altar of the church, then let your young people leave the church if they choose, find out how lost they really are and get saved. Then, maybe they will help bring the fire of God back into the church or maybe end up in some other good church, but they'll know that they are saved by the Lord, not kept by the programs."

In 1966, I was 31 years old, delightfully ignorant of politics, and a bit brash maybe, but bold. Then I presented my question.

"I know you expect me to qualify scripturally as your Pastor and I feel in all sincerity that I do. Do you five Board members qualify scripturally as Deacons?"

One of them said, "What do you mean Pastor?"

I said, "I mean do you qualify according to Acts 6:1-6 and 1 Timothy 3:8-13?"

Well, they didn't really know apparently, what these verses stated as qualifications, so I said, "Well, for instance, since this is a Pentecostal church you would understand if I asked how many of you are filled with the Holy Ghost as in Acts 6:3?"

"Can you be more specific in what you mean Pastor?" the spokesman said.

"How many of you have been baptized in the Holy Ghost and speak with other tongues as the Spirit gives utterance?" I asked. One of the five raised his hand over his head and one tentatively raised his hand to his shoulders. "Do you two brethren have liberty in the Spirit? Do you actually carry on in this gift, for instance, by praying regularly in tongues?" I asked. The one with his hand to his shoulder put it down and the other brought his hand down from over his head to about his shoulder. I gave a short exhortation on the difficulty of walking in unison in the leading of the Spirit, if we were not all filled with the Spirit. A couple of the brethren then asked if I wanted them to resign. I responded adamantly, "No! I don't want you to resign, I want you to qualify. I need Deacons, but I need qualified Deacons."

Well, whatever your convictions may be on the Baptism of the Holy Ghost, I am sure you can see the difficulty my expectations caused. I don't apologize in the least for my stand, that all leadership in the church should be scripturally qualified leadership, especially since those qualifications for offices, such as Pastors and Deacons, are so clearly stated. I partially apologize for my youthful zeal that stretched the qualifications of "wisdom from above" (James 3:17). I know God sent me to this church, because He knew my character and ministry and at what stage of growth my wisdom was.

As I see it now, this church had experienced some of the best preachers for decades and the church problem (of which I was blissfully ignorant) had outlasted them all. This was not the time for more diplomacy of which I lacked, this was the time in the church's growth curve for confrontation. I assure you, that I never purposed in my heart, schemed with my mind, or set any plan in motion to cause confrontation. But, my determination to hear the voice of God and obey, and not be confused by any other voices, caused the bumping of heads constantly. I wouldn't want to offend the church people for anything, for there were some real gems in that congregation, but I have described my five year stay in this church as two and a half years of hell and two and a half years of heaven. I was just as happy during both periods and didn't really analyze the difference until after I left.

Good people, with some bad unscriptural habits. There was that same old historically recurring problem of a Jezebel spirit that starts with everyone demanding to get their own way, the flesh, and then the demonic blindness goes on and Satan can then manipulate well -meaning people into 'strife'. Nothing new! Same-o, same-o! That strategy is as old as the devil and hell, but far too common in local churches, as well as denominational organizations. It is the main reason for the unlikely success of a voting democracy in the churches to ever get the will of God.

Democracy will only be successful in the church when 90-95% of the church are in prayer meeting. The church is a theocracy where people stay in prayer, ten days, 120 days or whatever it takes, until they hear the voice of God and unanimously agree to obey.

47

God's Grace During Historical Board Meetings

―――――⸱⸻⸱―――――

To further explain and clarify one of the problems of a non-Spirit-filled Board that had become accustomed to being the boss (despicable word in a church), let me tell a couple more stories of historical Board meetings.

One of the early Board meetings was in my living room. Other than the normal business that needs to be aired once a month, the spokesman, apparently had been designated to present a specific agenda or job description for the Pastor, including his daily schedule, etc.. There was actually a fair list of demands, I'm sure presented in all the sincerity and naivety of what they had been allowed to think was normal business relationship.

"Obviously there is a misunderstanding here", I said. "There is obviously a lack of understanding of your responsibilities as Deacons and of mine as Pastor. Your job is to 'serve tables' or pay bills, or keep up the repairs etc., or whatever it takes to keep the plant running, so that I have a place to gather the people together and perform my calling of spiritual ministry and leadership to the people. There are no bosses in the church! There are callings and giftings that are directly governed by the Word and led by the

Holy Spirit. I'm not your boss and you're not mine. You are Deacons, so you 'deek' and I am the Pastor, so I'll pastor. If you feel you are called to be the Pastor, then it must be for somewhere else because God called me to pastor here right now. Don't confuse the situation by ever having the path of the Deacon interfere with the path of the Pastor. The Deacon is to serve in such a way as to relieve the Pastor of jobs that would deter him from giving himself 'continually to prayer, and to the ministry of the Word'." (Acts 6:4)

There was a little rumbling and grumbling and the suggestion was that they paid me, so it was their 'responsibility' to tell me what to do.

My answer was fairly, and I guess shockingly, to the point. "You can keep your money if you wish, it won't change my calling. I can't be hired, so I can't be fired! God called me here, and I'll be here, with or without the $50.00 per week and $5.00 extra for janitoring, until God calls me away. I'm not a hireling! You're not my boss! As far as the suggested schedule with certain days off, I will minister to the people of this church and the people of this city every waking hour and respond to every need as God leads, and I challenge any one of you, or all of you, to try and follow in my footsteps. When I'm tired I will rest. If I need to get away, I will take the necessary time. I'm not lazy and all the spiritual leadership falls squarely on my shoulders. If I need help, I will ask some spiritually qualified people to help."

The awkwardness after that Board meeting subsided after a while. Every one of those Board members would qualify to manage their individual businesses very well. That was never a question. They had either been taught or allowed to believe, that the church was a business and they, the Board of Directors, were the boss of the chairman. God bless them! (Besides, countless other churches that have degenerated into businesses, have lost the leading of the Holy Spirit).

When the church loses the authority of the Holy Spirit, they historically have endeavored to replace it with political authority (whoever gets the most votes). As I was young and relatively ignorant of how to lead a church politically, I was dependent on the leading of the Lord and spiritual obedience.

Six months of ministry in this church had passed, when I received a phone call from a good friend and Pastor in Calgary. I would love to give you his name, but feel for wisdom's sake, I'll just share some of the conversation on the phone. Even then those who know this well respected Pastor will recognize him from his style.

"Brother Carbert, Hallelujah! I hear some good reports of your ministry, but I hear you're a little heavy on the Holy Spirit! You'll have to be careful, Brother Carbert, those people aren't used to that you know. God bless you! We'll have to get together sometime. Glory to Jesus! Keep pressing on my Brother!"

Well, that phone call made me go to prayer (as all advice or criticism does) and ask the Lord to forgive me if I was wrong. He brought to my remembrance all the preaching I had done in this church, even back to October 1965. My Brother Pastor was right. I hadn't intentionally steered my preaching that way, but I had faithfully ministered the messages the Lord laid on my heart. Sure enough, as the Lord brought them to my attention I could see, that I seldom preached without a strong calling for surrender to the Holy Spirit. I don't think my Pastor friend was speaking disparagingly of former ministries in this church, but was recognizing the different administrations of those giftings. One may serve with the left hand and another with the right, but they both offer the glass of water.

48

Taking a Stand

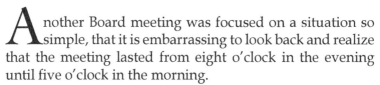

Another Board meeting was focused on a situation so simple, that it is embarrassing to look back and realize that the meeting lasted from eight o'clock in the evening until five o'clock in the morning.

As far as I can tell, for the history of this church building at least, the piano and the organ were up on the platform. When the preacher was at the pulpit, the organ was behind him slightly, facing the people. The upright piano was on his left, positioned to see the organist, who it seemed had been accustomed to leading the singing by the organ. As I prayed about the situation, it seemed it would best facilitate my ministry if the piano and organ were off the platform on the church floor, facing the pulpit. , That way the instruments could follow my leading, as I endeavored to follow the leading of the Lord in worship and praise.

There was more than one element, I felt, that needed changing to accomplish the change in leadership of the worship time. I felt that the organist looking down on the congregation caused added intimidation, concerning decisions that may desire to be kept more confidential for a time. I felt that the Lord had given me some strengths in music ministry, that would be better enhanced by the instruments in an accompanying role rather than a dominating leadership role. The one thing that also seemed so practical was the needed space on this small platform. I could hardly move around, as I was prone to do at times.

Well, the historic Board meeting was convened out in the country at one of the Board member's homes. After all the monthly niceties and necessities were handled, I presented this situation of the piano and organ being moved to facilitate my ministry. Besides the fact that the organist was a Board member's wife and the instruments 'had always been' up there, my naivety of thinking there would be no problem of moving some furniture in the church, and not catching on to the situation, that I had polarized the Board with my undaunted boldness, caused a little 'kafuffle'. I was slowly, oh so slowly, catching on that my five Board members were divided such that two seemed to love their power and voted against the Pastor's wishes; two tried to determine the Pastor's wishes and, if they felt it was wise, always voted support of the Pastor. The other member seemed to listen carefully and try to decide who would win and vote that way.

I tried to explain that this wasn't a voting matter, since it was strictly to do with ministry and needed no expenditure. My intention was just to inform them of the change and give them the reasons. Well, I tried again to explain that that was what I was going to do to enhance my ministry and it didn't matter whether they voted (as this church, we discovered, had voted on everything, even the color of shoelaces to go to the Missions), I was just informing them what I was going to do, whether they wanted to vote all yes or all no, it was not directly their business or decision. The discussion would fire up again, they could not grasp that the preacher would even consider doing something without the consent of the Board. As the clock was approaching 5 a.m., I adjourned the meeting and told them that I would wait in the car because I had nothing more to say on the matter, except that I would be moving the piano and organ down off the platform when I woke up in the morning.

After a few minutes had passed, the brethren filed out of the house and climbed into the car to go home. I sat in the middle in the back seat. The brother on my left put his arm on my shoulder and said, "You know we love you brother, but we voted against your decision." I replied, "I'm glad you love me, but your vote changes nothing. The piano and organ will be moved down as soon as I get up in the morning."

Silence — blessed quietness, all the way home and then the cordial 'goodnight' as I got out of the car.

The next day, I went to the church to figure out how I was going to move the instruments down by myself, since I didn't expect any help. Surprise! A couple of sons of one of the board members showed up and we moved them down, as far as I know they are there to this day, almost forty years later.

I was informed that they didn't appreciate my actions and wanted to invite the District Superintendent down to a special meeting. I said, that would be great! I hoped they would have the gall to complain, so I could explain my stand to the Superintendent.

I had every confidence in the wisdom of the Superintendent to see through this longstanding (before I came) power struggle. If he didn't, I was confident I had acted in the interest of a move of God in that church and wouldn't be likely to change my decision. I never informed the Superintendent of any of the issues but invited him for a constitutionally called meeting on the following Tuesday.

We had a fair time of worship and then opened the floor for any discussion that might ensue. The Superintendent took the chair and tried to encourage some discussion of why he was invited to a meeting such as this. There were a few non-issues brought up, things that church members would be interested in when the Superintendent visited, but no mention of the power struggle. The Superintendent gave a good spirit-led inspirational exhortation and closed the meeting in prayer. Lunch was served, people filed out to go home, then the Superintendent reached up (he was a 'big' little man) and with his hand on my shoulder he said, "Brother, you don't have to put up with this. With a ministry like yours there are lots of churches available."

I burst into tears and said, "Brother, I have always respected your wisdom and spirit in leadership but, if that is how you determine the will of God, I am gravely disappointed! I came here because God called me, and I won't be leaving here until God tells me!"

I guess I was still in awe of his sensitivity. He somehow discerned the struggle, even though as far as I know, nothing had been said to him to betray that fact. We are friends to this day, with a mutual respect for each other's strengths, even though he slightly embarrassed me, by using my name in a message to the conference concerning 'the violent take it by force'. (Matthew 11:12)

The spirit in the services slowly began to manifest more and more of God's presence and power, even with the spiritual undercurrent in the church people were getting saved and filled with the Holy Spirit. Some greatly encouraging healings were taking place. New people were coming into the church. The dissenters were getting less and less of an ear.

49

Gospel Disc Jockey

W e carried on with the "Pentecostal Hymn Time" radio broadcast at eleven p.m. every Sunday night over C.J.D.V. The former Pastor had started the program years before. I enjoyed it tremendously and received lots of mail and phone calls of people being blessed. Two of the men who worked at the station made our church their church home. They took time to teach me what to do and stayed with me, until I was comfortable to be left alone in the studio. Then whoever finished their shift at eleven in the evening, would just turn the station over to me and go home.

We always started with a theme song from Revival Time Choir, "Jesus is the Answer", and a taped promo for Pentecostal Hymn Time. Then, we would come on live and do requests that either came by mail or live on the phone. We preached a little in between songs and encouraged people to phone for prayer. Some nights the phones were fairly busy. We had to grab the news off of the teletype in the other room, while the news promo was playing and get back to our microphone in time to read it, every hour on the half hour. Before I share a couple of interesting newscasts let me tell you of an interesting development.

We were supposed to sign off at midnight, shut the lights off and go home. However, I started going to prayer about five minutes before every sign off. One night we got into some serious prayer time and the phones started ringing as God was meeting some peoples' needs, so I just kept music playing in the background and kept praying. Before I realized it, the time was one-thirty in the morning. So I did a proper sign off anyway and went home.

I went in to explain to the station manager, what had happened. He just said that he didn't care. If I had a listening audience, I could stay on all night for all he cared. The transmitter was left on all the time anyway. I said, "Are you serious?" He said that he certainly was, but that I shouldn't get my hopes up for a listening audience at that hour.

From then on, I went from Sunday evening at eleven o'clock until Monday morning at six o'clock every week. The day shift man would come in and take over the regular broadcasting at six o'clock.

We promoted a little contest to come up with a name for the program after midnight and it became known as 'Light in the Night', the first and only live, all-night gospel DJ program in Canada. Wow! Was that an exciting experience or what! Five years of seven hours a week ministry over the radio, it just had to be one of the highlights of my stay there.

We still had to do the news every hour on the half hour and let me tell you two stories about that.

Most of the time, between phone calls and searching for special requests, I was pretty busy. We had to keep a log of every song played and the time, as well as a list of the phone calls. We didn't have the seven-second delay on the phone so whatever was said went over the air most of the time. I had the option of answering the phone first, before I put the switch on to broadcast it.

One night, I was rushed just at news time, so I pushed the news promo into the machine and ran, I mean like in a hurry, sliding around the corners, grabbing at the door jambs, got to the teletype machine and ripped the section of news off in one quick swipe, raced back for my microphone, just as the news promo ended and started reading the usual seven items. The seventh item of news was usually something on a lighter vain, just before the news sign off was pushed. I had been reading through each item carefully, because I hadn't had time to peruse it ahead of time. Item number seven went something like this: In Toronto today we crowned Miss . . . Miss Nude Canada. I paused slightly and said, "God help that girl and God help this sick country that condones such. Let's pray for them both". I launched into an impassioned prayer, with compassion for that poor misguided girl, and judgment on our nation that would condone such. I said, "Amen". Hit the sign off for the news. The phones all lit up and I fielded all the pro and con calls for 15 to 20 minutes while music played.

Another similar incident happened when I grabbed the news and began to read it. I only got about half way through, when I read some immoral, well maybe, amoral, position that a certain politician was promoting and I stopped in the middle of the newscast and started to pray, "God help that poor godless, ignorant man, and help our country to come to revival and back to the 'Faith of our Fathers'. Again, the phone lines were all lit up well before I finished the news. I hit the news sign off and started answering calls.

The very first one said, "What is this, news or a prayer meeting?" I just said, "Yup!" and hung up to take the next call. I figured by the tone of his voice, it might have caused a problem for me or the station. Sure enough, when I woke up Monday there was a call to see the station manager in his office at the station. I walked into his office. We greeted each other cordially and sat down. He said, "I got a phone call about two-thirty this morning." I said, "I wondered if you would, because I got several." He said that a man called complaining about me praying during a news cast. So the station manager said that he turned the radio on and listened to my program for the rest of the night.

His decision was this, "if they are complaining they are listening. Besides, I listened the rest of the night and what you did suits the character of your program. Don't worry about it." We spent the next few minutes reporting on the number of letters and phone calls that were coming in. I was told that for every letter I received I could count on approximately 1,000 listeners.

I received a phone call from some teenagers one night wanting me to play a hit song of the time by Glenn Campbell, "Who Will Answer?" I replied that it was not really considered a gospel song and that I only played gospel on this program. They coaxed me some more, so I invited them up to the station, while I played it and asked them some of the dark questions this song was asking.

I let them in to the station and put them in the next studio with their own microphone. I, of course, controlled the on-off button. I let them try to come up with the answers to the questions the song was asking. It wasn't difficult to show that Jesus was the only One who could offer the effective answer. Jesus' solutions were only qualified by faith in God's Word and receptivity to Jesus' Lordship.

One call came in after midnight from a phone booth on the highway passing through this town. A lady was crying in pain. She said, that they were just passing through town and were listening to the program. She had been trying to deal with some severe abdominal pain but decided to stop at the phone booth and call for prayer. We started to pray over the phone and I believe the call was being broadcasted over the air. When she started to shout that her pain was gone and began to praise the Lord, she shouted Hallelujah. She thanked us and hung up. I don't know the lady's name or any other details, but I got blessed hearing her praise the Lord!

I had the privilege of having a group of about ten young people from the Northwest Bible College in Edmonton come to the church for the weekend and I interviewed them on radio. The interesting lesson I learned from that, was that the average age of their encounter with God was approximately sixteen years of age.

When I would read the news, I always ended with the taped news sign-off and then added a phrase I had heard years before on a North Dakota radio station, "Well, that's the bad news, now, back to the Good News!" Then I would play some pre-recorded miracles from missionaries or reports of local miracles and hit the music button again.

The Radio ministry was an exciting blessing to me. Thirty years after the fact, I still had people introduce themselves to me because they recognized my voice. Which reminds me of the times when my voice would leave me, either from tiredness or laryngitis, and Kay, who is not a night person would come to the studio and talk for me. What a blast that era of our ministry was!

50

Airwave Surprises

Ora's mother was sick in the Calgary General Hospital. Ora asked if I would visit her mother, who was a good Salvation Army lady. I was busy all day and couldn't get into the hospital until about nine-thirty or quarter to ten . . . at the desk, I explained to the nurse my situation. She phoned up to the nursing station and they agreed to have me come up because Ora's mother was still awake. I walked in to the room to find her in the first bed on my left, a lady reading to the right and the back two beds had the curtains pulled. I spent some time with Ora's mother. I read scripture and prayed and she thanked me for the radio program because she listened every week. The lady to the right, who was reading spoke up and said she was a Baptist and listened every Sunday as well. All of a sudden there was a loud clatter-bang behind the one curtain. I wasn't sure if I should look behind the curtain or not, for fear of embarrassing the lady, but she was calling loudly for me to come with, "My radio priest! My radio priest! Please come! Please come!" So, I cautiously stepped behind the curtain prepared to help the lady. She was standing beside her bed. The noise was just the sound of her putting the sides down in a hurry, because she was afraid she was going to miss meeting her 'radio priest'.

She was a regular listener to the radio program and had recognized my voice. In her broken English she said that she was Roman Catholic. She explained why she called me her radio priest, even though I wasn't Roman Catholic. She said, in her broken English, that she could feel I loved Jesus deep in my heart, and she wasn't sure that her priest did. I thanked her and encouraged her to pray for her priest to experience a powerful encounter with the love of Jesus.

She then took a $2.00 bill out of her bedside drawer to give to me. I assured her that our radio program was paid for by sponsors, and that was the reason we never asked for money. She became quite adamant that Jesus had told her right here (as she patted her chest), that she was to give me that $2.00. I accepted it to buy a record of her choice, and I would play it for her on the following Sunday night. Then the lady across from her spoke up and said that she was a regular listener as well. Think about that! One room in the large Calgary General Hospital and four out of four ladies; one Salvation Army, one Baptist, one Roman Catholic and I'm not sure of the denominational preference of the other, all listened to "Pentecostal Hymn Time" and "Light in the Night". Who knows the eternal value of all those good gospel radio Programs.

It was possibly six months or more after we left this town, when I was hired to work on a paint crew at a Gas Plant in central Alberta. I got on the shift bus at seven in the morning and was welcomed by Art Lebsack who recognized me to be the new man he was expecting on his paint crew. I sat with him and chatted all the way out to the gas plant. After talking for several minutes, Art said, "I feel I should know you!" So we discussed where he had been and where I had been, but we had never lived in the same areas. All of a sudden Art ecstatically shouted, "Pastor Carbert! You're Pastor Carbert! I recognize your voice! I listened to you every Sunday night for years!"

I'm always amazed that so many people are gifted at recognizing my voice, sometimes years later.

51

A Child Set Free

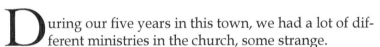

During our five years in this town, we had a lot of different ministries in the church, some strange.

One such ministry left us wondering about 'angels unawares' (Hebrews 13:2). We had booked an evangelist for a week of meetings. Our advertising was all done. Our preparation was in place for a 'God event'. Our evangelist phoned and apologized to us, because he had double booked and couldn't excuse himself from the other meeting. He wondered if we would forgive him and possibly make some other arrangements. The forgiveness was no problem, but it was too late to make other arrangements. So I began preparation to preach the week myself.

Two days later, another call came from my Calgary, Alberta Pastor friend, out of whose church the evangelist worked. "Hallelujah, Brother", he greeted me. "I'm sorry for the problem with the evangelist's schedule, but I have a brother sitting in my living room who would do thee good!" So he proceeded to explain to me the situation of this visiting brother.

He had never actually preached a series of meetings, but thought he should launch out and respond to an invitation to minister to a group of Charismatic Roman Catholics in Calgary. He was from Oklahoma, U.S.A. and had never been in Canada before. He apparently had a bit of a debt, and was counting on the finances from these meeting to clear his indebtedness. Well, the arrangement fell through and he was stranded in Calgary. No meeting, no money, so he called on my Pastor friend for help. The timing was right, so my friend sat him down in his living room and checked him out. Satisfied that this brother was theologically sound, the Pastor called me to see if we could use this stranger, to help out in our planned week of meetings. Some of the stranger's credentials were that he had been the editor for the publication of a well-known evangelist in the United States. I paused on the phone for a few moments and then said "Yes!" to my friend and suggested that he send him to us by bus and I would pick him up.

I met the brother at the bus depot (let's call him *Paul**) and thus the saga began. I tried to quiz him a little more on the way to our house, but sensed a strange attitude that I couldn't identify. We put him in our downstairs bedroom across the hall from my office, so that he would have the opportunity to be quiet and private. In the morning, he came up the stairs to inform us, in a fairly demanding manner, that he was a prophet and expected to be treated like a prophet, that is, Kay was to pick up his socks and underwear and make his bed. He had a colostomy, so he demanded certain foods. Well, he didn't get very far down the list before my 'great protector' mode kicked in and I fairly directly and succinctly informed him, that he was living in the house of a prophet (using the term a little loosely), and that we prophets picked up our own socks and underwear in this house, and the food demanded was way beyond our present means. If God provides it, we would be happy to serve it.

I suppose that encounter must have established a mutual admiration society between us. We walked together the rest of the time he was with us, even when he cast a bad spirit out of Kim, my three year old daughter. Kim started to throw a tantrum and he picked her up and took authority over that spirit. Well, whatever your theology may be on this subject, the tantrum was over immediately and forever, never to happen again. Kim became a peaceful, non-rebellious child, and grew up to be a woman of God and a preacher's wife.

Kimberlee Kay was born on March 22, 1967 (Canada's Centennial Year). She was an active child, running from her mother, at nine months. Possibly, she learned how to be active, because she always endeavored to keep up with her older sister, Candace. (Sometimes this was an annoyance for Candace, but at the same time, Candace always looked after her younger sibling).

Kim had a desire to 'conquer' whatever might be a challenge. She would climb onto the tray of her highchair and do her little 'dance'; or she would find a way to be on top of the upright piano; or even at one time, climb a slide that was approximately ten feet high . . . might I add . . . up the slide, not the stairs.

Her birth brought a new baby to the parsonage, since the last time a baby was born in the parsonage, was twenty years before.

52

Healing Through Gift of Knowledge

———————⌒✦⌒———————

One of the problems in my presumptuous heart was putting together these two facts: this man of God who talked faith and obviously moved in faith wore a bag on his hip because of his colostomy. I have my theological position on that, but I of course, will have to reserve final judgment, until I see Jesus face to face.

I believe the meetings started on Tuesday evening. Every meeting mounted with intensity. Brother *Paul** didn't really preach very well, but when the altar call time came, the altars were full. God used Brother *Paul** in an unusual manifestation of the 'word of knowledge' (1 Corinthians 12:8). He would start to pray for someone and just speak out their precise problem, privately if necessary for confidentiality. I knew these people, and when God would give Brother *Paul** the 'word of knowledge', I had no problem acknowledging its verity or its source. I certainly wouldn't share anything about anyone to such a ministry, and he had never been in Canada before, let alone in this town. Some awesome things happened.

My deacons were still struggling with some of the Holy Spirit things on which I felt led to challenge them. *Paul** didn't even know who my deacons were. He pointed at one of them and began to prophesy. The brother turned pale as a sheet and headed for the door. *Paul** pointed his finger at him, as the brother stood with his hand on the door, and said that God had shown him the brother was suffering from an incurable disease, and that he should make his decision now, to either walk out the door and die of his disease or turn around and be healed. The brother hesitated but a moment, and then turned about face and back up the stairs and, white and shaking, made his way to the altar and was healed. Thirty-five years later, the brother still walks in health in body, soul and spirit to the best of my knowledge.

There were several healings, spiritual, physical and emotional. There were some who received the Holy Spirit infilling. Some of the charismatic Roman Catholic people from town came in and some of them received the infilling of the Holy Spirit.

Another memorable encounter was when *Paul** approached one of the deacons and started to prophesy over him, and then stopped and asked him if he could speak with him privately. The deacon became quite agitated and adamantly refused. So I intervened and advised the deacon to accept the offer. *Paul** had been gracious and prudent enough not to say anything too personal publicly, so why would the deacon refuse to hear him out. The deacon made the excuse that the time suggested for the meeting at his house was not convenient, because he had a school bus run. I offered to sub for him at no cost to him (as I had done before), but he said someone had complained about me parking the bus on the railway tracks the last time I drove for him. I laughed at him and told him that either he was lying or someone was lying to him, for I had never stopped a school bus on the railway tracks in my life. After all the excuses were exhausted, the deacon finally agreed to meet with him privately for one hour only. I drove the school bus while *Paul** and the deacon met. When I returned from the bus route I waited and visited with the deacon's wife. In a few minutes out came *Paul** shaking his head and went right to the car. Then came the deacon just fuming with anger. He threatened to take *Paul** to court and sue him for slander or defamation of character or something. I tried to calm the man down with the revelation that *Paul*'s* spirit had been right by keeping, whatever the 'word' had been for him, private. The deacon's spirit was obviously wrong in deciding to take Brother *Paul** to court. (1 Corinthians 6:1-8).

I got into the car to drive *Paul** as he was just fussing and questioning. I asked him how he perceived the meeting had gone. He just said, "Brother, I don't understand it. Every time God has given me such a definite word for someone it has been right on but this brother strongly denies everything I told him". I then shared my experience upon one of my first encounters with the brother. I had never told anyone or acted on the whisper in my spirit. I kept looking for an occasion, when what the Spirit had whispered would be manifested. Then I explained what I suspected *Paul** had discerned to be the problem within the brother. *Paul** started to weep and shout "That's it, that's it!" Well, I want you to be encouraged to know, that I was not present, if and when the deacon dealt with this matter, but I never again sensed any hint of the problem and feel confident he is my friend to this day.

**1968, Lyle and Kay with 6 ½ year old Candace,
1 year old Kim, and 3 month old Gordon**

53

Prophetic Word to the Church

The closing Sunday morning service (I really don't remember the Sunday evening service. It may have been warm enough for Drive-in Church, but I don't remember), Brother *Paul** started to preach, but let go of preaching and began to prophesy, just like the words right from a Prophet's mouth.

Now remember, this man had never been in Canada before or ever heard of this town. I didn't tell him anything, but what he said gave an enviable list of the preachers that had pastored in this town during its history, not by name, but in order as the church had experienced them. He told family details and related the before and after of several pastors, and how the church was responsible for the way they had treated them. Then he turned and pointed at me and told them, I was a man of God and they better not dare to mistreat me, etc. Then he explained what had happened Saturday, while he was walking in the park by the river. God spoke this into his spirit, and told him that this church was stingy. He was not to take one red cent from this stingy congregation, and they wouldn't be blessed until they repented. God showed him a vision of a lady, not from the church, putting an envelope in his coat pocket which would more than meet his need.

Then *Paul** turned and walked off the platform via the side door which led to the basement. I was sitting in the second row sobbing, as I was aware that God had just spoken through the Prophet, a message that everyone in the church would know as true. I didn't know how to close the service. I just sat there with my face in my hands. I heard *Paul** go down the couple of steps off of the platform, and then proceed to the first landing where he could either go out the outside door or turn and go down to the lower auditorium. Then he stopped for a few seconds and came directly back out onto the platform. Remember again, that I never let on who my deacons were. He pointed at one of my deacons and said that God had told him, that brother was the one to close the service. Well, my quick assessment in the light of what had been said was, that he had picked a good-spirited brother and probably the only one who could have closed that meeting.

The deacon came up and stood in the pulpit, for a time, sobbing and then exhorted the people to listen. He assured the people, that it would be out of character for me to have told this preacher anything, and that they knew that they had heard from God and had better make things right with God and one another. Then he confessed, that he had to repent and apologize to a young brother before he himself could leave this church service. He closed in prayer and went directly to the young brother. They embraced in tears and a chain reaction rippled through the people as brother with brother, sister with sister and brother with sister, did some house cleaning. As I see it now, that may have been the turning point in the spiritual health of the church.

But the story about this strange preacher continues. We were leaving for the District Conference on Monday morning. We received a phone call from a Spirit-filled Roman Catholic widow, who heard we were going to Edmonton. She had to go to Edmonton as well, but did not enjoy driving her big Buick in the city by herself, and wondered if the guest preacher was going as well and would he drive her car for her. I asked *Paul** if he had a qualified license and was he willing to help her out. He agreed.

We left town in our 1968 Mercury with just enough gas to get there and $7.00 in my pocket for the return trip. We were being billeted at a former church member's home. We were driving along Kingsway just before the turn south to Central Tabernacle, the site of the conference, when the clutch went out of my car. We pushed the car to a Shell service station and phoned the church to try and get a hold of our host, who at that time was the custodian there. Our host came on the phone and sounded so excited to hear from us, because there was a brother standing on the church steps waiting anxiously for me. I explained my predicament and our host arranged to pick us up and get us to the church, where he would put us in touch with a mechanic in the church. We arrived at the church, and there on the steps was Brother *Paul** in tears with an envelope in his hand. He told me how the Lord had fulfilled the vision of provision. He just got in the car to drive this lady to Edmonton, when she took an envelope out of her purse and slipped it in his coat pocket. She explained that the Lord had spoken to her in the night to put that precise amount of money in an envelope and do as she did.

Brother *Paul** didn't know how much it was until he got out at the church and counted it. The amount was exactly what he needed to get out of debt plus enough for the tithe. He said that God told him to give the tithe to me. He hugged me and gave me the envelope with an exhortation and a commendation written on it. I was so blessed, to see how God had worked, again. Oh, He is faithful!

We attended the conference sessions where a pastor had heard of some of the rumblings from our meetings. He wanted to know, if I would recommend Brother *Paul** for meetings in his church. I confessed that I knew very little about him, but confirmed that the stories of God stirring in our church were true. Then I simply assured him that if God was able to use Brother *Paul** in his church, as he did in our church, that his church may just get shook up. He invited Brother *Paul** for meetings and I never saw him again.

Sometime later I received a strange phone call from Brother *Paul**, asking me to please write a letter to his wife because he didn't think she believed what happened. I felt strange about doing that, so I procrastinated until I received another phone call from him saying that it was alright now and not to bother writing. "She believes! She believes!"

The tithe *Paul** gave to me paid for my car repairs almost to the penny and my $7.00 got us safely back home.

That Roman Catholic lady then approached me to have Bible studies in her home every Thursday and teach on the Holy Spirit. That was a thrill! She had asked her priest, who was not Spirit filled to come and teach them, but he wouldn't do that, so the lot fell on me. Every Thursday you would see these Roman Catholic people coming in with all shapes, sizes and translations of the Bible, which they recently had been given the Pope's benediction to read.

They would ask naive but sincere questions like, "Did Jesus really have brothers and sisters?" God gave me the wisdom not to give them my opinion, but to turn them to the different scriptures and let them read them for themselves. (Matthew 12:46, 47; Mark 3:31, 32; Luke 8:19, 20; Matthew 13:55, 56; Mark 6:4; and Galatians 1:19). The response from one lady was both humorous and sad. She exploded with, "You mean he (the priest) has been lying to us all this time?" I suggested he may not be lying, but just reporting what he was taught was the truth.

Questions upon questions concerning things they didn't understand from the scriptures. I was thrilled and honored, to be called upon to teach the Word to these sincere, mostly newly filled with the Holy Spirit, people. At first, they would ask me to say prayers, which I would explain I never do. However, I would be happy to talk to Our Father in Heaven in the Name of Jesus from my heart, and have them join me. So I was privileged to teach the simplicity of coming "boldly unto the throne of grace that we may obtain mercy, and find grace to help in time of need." (Hebrews 4:16).

54

Caught by a Con

A nother, different kind of strange preacher approached us for some meetings. He had letters of recommendation from some notable people, who probably heard him give his testimony and preach his fire and brimstone sermon, but never had the opportunity to check him out closely. I agreed to have him come and give his testimony of twenty-five years in Prince Albert Penitentiary in Saskatchewan, how he became saved and wanted to help others find Christ. There was a little response at the altar, but I sensed something wrong from my first contact with him. I felt a little hesitation by his approach, but thought it was likely just the roughness attached to his past. I told him I would pick him up at the bus depot and look after housing him. When I got to the bus depot, he was nowhere to be found. When I arrived home there was a phone call from him, to let me know he was already booked in to a motel. Why did he go the opposite direction from our clear arrangement – RED FLAGS! I went to see him at his motel, to let him know that the church wasn't prepared to keep him in a motel when accommodations were already provided. He said that he lived by faith and wasn't concerned about that, but just wanted to be alone. This put me on the alert, so I watched him pretty closely.

He was scheduled for Sunday morning service. I picked him up for church and gave him liberty in the pulpit. He was pretty glib of tongue and could wax eloquent on his bad past, and how he had given his life to Jesus and that everyone should or they would go to hell. As I said, there was a little response that kept me busy at the altar just long enough for him to get to the door ahead of me. I slipped back there quickly and overheard the conversations at the door between this preacher and some of the sweet elderly ladies: "Brother did you sleep well last night?'

"Well, I would have, but I needed more blankets," he said.

"I have a blanket I would be glad to give you," said one lady.

"I sure missed my bacon and eggs this morning!" he said.

"I would like to give you a dozen eggs and a pound of bacon," another lady said. "Wait here and I'll be right back".

"Well, I would need a hot plate and a frying pan to cook them on anyway," he said.

Then I took him aside by the elbow and began my dissertation. I told him I believed in living by faith, but that meant if you have a need, you tell God about it and believe for God to supply. What he was doing was called common 'panhandling' or 'conning' old ladies into feeling sorry for him and paying his way. So, I informed him that would be the end of that. He had rejected our offer to care for him and would have to figure out how he could pay the bills he had incurred. We gave him the love offering, which was not very large and offered to take him to the bus depot. He then informed me that he had lined up a Sunday night meeting at the Baptist church and was going to stick around for a while. RED FLAGS were going up again so I phoned the Baptist minister to caution him about this man's extra-curricular activities.

I had a friend in this town, named Stan, who was an alcoholic and a heart patient. I spent some time with Stan in the bars and elsewhere endeavoring to help him. I'll get back to this preacher shortly, but let me tell you one of the times that my friend Stan called me in the middle of the night, two-thirty to be exact. He became involved in some kind of religious discussion in the bar with two guys that had just gotten out of Prince Albert Penitentiary and had come back to town. The bar was scheduled to close at three o'clock, so there wasn't much time left and Stan had told these two guys that he had a friend, who could answer any question on religion that they could ask.

I was that friend! Stan warned me, that I didn't have to come if I didn't want to, because these were the two toughest guys in town and he didn't know how they would react to a preacher. I went!

As always, when I went into a bar, I sat down at the table and pushed all of the glasses and bottles away from in front of me and put my Bible in their place. Stan introduced me to these two men and they started firing the questions at me. They weren't sloppy drunk, but well lubricated so their tongues were fairly expressive. God gave me wisdom to talk to them, and gave me a rapport with them, so that the opportunity to share the love of Jesus was awesome. Three o'clock came and the bar was being emptied so we had to leave. Stan's two friends invited us over to their little old house for steaks, so that we could continue the conversation. I accepted the offer, but asked to be excused from eating steak at that hour of the morning.

We talked until five in the morning and then prayed together. One of them jumped up and said that he was starving so he put on the steaks. I again tried to gently refuse a steak without offending their hospitality, but they wouldn't hear of that and put one on for me. The problem in my mind, was that I had been fasting for some time, and for me to eat a steak could be potentially dangerous to my digestive system.

I had done some reading and seen the kind of thing that could happen. The villi in your intestine virtually go to sleep after several days of fasting and to abruptly put meat or roughage into your system would have a tendency to rupture them, causing bleeding and sometimes bloating. I didn't know how to explain this to them, so I prayed and asked God to protect me so as not to hinder my friendship with these two men.

Maybe this would be a good place to explain a long standing hang-up I had, concerning letting anyone know about my prayer life or fasting.

Early in my walk with the Lord, I had read Matthew 6:1-6 especially emphasizing the fasting element in prayer. I had taken it to mean that we should keep it a secret and that it was wrong to let anyone know I was fasting. I'm embarrassed to say how many times over the years, that I would kind of lie or at least mislead people to keep them from finding out I was fasting. I have learned over the years the difference between bragging and just explaining when necessary, but I confess to the fact that to this very day, I find it awkward to reveal my prayer life or fasting.

Now, you understand how awkward it was for me to turn down a generous offer of steak at five in the morning, from these men who were insistent that I let them show me their hospitality. From the eternal perspective, I never saw any long term results from that visit and the steak never made me sick, THANK YOU JESUS, but those two men did offer me a friendship that kept the door open.

Now, back to this preacher! I had expressed my concerns for his genuineness to Stan. Stan, being an alcoholic con himself, didn't feel comfortable with him either. Stan suggested that we set up a meeting with our two convict friends and this preacher and let them check him out. I thought that was a great idea, so I lined up this preacher to go witnessing with me at the bars on a particular night. I took him to the table to meet Stan and our two friends. When the two fellows, recently released from Prince Albert Penitentiary saw him, they laughed and greeted him with, "Judy, Judy, what are you doing here?" Apparently this man was well known in the Pen as a homosexual, and loved young men. All this did, was make me extremely cautious, hoping that this was all in the past for him and he just needed a little refining.

Well, it wasn't many days until I realized that this man had used my name and the name of the Pentecostal church to open lots of avenues for his con game. The other ministers in town started phoning me with a lot of concerns and questions. This man had made the rounds to all the churches, and conned people out of a Volkswagen bus and had them equip it for living in, by supplying everything necessary for him to travel independent of any one. So, I chased him down and let him know that he had better come clean or else I would do it for him. That was the wrong approach, for within days he had disappeared. I did what I should have done at the first suspicion; I called my friends, the police. They called me back to inform me that there was a warrant out for this man's arrest but the last word they had, was that he was heading through Saskatchewan towards Manitoba. After the fact, I found out the reason he wanted a private room. He wanted to have young men come and visit under the guise of helping them. I also learned that he had talked one young man into traveling with him heading east.

I apologize in hindsight, to all the people, ministers and churches, etc., who were taken in because of my naiveté, but pray I won't ever swing the pendulum to cynicism.

55

Bar Ministry

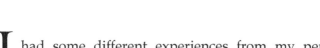

I had some different experiences from my periodical tour of the bars. I obtained some of Don Gossett's, *"Ho, Everyone That Thirsteth – Something Better Then Beer"* gospel tracts. I often would just go through the bars, looking for a prospect to witness to and leave one of Don Gossett's tracts on the table.

One of my trips through the bars, I was slowly walking through, talking to this one and that one, leaving tracts and moving on . . . . I just happened to glance across to the left and caught a glimpse of a lady ducking under a table over in the corner. It was one of the daughters of a long-standing family in the church. I turned at the end of the bar to come back towards the door. I glanced over in the corner again but couldn't see the young lady. She apparently was hiding under the table. There was an older man drinking alone at a table, so I sat down to talk with him. His table was situated right at the corner that this young lady would have to go by to leave the bar. In a few minutes, I could hear some razzing going on in the corner, as this young lady's friends started teasing her about her pastor seeing her. Shortly thereafter, she and her friends tried to slip by my table to leave. I looked up, and she sheepishly whispered, "Hi, Pastor!" and left. I finished talking to the older gentleman, left a tract and proceeded across the street to the next bar.

Can you imagine the consternation of the young lady, when she saw me walk into this bar? I tried not to embarrass her by looking at her, but when I next looked up she was just leaving. This young lady is definitely serving the Lord today, almost forty years later. I would be surprisingly honored, if my bar tour helped in any way.

On another occasion, I went into a bar to look for someone who I heard had backslidden and 'fell off of the wagon'. I spotted him right away, and went over with my normal approach, move all the glasses and bottles to his side of the table and place my Bible in front of me on the table. The bar maid was busy, with her back to us, loading her tray to serve. When she turned around and spotted me and my Bible she started to shake so badly, that she had to turn around and put her tray down until she regained her composure. She then proceeded to turn and take her tray away from us. My friend at the table noticed and said, "Why don't you get out of here? You are making the bar maid nervous!" I laughed and thanked the Lord and stayed with my friend until he decided to leave the bar and I drove him home.

A comparison just came to my mind that might not have been experienced by the majority of readers.

Often, when I would tour the bars with my eternal ulterior motive, I would get a reaction from people who recognized me or saw my Bible. Sometimes, people would try to hide (as the young lady in the previous story). Sometimes, people would quickly push the glasses and bottles etc. in front of whoever else was at the table and assure me that they weren't drinking, but just visiting. Sometimes, some inebriated backslider would invite me to their table and proceed to introduce me to everyone with glowing terms of admiration and affection. Then they would use me as an excuse to preach hell fire and brimstone to their fellow drunks, quoting scripture and waiting for my altar call or something. I even had some make appointments to come and see me in my office, so they could talk privately and some even kept their appointment.

The interesting comparison is my visits to mental hospitals. Practically every time I went to see someone in a mental hospital, there would be a reaction from the patients as I walked by. Of course, most of them had no natural way to know who I was, but would react in a similar way to the people in the bar.

For clarification, I would like to state that all psychiatric patients are not demon possessed. However, a large percentage of the chronic incurables are troubled by demons or evil spirits. I am suggesting strongly, that these patients who have no natural way of knowing who I am, but react as though Jesus or one of His representatives just walked in, have a reaction because of the conflict within them. The evil spirit feels bothered when the Holy Spirit is present. They would quote scripture by the yard. They would verbally attack me, as if I was Jesus. They would plead for spiritual help as in Matthew 8:28-34.

I just thought that there was an interesting comparison between the bar and the mental hospital.

It would seem from my very unscientific examination that the same spirit is predominant in each.

56

Drive-In Church Experiences

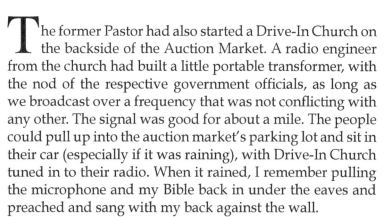

The former Pastor had also started a Drive-In Church on the backside of the Auction Market. A radio engineer from the church had built a little portable transformer, with the nod of the respective government officials, as long as we broadcast over a frequency that was not conflicting with any other. The signal was good for about a mile. The people could pull up into the auction market's parking lot and sit in their car (especially if it was raining), with Drive-In Church tuned in to their radio. When it rained, I remember pulling the microphone and my Bible back in under the eaves and preached and sang with my back against the wall.

I enjoyed this means of evangelism so much, that I never missed an opportunity for twenty-five years to have Drive-In Church on a Sunday night when the weather would allow.

I am sure, I could not begin to tell you a small percentage of the happenings at Drive-In Church, but let me share a few of the outstanding memories.

We were not able to accommodate the outreach at the Auction Market, besides the transmitter broke, so we would get permission to use different sites with good exposure.

Country and Western or Blue Grass music would attract the largest crowd. The Kuhn Brothers, out of Calgary, always filled the lot or the church. Folks from different churches would attend, so I endeavored to have preachers from different denominations join me. I distinctly remember one time when the altar call was given, a 300-pound man led a 90-pound blind girl by the hand, as they came to the platform to give their lives to Jesus.

Another time, we were set up in an I.G.A. store parking lot, when three sisters drove in with their Chrysler to pick up some baby food. They saw all the cars and presumed the store must be open. When they found the store closed, they walked back to their car and stood out front of the car for the whole service and then came for prayer.

Another occasion happened, when a native family, a truckload, pulled in to the parking lot, because they thought this gathering was an extension of the annual Rodeo, which was only two blocks away. The whole truckload came to the church afterward and gave their hearts to the Lord. We had a native lady in the church from that same reservation, who interpreted for us, as this man pleaded with us to come to his reservation, and preach that 'same kind of Christianity' that we preached in the parking lot. Thus began a longstanding relationship with the Stoney speaking First Nations.

We have had people who opposed the gospel being preached outside the church. One place took a petition up and down the whole street that ran adjacent to our parking lot. Then they found out that the majority of the people refused to sign the petition, because they enjoyed the service every Sunday night of the summer months. We found out, because a few of them, although they lived just across the street and could listen from their own property, loaded up their cars and trucks and drove across the street to make a statement to their neighbors and to let us know how they felt.

One family, in another place, yelled at us from across the street to shut it down. We didn't, so he sent his husky young son in his early twenties to threaten us if we didn't shut down. I left the group singing on the platform and jumped down to talk to him. I walked with him back across the parking lot and apologized if we were offensive. I volunteered to lower the volume if that was the problem, but he just shouted right back at me that it didn't matter how loud or quiet it was, he just wanted it stopped. I, as gently, yet firmly as I could, explained to him that there were other people besides him out there, that needed to hear the good news about Jesus, so we wouldn't be stopping. He then threatened to call the police and stormed across the street to his place. A few minutes later the police drove by and waved at us and we waved back and carried on.

Another man walked four blocks to explain to me (no, to lie to me) that it was so loud that he couldn't even talk on his telephone. I checked it out, only to find out that he was of a particular religious sect, that didn't want us preaching on the street. You couldn't hear our sound even two blocks away. He called the police who dutifully drove by to check it out. They waved and we waved back.

There was one more lady, that I remember, who complained to the I.G.A. manager in one town. She threatened to not shop there anymore if he didn't get that religious stuff shut down. He sent his son out to apologize to us. Although he was in favor of what we were doing, he felt he couldn't afford to lose customers over it. So we moved to the Community Center parking lot, which was a better location anyway.

Of course, there were those that gave us favorable notice. Some wrote articles about us in the local newspapers and some sent requests for us to sing certain songs, because of people who could hear us, but were crippled or shut-ins who couldn't attend.

The gospel should stir people first of all, to come to Jesus Christ and then for the enemy (who is Satan, never people) to get mad. You know you must be doing something right when some love you and some hate you for the same message.

57

God's Healing Power

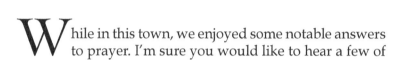

While in this town, we enjoyed some notable answers to prayer. I'm sure you would like to hear a few of the HEALINGS.

The town Ministerial decided to cooperate with a city-wide evangelism crusade, with a nationally known preacher and his soloist. The meetings were held in the school auditorium in the downtown area. One of the Pentecostal men who attended, had enjoyed a recent encounter with God. He had been praying every morning in the church, before he went to work. He had a long history of heart trouble. One morning, as he was alone praying, he heard the Lord speak healing into his body. He was so excited, that he made a special trip that day to tell me all about it.

During the first part of the city-wide outreach, this man started to lose his balance and had to be helped out of the meeting by two men. His feet were in a running motion sideways, as the men picked him up and carried him out. The ambulance came and took him to the hospital. The first thing they did, of course, was check out his heart. They could not believe the results, so they checked his heart and complete circulatory system two or three times. They brought the charts to this man to show him the conundrum.

His heart, blood count, etc., were all perfectly normal for the first time that he could remember. He was quick to testify to the medical staff, how the Lord had met him one early morning in the church.

So what was wrong with this man? After much testing the doctors discovered an arthritic condition that was pressing on a nerve at the base of his skull. He asked for prayer and the Lord healed him.

The following Sunday morning, I preached on James 5:13-16. In short, the emphasis was on the absolute of faith:

– The believer has a problem
– The believer calls for the elders
– The elders anoint with oil and pray the prayer of faith
– The Lord SHALL raise you up, etc.

Monday, mid-morning, I received a phone call from this brother. His wife, had a spinal fusion that went bad. She had missed the Sunday morning service, because of excruciating pain every time she moved. Her teen-aged daughter had stayed home with her, just to help her in and out of bed and to care for her. She had to keep her back arched or she would yell with pain.

Apparently this brother had gone home after the Sunday morning service and preached the James 5 message to his wife. They prayed about it, and came to the agreement that they should be obedient and call for prayer.

It was kind of a cute occasion and another lesson of faith for me. The two evangelists were staying with me and had a different persuasion concerning healing. They were good brethren and men of faith, but had been taught uncertainty about the will of God to heal.

They were always teasing me, about my Pentecostal ways. They thought that Pentecostals just used 'Amen', 'Praise the Lord' and 'Hallelujah' as punctuation habits. I agreed that some did, but that I would appreciate them checking up on me, so that wouldn't be true of me. They would tease me with "I'm not sure about that one!" or, "Oh, that was real!"

We had some discussion about healing, when this brother phoned and explained the situation, and requested me to come and anoint his wife with oil and pray the prayer of faith. Well, when I hung up, I turned to my two friends and said, with tears, that I was going to pray for a lady and she was going to be healed, and would they like to come with me. I know that the Lord dropped the gift of faith in my heart that enabled me to talk that way. The two brethren turned me down politely, and said that they would pray for me.

I arrived at the house and this brother and I walked straight into the bedroom where his wife lay in pain. I read and exhorted one more time on James 5 and anointed her with oil and prayed the prayer of faith. Nothing happened!

With my arm on this brother's shoulder, we turned to walk out. We hadn't even reached the kitchen yet, when his wife came running and yelling, "I am healed! I am healed!" She wrapped her arms around her husband's neck and wept with joy. She explained that she felt nothing as we prayed, but as soon as we turned to leave, she felt the Lord speak into her spirit, that she should put her feet in her slippers and she would be healed. She did and she was!

The confirmation of this healing came in a strange way. A few weeks later, this lady was in a car accident and they immediately checked her back. The x-rays testified for her that God had healed her back.

I have forgotten some of the details concerning another Brother's healing. I could ask him, for he is still alive at this writing. I'll tell the important part as I remember it.

This brother was a farmer. He was having some problem with a stiff neck, which I think, had been diagnosed as arthritic. He asked for prayer and was wonderfully healed.

However, in the excitement, he forgot to ask for prayer for his arm. He apparently had torn the muscle from the bone at the top of his arm. He couldn't lift his arm properly, and besides the pain, it hindered him working around the farm. So he came back a second time and asked for prayer again. God healed that arm, so that it was as good as the other one.

On another occasion, we had invited the Northwest Bible College to send us a group to minister for the weekend; Friday through Sunday night. We specified for them, to include their hockey team, because we had a hockey team in our church that would like to challenge them at nine o'clock Saturday morning on the outdoor rink in a small village near this brother's farm. They were going to supply the chili, etc. (that's reasonable since they had their sons Tom and Richard playing).

We had a good service Friday night at the church, but most of the hockey team couldn't come until Saturday morning. We went out to the rink and started playing hockey amongst ourselves and a few of the Bible school students came at nine o'clock Saturday. The rest of the hockey team didn't show. We played some more. They didn't show. We went for lunch. They didn't show. We went back to playing hockey. They didn't show. About three or three-thirty in the afternoon, in came the rest of the students.

Apparently they lost control and had a gentle roll-over in the ditch full of snow. They worked at getting the car upright. Nobody was hurt, so they continued on and got directions to the rink.

We then started the official church versus Bible College game. We had been skating since nine in the morning and were a little fatigued. I don't remember the score, but I either got hit or lost it at center ice and landed on the tip of my shoulder. It was pretty painful, but I kept going until the game was over. The farmer's wife and Kay, my wife, with some help put on another feast and we all went home to get ready for Sunday.

Sunday morning service was great with all these young people on fire for God. The only problem was, I was in pain. I was on the platform when the spirit of worship was so great, that I felt the Lord prompt me to just raise my hands to praise Him and I would be healed. I started tentatively to raise my hands in obedience, oh, ouch! I put them down again. That just accelerated the pain. One of the students preached a message in the morning.

After the morning service, I went home and called our family doctor. Since he lived just down the back alley from us, he said that he would come over and take a look at my shoulder. He examined it every way he could, and was convinced that I had broken it. That seemed a little obvious to me when he showed me the obvious bump via the mirror. He said, that there was nothing he could do for that type of break on a Sunday afternoon, but to come in to the x-ray clinic in the morning and they would decide what to do then. In the meantime, he encouraged me to either put my arm in a sling or support it with my other hand.

There was another student who preached in the evening service. I don't remember for sure what the message was, maybe "Send the fire! Send the Fire! Send the Fire!" Anyway, I was kneeling at the altar to the left of the pulpit when the student who ministered laid his hand on my back and shouted "Heal him Lord!" I felt a jolt of faith and both my hands went straight up in the air without pain. I shouted and swung my arms all around and testified of God's power to heal.

Monday morning, I dutifully went for my appointment with my doctor. He had me x-rayed and then came in to show me the pictures. He said that the x-rays showed that the bone had been broken, but it was healed, so I shared what happened.

Later, when there was some difference of opinion, concerning the time of birth for our second girl, Kim, the doctor decided to try induction and if that didn't work then he suggested that Kay get her husband to pray — "that seems to work".

Another result of that weekend wasn't known to me for several years. A father of one of the young men that played hockey, came to me in the pool at Banff Hot Springs several years later. He was visibly stirred as he said that he felt he should tell me about his son.

The father was a well-known minister in Alberta. His son was a big boy, probably 6'3" or 6'4" and pretty well built. He apparently had developed some disdain for ministers. He thought most preachers were wimps, but something that happened that weekend apparently turned him around. The last that I heard, he was traveling the world as a missionary-evangelist.

58

Sunday School Salvation

There were many souls saved while we were in this church, but the one I would like to share with you had some special wrinkles to it.

One of our deacons was teaching the Junior Boys class at the time. This particular Sunday morning, the deacon felt led by the Lord to give the boys a chance to make their decision for Jesus. One of the boys that he prayed with that Sunday morning, was one of the *Jones** family. I'm sorry, I don't remember his first name.

Sunday afternoon, I received a call from the *Jones** family. This young man, who just hours before had given his heart to Jesus, had been kicked in the head by a horse and died. Besides the mixed emotions of the loss and the testimony, I was praying for wisdom, as I drove out in the country to visit the bereaving family. The father had rarely, if ever, attended the church, although the mother and several children had attended for some time. An additional note of interest was that a young man, David from the West Indies (Barbados), was interning with us for the summer between Bible College semesters. I took Dave with me as I headed out to meet the *Jones** family, especially the father, who I barely knew.

My uncertainty as to how Mr. *Jones** was going to receive me at such a time, or how he would react to such a loss apparently had left some doubts in Dave's mind concerning what to expect. Thus, a memorable experience as we knocked on the door, for Mr. *Jones** opened the door with a butcher knife in his hand and his eyes staring with grief. Dave thought for sure he was going to have to help rescue me.

As it turned out, Mr. *Jones** was just in the middle of carving some meat for dinner. Dave still remembers that occasion many years later as part of his preparation for ministry.

59

Ministry of Helps by Caring Saints (Kay Calls them 'angels')

S ome of the most outstanding memories for Kay are the 'angels' that God sent along at just the right time.

In one place, we had a whole congregation of 'wanna-be' grandparents. Upon the birth of our daughter, Candace, every one gave her special attention to help relieve Kay. Kay was on the piano for every service and at my side for every aspect of ministry, without missing a Sunday, even for the birth of our daughter. But, of all the angels in this church, Edith, Eva, and others, there was one who few (if any), would know about. She used to quote, "Let not thy left hand know what thy right hand doeth" (Matthew 6:3). So, few people knew the little things she did in private. She was in her late seventies but seemed to never tire, between caring for her own children and grandchildren, in ministering to Kay and I, in the right way at the right time. Gertie will probably only be famous in heaven.

Gertie's faith, for example, was manifest when she was baby-sitting her grand-children and broke her ankle. Her son was so supportive, that he was going to call another baby-sitter and get his mother some medical help. Gertie said, it would be alright, because she would pray and God would heal her. Her son and daughter-in-law scolded her and suggested that she should use common sense.

Well, she prayed! The Lord told her to put her shoe on that swollen foot and she would be healed!

Gertie didn't hesitate (like Peter walking on the water) but just thought she would try to get her swollen foot into that shoe! As soon as her toe went into her shoe the swelling went down and her broken ankle was healed. She never even had to use a cane.

Well, this church was also blessed with angels. Gramma had a way of knowing, when to show up to do the ironing, etc.. The introduction to this world of Kimberlee, and our new addition, Gordon David Lyle, born September 29, 1968, put a fair amount of pressure on Kay with multiplied laundry and other sundry pressures.

So, God spoke to Gramma who would show up uninvited, at just the right time. *Amy** had the ministry of stepping in at the right time as baby-sitter every Wednesday, her day off from her job (but other times as well). This gave us a chance to get away for a break, or to go and make pastoral visits. Another valuable baby sitter was Edna, who looked after Kimberlee and then Gordon during church services. After Gordon came along, Linda used to look after Kimberlee during service as Edna took the responsibility for Gordon. Thank God for these people.

One of the deacon's farm seemed at times to be our second home, which either provided a place for the three kids to make memories or the whole family to ride horseback, collect dinosaur bones, or even hunt deer.

Another couple who eased our load with their talents was *Jerry** and *Daisy**. *Jerry** helped with the bulletin which was a constant need. *Daisy** came as needed and typed all my correspondence, which saved Kay from taking the extra time to do it. There were probably many others who were just faithful helpers in myriads of ways, which the Lord rewards when, sometimes we take it for granted.

60

Ignorance is Not Always Bliss

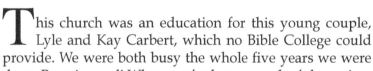

This church was an education for this young couple, Lyle and Kay Carbert, which no Bible College could provide. We were both busy the whole five years we were there. Busy is good! When you're busy, you don't have time to worry about little details that could grow into mountains, when the ingredient of worry is added.

During the first two and a half years, I had the rare privilege of tearing up two petitions to get me out of there. In both instances, someone had filled a page with complaints concerning my ministry in the church. Then, they proceeded to pass it around among the congregation for signatures, so they could send it into the District Executive and get some action. In both instances, it ended up in the hands of new converts who promptly, with tears, came into my office to ask what they should do. I took a quick perusal of the contents and tore them in little pieces and threw them in the trash can. I encouraged the young converts not to pay attention to such unimportant stuff, but to concentrate on serving the Lord with all their heart.

I rehearse these incidents, so that you may understand that when your spirit is right, even though your method and manner may need some improvement, God can use you where He places you. If your spirit is wrong, it does not matter if everything else seems right in your mind, you are wrong and God can't honor that. ATTITUDE IS EVERYTHING!

God did some unusual things to us and through us while we were in this church. We have learned, I trust, and still are learning, to be obedient servants of the Lord and not live for specific results.

When you start setting goals and agendas, you had better make sure that God established them and that they are not the product of any other motivation. I am sure that we are not always aware of the thousands of voices that Satan is happy to use to get us busily side-tracked. That is: selfish ambition, born out of an active mentality to make an impression of success on others; the same ambitions some times to buoy up our 'raison d'être' or self- importance; the subtle influences of being raised in a culture of family and friends that have been built in a preconceived notion of what constitutes success or failure; the demands of society which lay expectations at your door on how to act or react in any given situation; etc.. All of this complicated structure of human ideas can be so simple, if you can only learn one absolutely essential element in your walk with God.

Allow me to state again. Ephesians 5:17 says, "Be ye not unwise, but understanding what the will of the Lord is." Carbert's colloquial version says, "Don't be an idiot! Before you do anything, find out what God's will is and do it!" In a more refined evolution of that verse, I would say, "After you are born again, there is absolutely unequivocally nothing more important than to know the voice of God and obey!" Everything else is just stuff!

The will of God will not always look sensible or accomplish what may be generally accepted as success, but when obeyed, the results are personal peace. If it was any other way, you just might be tempted to take some of the credit for what seems like success and the blame for what seems like failure. When you know that you know you've been obedient to the voice of God, the results are HIS! PRAISE THE LORD! What a profound truth that has proved to be in our lives.

Another vision that God gave me to get my attention to do His will, was another farm scene.

I saw the seed drill making its rounds on the large prepared field. The seed drill, is the implement that the farmer uses to put the seed into the ground in strips, many rows across varying in number according to the size of the drill. The field was completely seeded as the seed drill began to go over it again. God was able to get my attention quickly this time, as He gave me this vision of a stage in the church being completed. For the same implement to go over the same ground again, would keep the drill busy, but keep disturbing the seed so that there would never be a harvest.

I resigned immediately and started making preparation to hand the reins over to the next ministry. I no sooner had announced my resignation, than a lady approached me with this proposition. "If we took up a successful petition would you consider staying as our Pastor?" She was the wife and mother to one of the newer families in the church. She was a sweet sister, who just loved Jesus and thought, as has become normal in the churches, that the will of God is determined by the majority. Of course, I declined the offer and counseled how to know the will of God.

If you remember the story, this church had dealt with thirty-five names before they invited me to come as their pastor. So, we immediately began teaching on how to know the will of God and praying for God's will ourselves.

Immediately upon informing the church and the District of our resignation, names started to circulate that might be candidates to pray about. We were given three names that apparently had made their desires known to the District. I only knew one of the three, and felt a real check in my spirit concerning him becoming the pastor. It was nothing personal concerning the brother or his ministry. As a matter of fact, he was young, dynamic, musical and the son of a respected minister in Alberta. He also has since become a world-wide evangelist. God just said 'no' to my spirit even though he would likely be the favorite candidate from all outward appearances.

One was from British Columbia and I felt no leading towards him as the one either.

The third candidate I knew nothing about except where he was presently pastoring in Alberta, but felt strongly that he would be the next pastor of the church. Kay prayed independently of me and received the same word from the Lord. The District Superintendent, without conferring with us, the church or the pastor, later told us that he felt the Lord had planned for this brother to become the pastor. Just to complete the circle, we found out later that the Lord had put this in the heart of this pastor and he wondered why, since he didn't even know I had resigned.

After teaching for weeks on 'knowing the will of God', we called a meeting to decide on the new pastor. I decided to follow procedure as far as my convictions would allow me. I gave the Board the opportunity to decide, in which order the three names would be presented for a vote, one name at a time. To encourage the people to vote simply and not confuse the issue of comparing brother to brother, we would only let the congregation know one name at a time. I was careful not to reveal my understanding of who Kay, the Superintendent, and I felt was the man God wanted.

It was my opinion, that if the Board had the will of God, they would probably put the right name first on their list. Well, they didn't. They put the young man's name first. I was praying something like this, "Lord, I was sure you said it was not to be this young man but the other brother". "How are the people going to learn your will, if the Board members haven't got it straight?"

So the Board decided the order of presentation would be the young man first, the pastor from Alberta second, and the pastor from British Columbia third.

We opened the congregational meeting with a good time of worship and a strong exhortation on James 1:5-8, "If any of you lack wisdom . . . a double-minded man is unstable in all his ways." We encouraged the people to listen for the voice of God, or the still small voice in their spirit and write down a 'yes' or 'no' on their ballot. Whatever the first impulse was in their spirit, they were to put it down on the ballot without debate from within or without. After all, we were going to pray for wisdom. God was going to give that wisdom liberally and we were going to act in faith without wavering.

I obediently presented the young man's name first. The vote was split and not in his favor. Whew! That was a relief!

Then we presented the name of the pastor from Alberta. The vote was within three votes of being unanimous. The one young couple came up, troubled, to explain to me that their first impulse was to say 'yes' but they thought, for some unexplained reason, that I would want the third man and they were trusting what they thought to be my judgment and voted 'no'.

Well, that explained at least two of the three votes that kept it from being 100% and may be even the third one.

The whole meeting, worship, preaching, voting and all took just one hour. Maybe the people had finally learned, to hear the will of God and do it. The new Pastor, became the pastor and remained their pastor for ten years, until his health became a challenge for him.

61

Another 'In-between Time' With Some Questions

O ver a year earlier, at the District Conference, the churches were asked to pray for a needy town. A Pastor was being sent there to start a new church. Apparently, a group of about forty people had contacted the District office to send a pastor. The people had a commitment of approximately $40,000.00, and wanted to start a Pentecostal church. The Pastor was interested, because his wife had a couple of brothers living there.

I brought the report back to the church, and it was faithfully prayed for, out loud every week by someone at the prayer meeting. I encouraged it, because it caught my attention and fit my vision. I never once thought of me going there, because I didn't know I was going to be free to do so, and besides, this Pastor was a good, gifted preacher who had already gone there.

After I resigned from my church, we of course, began asking God for direction. The name of this needy town kept coming to our attention, so Kay and I decided to confer with the District Superintendent to see what was going on there. Surprisingly enough the Superintendent said 'Nothing'. I asked what had happened to the Pastor. The Superintendent explained that he had only stayed a couple of weeks and decided it wasn't the will of God for him. So I asked the Superintendent if the District would mind us looking at it, since it seemed there was a tug on our hearts. He informed me that he wasn't sure that the opportunity was the same now, but gave me a couple of names to contact and agreed to meet us there for breakfast on a Tuesday morning.

We borrowed a little tent trailer from a Baptist brother, who had received the Baptism of the Holy Spirit in our church. Kay and I, with our family, drove there on Monday afternoon. We put up the tent and proceeded to tour the town before bunking in for the night.

Tuesday morning, we met the Superintendent, at a restaurant for breakfast. We always enjoyed fellowship with him and this certainly was no exception. After breakfast, we proceeded to the real estate office, owned by the man who had headed this group of people interested in a Pentecostal church. We had a pleasant introduction and discovery time, as the man voiced his continued interest, but reticence to promise any sum of money or number of people. The people seemed to have scattered some, which left the $40,000.00 or so, that seemed to have been pledged, in an uncertain state. That information didn't change the tug in our hearts, but the meeting with that man caused some concern.

We walked out of his office and I said to the Superintendent, "That brother has an alcohol problem." The Superintendent said that apparently he used to have an alcohol problem, but was saved and delivered through a meeting of the Full Gospel Business Men's Fellowship. I still felt a little uncertain about him being in leadership, for I felt some underlying problem that I didn't understand. We gathered two or three names and contact places and then the Superintendent had to leave.

One of the names was the Pastor of the Full Gospel Church who had been there approximately eighteen years. Kay and I drove over there to chat with him. However, when we found his place, Kay decided to remain in the car with the children. I went in to visit with the Pastor, who had a friend of long standing visiting with him from Calgary.

I proceeded to explain that we had been feeling a tug on our hearts to come to this town, which we were still praying about. I assured the Pastor that we would only be coming if God made it clear that we should. I explained, that it was not my intention to set up opposition to what God was already doing if we did come. I suggested that if God called us possibly it would be to walk along side of the Pastor, but that we would know when and if the time came.

I didn't understand why I was so unsettled after visiting with the two brethren for over half of an hour. We talked, and the only thing that stayed in my mind of the conversation was when the Pastor said, "Brother, the Lord knows His vineyard. If He places you in this vineyard, He knows what He is doing".

We prayed together and I went out to the car.

My first words to Kay went something like this, "That man either knows something that he's hiding or at least he's not being completely honest with me". (Remember those words.)

We drove away from this town more confused and troubled than when we arrived. Why would a group of people being led by a man who troubled me want to start another charismatic type church in a small town where a man had labored for approximately eighteen years and seemed to have gathered a fair-sized congregation. Besides, this Pastor had spoken eloquently, some seeming, very wise words, (re: the vineyard etc.).

We drove home, returned the trailer with appreciation and proceeded to store our stuff, so as to head for Red Lake, Ontario, to spend some time seeking the Lord and working to pay off our indebtedness.

62

*No Paycheck is Big Enough –
Only God*

Another interesting lesson we learned, was that no matter how big (or small) a regular pay check is, that you shouldn't cut God off by trusting in your pay check. Keep your trust for provision in JEHOVAH JIREH, the Lord our Provider, not in ourselves or others. That may seem very impractical, but this is a spiritual lesson we had to learn. We had never had a paycheck in ministry for five and a half or six years. We truly had learned the excitement of living 'by faith' knowing that God would provide if we would obey. Well, something happened when we arrived in that old established church, which supplied a parsonage and $50.00 per week plus $5.00 extra if we did the janitorial work. No matter how hard we tried to budget we got deeper and deeper in debt. Until the Lord showed us that we had stopped trusting in His provision, which was limitless, and limited our faith to how much the church could pay, which looked like a lot to have guaranteed every week.

We never had any guarantee before this, BUT GOD. (Ha! Ha! Ha!) Does that sound funny to you? Just check and see who or what you've put your trust in and presumed that was God's limit on your income.

In Red Lake we helped my Dad, by fixing up his basement to accommodate this little family of five, Lyle, Kay, Candace, Kim and Gordon.

Mom and Dad were both still working, so Kay did the housekeeping, cooking and babysitting. I worked on construction as many hours as possible to get completely free of debt, before we took the next venture. We helped out in the home church for September, October and November of 1971. Candace got into the Ontario school system and everything temporarily seemed satisfactory. But, there was never a day, hardly ever a moment, when Kay and I weren't saying, "Lord let us hear your heart. Where do you want us to go? When and How?"

I was invited to consider the Grace Church in the city of Winnipeg. Now that would be neat, to be in the city of my birth and also my spiritual beginnings, near to my parents and relatives, another established church with a regular income, and some ministerial recognition (oh, I know that must disappoint you to think I actually considered that). Well, with all my natural reasoning, I couldn't get God to say anything but absolutely, "No!"

An invitation came from London, Ontario to plant a church in the University area of North London. Wow! It was like a dream come true! I would love that. I had vision for ministry amongst the University crowd, I had free room and board offered us at my friend Gordon Linton's, we would be only thirty-five miles from Kay's hometown, Tillsonburg, and about seventeen miles from one of our earlier church plants. I had lots of friends and support in the London area, a dream come true, but, without any reason that I could understand, God would give us no peace about that opportunity. God said, "No!"

We had a variety of other options that are barely remembered because they were not a struggle. They were quickly decided as not to be the will of God.

The one, may I say, nagging in my spirit, was that needy town, which made no sense. Why would I go to a place like that, to start a church where there already was a Full Gospel Church? Why couldn't I get peace about the Pastor there?

One day near the end of November 1971, I was nailing drywall in the living room of a new house, not more than a block east of Mom and Dad's, when I was overwhelmed with a burden for that needy town. I began to bawl and shouted at the top of my lungs, "Yes, I'll go to that needy town!" Well, my Italian friend, Pasquale, came running out of the kitchen to see what was wrong and I explained to him that I was just talking to my heavenly Father. He looked at me a little strangely and went back into the kitchen.

I finished that job, talked and prayed with Kay and headed down the highway for our next venture.

I had one phone number of the man to whom the Superintendent introduced me. I called him to tell him of my decision. I was immediately welcomed to stay at their house, with the hospitality of free room and board and free fill ups for my car.

After paying my bills, etc., I had thirty-five dollars left in my pocket. My Dad loaned me his Shell credit card to get me there and Kay and the kids stayed in Red Lake until I could find out what was going on.

I drove 1,100 miles, virtually non-stop, in tears the whole way, gospel tapes playing, shouting and crying saying, "Okay, God, I said 'yes', now what is this all about? Why am I going to this place?" The answer seemed loud and strange but repeated several times, "Because Jesus is Alive".

63

Jesus is Alive!

I arrived December 2, 1971, Thursday evening approximately nine-thirty in the evening. The folks welcomed me with enthusiasm and hospitality. He sat on the chesterfield and she sat beside him, cuddle-like and they started firing the questions at me. I was enjoying sharing my convictions from the Word. I could sense some uneasiness, but didn't know what it was. One of the things I said, that drew some unguarded looks, was my conviction that deacons had to qualify, according to Acts 6:1-8 and 1 Timothy 3:8-13.

There were a few other questions that brought forth answers which seemed to bring a little tension. I was naively innocent. I knew nothing and could answer questions and state principles from the Word. The next clue might have been the prophet's chamber they had prepared for me, a comfortable bed, a small T.V. etc. in the wine room. His hobby was making wine. Whatever your convictions may be, concerning 'sipping saints', this was a bit of a shock to this conservative teetotaler.

Friday morning everybody was hospitable, but a little tense. Breakfast was great! Then a question was asked that led me, I believe, to respond with a caution. I said, "My brother, you are a born leader and successful in business. If there is such a thing as choosing deacons, you would automatically be chosen as number one deacon, except that I would hope you would have enough principle to decline, until you qualified scripturally. I appreciate your hospitality and zeal to encourage whatever God has called us here to do, but I don't believe you at present qualify for leadership.

They went off to work and left me quietly alone. A knock came to the door. It was a brother, who became a faithful encourager right to the day we left that place, whatever idiosyncrasies might have accompanied his giftings.

This brother had been prophesied out of his marriage by a self-made prophetess. He was a hard working handy man, with expertise in plumbing and heating. He was not a young man, but seemed to have the energy to work long hard hours and then fight sleep in church (for which the teen-agers a few years later used to enjoy teasing him). His head would start to nod and his eyes close, and right on schedule one of the teens would tap him on the shoulder and ask him the time. He would startle and give them the time. After a while he would catch on and say, "I wasn't sleeping I was just praying."

This brother suggested that I should go with him for a drive, because there were at least three people he thought I should meet.

I believe the first stop we made, was at the home of *John and Karen Smith**. I don't remember anything about that visit except that I felt inquisitive and cautious. The next place I believe was the home of *Neal Green**. We weren't there very many minutes, before they shared the shocking news. Apparently, their Pastor, who had been there for eighteen years, had, on more than one occasion, been sexually indiscrete. The last time was causing a break-up of his family, and the *Green's** was one of the three, who had to make the decision to finally dismiss him on Sunday, December 5, 1971.

Well, I was shocked, and a little concerned, that it looked like I was an opportunist when the truth was, I had no former knowledge that there was such a problem. Flashback! From the Pastor's home back in the fall I went out to the car and said to Kay, "That man either knows something that he's hiding or at least he's not being completely honest with me."

We all joined together in prayer for wisdom in their decision and comforting in their grief, because they obviously loved their pastor.

We then headed back into town. I was determined that I was going to shut myself in my 'prophet's chamber' and fast and pray until I heard from God.

On the way to the house, the brother wanted to stop and see another friend about something, but I wanted to wait in the car. He said to please come in, because these people would like to meet me. I yielded to his wish and went in to visit *Richard** and *Jane**. We had one of my kind of visits, where we just talked about the things of the Lord. There was a little of the firing of questions that I was delighted to answer. Their daughter, visiting from Halifax and I believe, 21 years old, was serving the orange juice, coffee, cookies etc. from the kitchen, but never sat down in the living room with us.

We finished our visit, prayed and went home (where I shut the door and determined to hear something clarifying from God).

One month later, *Richard** showed me a letter from his daughter. While we were talking about the things of the Lord in the living room, the daughter got so under conviction that she went into the bedroom and wept her way through to salvation and was now attending the Pentecostal church in Halifax, Nova Scotia. I was able to confirm that with her pastor, Ralph Rutledge.

December 4, 1971, in the morning, my host and hostess slept in a little later, I suppose because of the weekend schedule. I stepped out of my door and my hostess spoke up and told me that they had a discussion about me. Their position was explained like this:

1 — they were sure that I was the man of God for
      this town.

2— they would offer me continued hospitality as long as I needed it, and I would always be welcome in their home.

3— they wanted me to know that they would help me anyway that they could including, finding a place to rent for my family, but, they would never attend our meetings.

Well, I spent all day Saturday in my room asking God for definite leading.

64

The First Service

————⟨◦⁄⁄◦⟩————

They suggested, that I use their home for our first meeting on Sunday, December 5, 1971. They were going to spread the word around, but they had business in another town, fifty miles away, and wouldn't be there.

Seven o'clock Sunday night, I was alone in the house. I took my guitar and started to sing and praise the Lord.

A man came in and joined me. He told me his background was Baptist, but that he had experienced the baptism of the Holy Ghost accompanied by the speaking in other tongues. He was zealous for the tapes and books of Kenneth Hagin. We spent most of the night, until ten o'clock, discussing demons and the power of speaking in tongues. His suggested solution for this town was to gather half a dozen people who would join us and speak in tongues for six hours a day until the Holy Ghost moved through this town. It might have worked, who knows, it just wasn't my mandate from heaven, so I never tried it. This brother was loyal and faithfully attended every meeting for about six months but decided that I wasn't listening to his advice enough and joined the Lutherans. He died my loyal friend. Whatever you may think of how I have presented him, I would love to have a church full of men and women with his zeal for the

Word and the Spirit. We can handle idiosyncrasies with life, but you can't steer a parked car.

My host and hostess, true to their word, left in separate cars. I saw them go by the house two or three times, but wouldn't come in until the meeting was over. My host assured me, we could have the Legion Hall for December 12, Sunday evening and he would see that it got in the paper.

He kept his word again, and we went in and set up about forty or fifty chairs.

The service was advertised for seven o'clock. About quarter to seven people started to trickle in. There were between thirty-five or forty in the congregation.

I had my guitar and some hymn books that I had gathered and began to worship in song, exhortation and prayer. I preached on 'Praise the Lord!' The response was a little bit dry, even though I thought I was free, anointed and blessed. I took up an offering to cover the hall rental and found out my host had paid for the first one (even though they did not attend).

I stood at the door to shake everyone's hand and introduced myself and then I would say, "Praise the Lord!" I heard one brother (I learned later he was a returned missionary) say "I hope that preacher doesn't think that noise is power!" I just kept shaking hands and saying, "Praise the Lord!" But, when *Andy** shook my hand, for some reason, I held on to his hand and repeated, "Praise the Lord!" three or four times, louder each time until *Andy** was shouting, "Praise the Lord!" It may seem strange, but that became *Andy's** release and he got such liberty in the Spirit that he became the worship leader and a few years later our first qualified deacon.

*Andy** was a story of his own. I had forgotten that about eleven years earlier, I had driven out to Lethbridge, Alberta from Red Lake, Ontario, to attend a wedding in which his daughter and my wife were standing up with the bride, Miss Joy Hazlett (the pastor's daughter), and Mel Jenkins.

While I was in my former church, I had helped *Andy** build roof trusses for his cottage at Sylvan Lake. I didn't get to know him very well, but just pitched in because of Mel Jenkins. I didn't know that he had moved up to within sixteen miles out of this town.

On the way in to town, I decided to stop and visit the Pentecostal preacher in a neighboring town. He told me to be sure and stop at the *Baldwin's** house right on the highway on the way to town. He gave me directions and I stopped by. *Andy's** wife, was not there, because she had been hospitalized with a recurring problem that became very serious the next year. *Andy**, his teen-age daughter, and his son were home and we had a great visit and time of prayer. *Andy** said he would pray about coming in to town for church but was attending a Missionary Church right now. As it turned out, *Andy** attended that church in the morning and started driving into town for the evening service for some time. Eventually, *Andy**, his wife and family became fully committed and very faithful to what became the Pentecostal Church in that town.

After our first meeting of December 12, 1971 in the Legion, our crowd dropped immediately to about fifteen or so. The December 12th crowd was composed of some 'tire-kickers' (people just looking with no intention to get committed), some hurting sheep, some unsure checkers of the new thing in town and some with vision that remained with us for many years.

We started a mid-week prayer meeting with some study in the Word, meeting in different homes. The crowd fluctuated some, but developed into what seemed like a relatively committed core.

One of the families which started attending was the *Harold Dodge** family. On Friday, December 3, 1971, I stopped at my host's real estate office for some reason. While I was waiting in the reception room, I struck up a conversation with a young man. Somehow he learned that I was the new Pentecostal preacher and I learned that he and his family were driving twenty-five miles out in the country to a Full Gospel Church. So, I boldly asked, "So you are born again then?" He answered, "Not yet!" Because I now know the man fairly well, I realize he, with his unique sense of humor, might have been baiting me to check me out. Well, he got the exhortation anyway to get his act together with God. He and his family, started sharing their time with us.

Our host and hostess lined up a rental house for us, that I felt we could afford, since I had found work on construction.

I headed back to pick up our stuff out of storage. Two young men, sons of deacons, were our moving crew with one of their trucks. When we arrived at the little rental house, *Harold** met us and helped us unload and I left immediately for Red Lake, Ontario to celebrate Christmas with the family and pick up Kay and the children to move to our new home.

65

Miracle in a Dryer

W e arrived in town late in the evening and quickly waded through the piles of stuff to set up beds and cuddle in for the night. First thing in the morning, we rose for breakfast only to realize there was no cereal or milk etc. and our finances had run out. We decided to set up the washer and dryer and put the house in order. Do you remember the story of Jesus sending the disciples to look in a fish's mouth for money?

Well, as Kay cleaned out the dryer to get it ready for use, she found enough money to buy groceries for breakfast.

The house was handy to the school so that Candace only had to walk across the street. No matter how we adjusted the furnace, we were never able to get the basement bedroom above fifty degrees Fahrenheit. We immediately started praying and looking for some place to buy. Actually, on the way into town, I had spotted a little house on a big lot right on the main thoroughfare, which I commented on as a good spot for a church. Kay got all excited, because it was the picture she had seen in her dream. We talked about this property to our host, the real estate man. He said it wasn't for sale, but that he knew the people who owned it and would check it out for us. Sure enough! He talked to the group that owned that property (I believe he was one of them), and they accepted our offer of $3,000.00. We had no money, but I had just been hired on as a safety man. That's a cute story in itself. I felt the Lord impressed me to get a job and to keep Kay free to raise our little family. I had talked to our real estate man, when I first met him, about the potential outreach in this town. He mentioned some of the development in town and in the conversation, he casually mentioned the construction crew of about 500 men at a Gas Plant, almost 37 miles south of town. Just the thought of a 500 man construction crew tweaked my interest for outreach, but I had no idea how I could ever reach them (maybe have special services in their construction camp? maybe?, maybe?). I didn't know what to do.

I was shopping through the local paper and the phone book for construction companies, because I figured with my experience in construction that would be the best opportunity for work. I spotted a contracting company and phoned them. I was invited to their office for an interview. The owner and his right-hand man, quizzed me for about 15-20 minutes. One of their questions was, "What kind of construction were you thinking of doing?" I replied that I had quite a bit of experience in house construction. Well, they laughed and informed me that they didn't build many houses, but wondered what I knew about gas plants. I knew nothing along that line, since I had never been close to a gas plant. They said that they would let me know if they had a job for me or not. I informed them that I couldn't work on Sundays.

The following Sunday afternoon they phoned me and asked, that if I was still interested in a job, be ready to be picked up at five-thirty on Monday morning. They hired me, to complete the crew of three safety men for that Gas Plant construction. They told me they were having trouble controlling this crew of 500 men, who wouldn't obey the safety rules at this volatile H2S (sour gas) gas plant. They reasoned, that I was a pastor and relatively mature and 6'2" and 200 pounds that maybe I could handle this situation. Wow! What a strange introduction to the oil and gas industry and what an answer to prayer for the job God gave to be right in the midst of 500 men as a mission field.

So, I had a job but still had no money for a down payment on real estate and no equity that would qualify me for a mortgage. "Give me a day or so to work on that", said Mr. 'Real Estate'.

A couple of days later, they informed me that there was a retired Presbyterian man in a nearby town, who would finance the whole thing, including the down payment if I was still interested. Kay and I didn't have to pray very long to know that God had just given us favor and we agreed to purchase that property. That was the beginning of our eventually owning that whole block of approximately one half acre consisting of three lots with three small houses. This was one of the ways that God used my hosts, even though they never attended a service.

66

Services in the Legion Hall

————⁓————

We continued holding Sunday evening services at the Legion. Another group had it rented for the morning, so we went to the other churches in town in the morning and were limited to our own meetings on Sunday evening and Bible Study and Prayer in homes during the mid-week.

Attending other churches has many times produced some interesting experiences. When we attended the First Church of the Nazarene, we ended up sitting on the second or third pew from the front on the piano side. I guess Kay and I were used to singing out in harmony and must have been heard by the Pastor's wife at the keyboard. She came right back to us after the service and thanked us for singing and welcomed us, and then asked us all those interest showing questions like, "What do you do in town?" We answered candidly that we were the new Pentecostal preachers in town. Well, I don't know if she thought it showed, but the look on her face was memorable. It seemed to record a little shock and indecision as to what to do with the hand-shake. She and her husband became our friends very quickly.

For some reason I attended the Christian Reformed service alone. I caught myself shouting 'amen' two or three times to the excellent preaching of the Pastor, as he had chosen to do a dissertation on 'Pentecostalism' for that Sunday morning message. My 'amens' seemed to bounce off the walls. By the third 'amen' people were starting to turn their heads to see who this strange person was that was attending their quiet church, so I restrained myself.

At the door, I had the distinct impression that the Pastor thought this well-dressed young man was a good catch for his church and asked me those same interest-showing questions. When I explained that I was the new Pentecostal preacher I saw his eyes light up, he swallowed and said apologetically something about his message and its timing. I assured him, no apology was necessary, since I agreed with most of the critical assessment of 'Pentecostalism' in its error, but wished he had given me about five minutes to sum it up with the positive. We became good friends in the Ministerial, to the point of him sticking up for me when the Ministerial decided to have each of us share our history and doctrine.

(Front and Center) Original house at our fourth place of ministry. On the right side are some windows of the Miracle church behind. On the left side is seen the new house, a gift from God.

I attended the meeting of the folks from North Battleford, Saskatchewan. The brethren flew down to our town, every Sunday for a season, and conducted meetings in the Orange Hall for a few people of that persuasion, some of whom were attending our services from time to time. That became an excellent illustration to me of the supreme importance of that gift from 1 Corinthians 12:10, "the discerning of spirits". Sometimes in our zeal, we can get confused between what is genuinely of the Holy Spirit and what is (however sincere), of the flesh, or human effort.

We kept using the Legion Hall, until one night at our home Bible Study, I presented our options. I had done some work on paper to present the possibility of building a basement church on our lot beside the house and then, as God moved, adding the main auditorium later. We were graciously offered the use of the former Full Gospel Church, owned by the former pastor, as long as we covered the cost of heat and lights. Or, we could try and find another hall where we could have more liberty to expand. I felt the Lord clearly prepared my heart to just preach as he directed and let the people decide what facilities we should look to. They unanimously chose to go back into the Full Gospel Church. I took time to explain what I felt the Lord had shown me that I would have preferred starting to build a place of our own with vision to the future. I explained that to go back into the old (semi-renovated former Presbyterian) Full Gospel Church was asking for one of two things.

It would either take ten years to lick the stigma on that church, or we would have to have a Holy Ghost revival that would blot out the stigma with an obvious testimony of God's presence. The people all said, "Let's believe for the revival."

Kay and Gramma Carbert painting one of the rental houses on the half acre God "gave" us

67

Easter Sunday in an
Unfinished Church Building

⎯⎯⎯⎯⎯⎯⎯⎯ ꧁꧂ ⎯⎯⎯⎯⎯⎯⎯⎯

E aster Sunday, 1972, we moved for our first service in
the old Full Gospel Church. Three or four families
attended including the former Pastor's wife and family.
She was an excellent pianist and played for us that service.
However, she was the first to come to me the following
week to explain that she couldn't continue in that building,
owned by her husband and filled with bad memories. By
the next Sunday, we only had one of those families return
and by the following Sunday, the former Full Gospel families had all left. We were left with two remaining faithful
families. The *Smith's** in the morning and the *Baldwin's**
at night.

The *Baldwin's** teenaged daughter became our regular pianist. Very slowly, I thought, new families began to
come in.

I would go down to this ramshackle old church, in the
process of renovation, about five o'clock Sunday mornings to start the furnace and pace the floor, laying hands
on all the old pews, the stack of used lumber piled behind
the pulpit and the piano, wipe the cobwebs down and take
authority over hell and its emissaries. I was giving full

account of ministry, and Kay and I kept seeking God for clear direction.

I had been in this town for about six months when one of those early morning vigils became a wrestling match with the enemy. He kept reminding me that we had gone backwards instead of forward, even though we had tried to be faithful to be there for the scattered flock, they had for the most part all left us, to do their own thing. So, I said to the Lord, "Okay, I've given my very best, I came here like you told me. I have been obedient, nothing more is happening. So can I go somewhere else now where you can use me more effectively?"

I was at the front of that dusty old church, when I was stopped in my tracks by a vision that seemed to flash back to the days on radio, when everything of news, etc. came in on a teletype machine.

Above my head and straight in front of me was a message coming in on a huge teletype:

"They that wait upon the Lord shall renew their strength; they shall mount up with wings as eagles; they shall run, and not be weary, and they shall walk, and not faint" (Isaiah 40:31).

Well, that verse was quotably familiar to me, so I was reading and repeating it, as it was revealed word by word. My spirit was saying, "Yes, yes, 'renew my strength, I need that, and oh, yes, mount up with wings as eagles', I love that, elation and thrilling experience, and 'run and not be weary', oh yes, that's exhilarating and exciting, and WALK, yes, I kept trying to finish the verse but it just kept repeating and getting larger each time, and WALK, *WALK*, and WALK. Then my heart just seemed to understand that walking was harder than flying and running, but that I should have peace right now, as I learned to "WALK AND NOT FAINT".

Immediately, a verse flooded my heart, that at that time I normally couldn't have quoted and didn't know where it was found:

"Therefore, my beloved brethren, be ye STEADFAST, UNMOVABLE, ALWAYS ABOUNDING IN THE WORK OF THE LORD, for as much as ye KNOW THAT YOUR LABOR IS NOT IN VAIN IN THE LORD" (1 Corinthians 15:58).

It was like a brand new understanding of God's faithfulness. My peace and confidence set my face afresh like a flint, to do God's will with excitement, no matter what the circumstances looked like.

Families started to come in one by one; and various and sundry visitors.

We started a boys and girls club, in our little home. We got up to twelve attending and had to tell them not to bring anymore because that already packed out our living room. We, as usual, had no money, but decided to try and build a garage behind the little house that would be big enough for a good club hall. The Trailer Court wanted to tear down the original big old house to make room for development. They said, I could have the old house for $150.00 if I removed it all from the property. I decided, I could tear it down and use the material to build my garage.

I talked them into having me remove it, at no cost to me or them and hauled all that old lumber to my backyard along with the windows and doors, etc. My wife and children, and several others who were not attending, and will probably never forget de-nailing all those boards, straightening the nails and sorting them for use again. We did very well until, one brother who was helping us put on the roof and he kept bending those old nails. He climbed down off the roof and drove away only to return with a few pounds of new nails.

68

The Garage-Church

————⌒⌒————

The garage got built, 20′ x 30′, with a sixteen foot overhead door and two man doors, one in the back and
one in the front, and four 2′ x 2′ windows on each side. I
kept thinking that we maybe could fix it up and use it for a
church, so that we could get away from the stigmatized old
Full Gospel Church, but, remember, I felt the Lord told me
to leave those kinds of decisions to the people. One family
came to me in the morning, and suggested that we use the
garage for church. A second family came to me in the evening suggesting the same thing. That settled it! We left the
side rails hanging down against the wall each side of the
sixteen foot overhead door. We built a 6′ x 6′ storage room in
the back corner with a 5′ x 5′ window towards the front as a
nursery. We built a three foot hallway across the back for an
entrance. We painted it all a pastel peach, or something like
that, and curtains to match, over the overhead door. A contractor in the church helped me build a little six foot wide
platform. We put a little heater on one side of the platform
and an organ on the other side. We could carefully place
sixty chairs in there. We covered the outside walls with
black tar paper and stucco wire in preparation for a nice
stucco exterior. We held our first meeting in there on Friday,
December 21, 1973 with a fellowship supper.

We never did get a car parked in there before it became our church. We never did get the stucco on the outside. We never did succeed in getting a sign painted. We called it 'The Good News Chapel'.

Within two or three months, people were filling this stucco-less, sign-less garage. People were getting converted, filled with the Holy Ghost and healed. The miracles were so continuous that we would step out the back door of our house and start to weep with expectancy, before we could walk the ten feet to the door onto the platform.

Several Sundays after Sunday school, we would let the children go down the alley to the playgrounds with someone to care for them, as 100 to 110 adults crowded into that little garage. That is where the revival broke out!

The "garage church," sold and on the move.

As a matter of fact, we had just gone through a time, when the Town Council had ordered us to stop having Church in our garage. I appeared a couple of times before the Council to ask their permission to continue, but they ordered me to stop.

So, I stated as gently, but firmly as I could, that I didn't believe they had the authority to tell me what I could or couldn't do in my garage, as long as it wasn't illegal.

So, I apologetically stated, that I was going to have to challenge their order, and continue to gather in my garage. Then I received somewhat of a 'word of wisdom', and explained that it was only temporary, until we could build a proper church sanctuary and finally use my garage for my car. "My garage is not a church", I stated, "but just a place for the church to meet until we could build a church." Well, you could see the tension drop in the room as soon as it registered that we were not intending for our garage to be the church. I even joked that they didn't have to worry about us asking for a tax exemption for our garage. So, they changed their objection and agreed to let us use the garage temporarily for our gathering place.

69

Miracles in the 'Garage-Church'

———————⟨◦⟨⟨◦⟩◦⟩———————

*H*arry* and his brother, *Art**, got saved, or converted, or born again . . . whichever term helps you understand. They were brought down from Norman Wells, N.W.T. by Gulf Oil through a Native training program. *Art** was pretty heavy into drugs and they both were heavy into booze and smoking. Jesus saved them, delivered them, and changed their lives.

*Harry** was fastidious in the care of his car. You couldn't get in his car, unless your feet were clean and everything else as well. There was a young lady with a little Sheltie Collie that she brought to church with her. For some reason, her regular ride wasn't available and she worked out in the country a few miles. Someone suggested to *Harry**, that maybe he could take her home, since her little dog was clean and would sit on its owner's knee. So *Harry** agreed reluctantly, and wouldn't you guess, the dog got car sick, just before he got the young lady home. *Harry** made her get out and walk the rest of the way home. Oh! He was upset!

Well, I tell you that story to explain, how the love of God finally got a hold of *Harry's** life.

One Sunday morning, in the 'garage-church', as we just started to worship, a man came in off the street. He didn't know where he was, but he heard the music and put his six pack of beer down on the lawn and came in the door to check on what he heard. He thought he was in a town about 50 miles away. He must have just awakened with a terrible hangover and didn't remember the night before. He stunk of human manure, as a matter of fact, it looked like he had been laying in it. He found an empty chair about half-way up on the one side.

That little 20'x30' 'garage-church' was not big enough and didn't have enough ventilation to hide the problem. Suddenly, there was a circle of empty chairs next to him (I'm sure you would understand and not be too judgmental of the people, there is a limit to what some people can stand). Well, the service went on. When the altar call was given, he raised his hand for prayer. He prayed the sinner's prayer and turned around and knelt sobbing on his chair. Now that was a great miracle, but the greater miracle was that fastidious *Harry** was the first one to kneel beside him, and put his arm around him and weep with him right through to faith. LOVE (GOD'S KIND) covers a multitude of sins and discomforts.

While we were worshipping in the 'garage-church', we would sometimes rent another location for large gatherings. The Northwest Bible College from Edmonton wanted to come with their musical group, so we arranged for the use of the school gymnasium. God moved in a wonderful way, and besides people coming for prayer for a variety of things, a cute story developed out of the altar call.

One man, nicknamed, 'Tiny', stood seven feet tall and quite heavy, testified to being set free from the bondage of homosexuality. As the Spirit of God moved mightily on him at the front, he started to sway back and forth like he was going to go down. Under his right arm stood a lady, a little five-foot Lutheran lady who was hungry for more of God. She testified that she felt the power of God all over her, and began to speak in tongues, which was already puzzling to her, but was having trouble concentrating on what God was doing, for fear 'Tiny' might fall on her. Well, God protected her from that.

After the service we invited everybody down to the 'garage-church' for lunch and fellowship.

The lady had a key to the Lutheran Church, and decided to check this 'tongues' experience out. She figured that, if it still worked in the Lutheran Church it must be real. So, she unlocked the church and went in and burst into speaking in other tongues. I will never forget her coming into the 'garage-church', just beaming, as she explained what she did and we all laughed with her as she loudly exclaimed, "If it works in the Lutheran Church, it must be for real!"

Here is a miracle testimony that we received years after it happened. Here is the email:

Dear Lyle and Kay,

The years go by so fast, it doesn't seem that long ago when my daughter and I stopped in to see you guys on your anniversary. It was too short a visit, but very memorable for me. What a joy to see you looking so good, especially you Kay. And Lyle when you gave me one of your bear hugs, I felt I had come 'home'.

I don't think you realize how much these years meant to me. Both of you were always there for me, as I searched for all the Lord wanted for my life. I learned so much from your example and your teachings. As I started to understand the ways of the Lord, they went from my head to my heart! I remember when I finally discovered what was meant by the "Joy of the Lord is my strength".

That day at your house, you, your family and friends prayed for me. The Lord knew my needs! The miracle I received, was not what I expected and I'm not even sure when I realized it. The Lord delivered me from bipolar disorder, a mental illness diagnosed and treated by a psy-chiatrist in Vancouver since 1999. I was fortunate to have a Christian Doctor, who was a believer. It took over a year for him to help me withdraw from all the psychiatric drugs. But, 'Praise the Lord', I am free.

I have been free since that day at your house. I didn't want any negativity, so I didn't tell the Doctor in Vancouver, but I will one of these days. Please share with anyone who will listen. There are people like me who believe the Lord can heal but a 'mental illness'. Who knew!

I hope you are both well.

70

Miracles Continue in the 'Garage-Church'

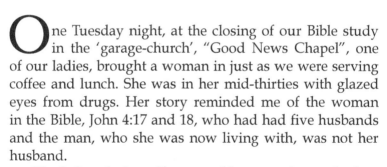

One Tuesday night, at the closing of our Bible study in the 'garage-church', "Good News Chapel", one of our ladies, brought a woman in just as we were serving coffee and lunch. She was in her mid-thirties with glazed eyes from drugs. Her story reminded me of the woman in the Bible, John 4:17 and 18, who had had five husbands and the man, who she was now living with, was not her husband.

The lady asked us, if we would stop and pray for her, because she really wanted help. We put our lunch down and went to pray for her.

While we were praying the tears began to flow, the glaze started to leave this ladies' eyes and God set her free from a life of drugs, psychiatric problems and sin, as she surrendered her life to Jesus. That was on Tuesday night and I was told she was baptized in the Holy Spirit, Pentecostal fashion, on Thursday night. Shortly after this, she was officially married.

This lady had lived a life of drugs and psychiatric problems. She had spent so many years talking to psychiatrists, that she knew how to play the game better than they did.

On one of my next birthdays, she gave me a card with a cartoon on it that said, "I have only been seeing the psychiatrist for two weeks, but I already have the left side of his face twitching."

This couple owned the Ambulance service and sometimes I would drive for them. On some of our trips, the lady would talk about some memories that were coming back. She had gone through several 'shock treatments' and it had affected her ability to remember and organize her thoughts, but God was healing that.

One such story that reveals her sense of humor, along with her desperation to have drugs, I will try to relate.

As my memory serves me right, she was in Ponoka in the Alberta Mental Hospital. She had been begging for more drugs to ease her problems, but they refused to give her more drugs.

Just as she was being turned down, the police pulled up with a patient in a straightjacket, which took both of the policemen to handle. So the police car was left unattended. She seized the opportunity, got into the police car and proceeded to drive all over the grounds with the lights flashing and the siren blaring. When they finally got her stopped, they were quick to give her some more drugs to quiet her down.

God did such a job on her that her religiously unemotional husband, was so impressed, that he phoned and asked me if I could come and see him. Of course, I said yes, and headed up the street two or three blocks to visit with him. You see, this man, was a psychiatric nurse and met the lady through his nursing career. They met through her repetitious drug abuse and psychiatric breakdowns and he probably continued thinking that he could help her.

She became so different for so long, that his first statement to me, as I sat down at their little round kitchen table was, "Whatever she got, I want!" He prayed in tears and invited Jesus into his heart that day. She continued to grow spiritually and he started showing up in our Pentecostal services. He had been brought up in the Christian Reformed Church.

Another miracle that happened to him was because of an accident. A motor fell on his arm and crushed it. I believe they had to put a plate or pins in it to help it heal. We had an Evangelistic Crusade which he attended. He came up to the front for prayer and God healed his arm! He grabbed the Evangelist and hugged him and lifted him off the floor as he testified of God's healing.

The Ministerial had a system, so that each Pastor took their turn at being the Chaplain at the hospital. One of the Chaplain's duties was to inform each Pastor of anyone registered in the hospital under their particular denomination.

The Chaplain called me one time concerning an out-of-town young man who had recorded his church affiliation as Pentecostal. I dutifully went to visit him. I teased and joked with him and told him the story of David and Goliath, and prayed with him and included the man in the next bed. I didn't feel anything unusual had happened, since the young man was released the next day and I felt, I had just done my Pastoral duty.

Some weeks, maybe months, later, the man who was next to this young lad in the hospital walked into the garage-church service and pointed at me and said, "That's him. That's the Preacher I was telling you about!"

His niece had been trying to get him to come to church with her for quite a while, but he just kept saying, "I would go to church, if I could find a preacher like the one who visited that young fellow next to me in the hospital". Apparently something had been said or done, that God had used to reach his heart, without me knowing anything about it. He got saved, delivered from drunkenness, witnessed to everybody, listened to gospel tapes and read his Bible for six months, until God took him to heaven. I learned that he was dying of cancer. Because of the change in his life, plus many other influences, the little church had a lot of his family attending. His wife, was a faithful servant of the Lord, until she passed away many years later. One of her unique gifts was, to be able to put experiences and gospel truths into poetry. One of her daughters, gave her heart to Jesus and one Sunday morning, with the garage-church packed to standing room only, her husband, a big man, was standing and leaning on the window ledge. In the middle of the service he started to weep and asked if he could have that experience in his heart that his wife had received. He gave his heart to Jesus and became a part of a chain reaction.

Besides the people in his family, who came to the church, he was involved with the organization of the Native Friendship Center and asked me to serve on the Board of Directors. I was honored to do so and later on, I was asked to sit on the board of the Kochitawin Drug and Alcohol Abuse Center. What an awesome privilege of ministry that became.

One of the ladies that gave her heart to the Lord through this exposure, was from the Big Horn Reserve, 68 miles west of our church and was married. She was very active in the Native organizations, and was a gifted interpreter for her native people, concerning Government dealings and court dealings.

Some years later, she became my interpreter on her home reservation.

71

Growth Meant Building a New Church

After several Sunday mornings of a hundred or more people in our 20' x 30' garage, it became more and more obvious, that we had to get the mind of the Lord on a building. I got together with my friend and parishioner and contractor, and after some prayer and discussion decided to go with the dimensions of 46' x 91'. It was immediately suggested that our congregation was made up of a large percentage of natives and metis, who weren't making very much money. The implied question was how could we expect to pay for the building? I remember having a flash of incredulity that anyone would even think that way, since we felt confident that it was God that told us to build, so it would be God that would pay for it.

Well, my idealism was put to the test many times. I don't remember all of the exact figures, but I think we had approximately $5,000.00 in the bank, when we had a ground breaking service on October 5, 1975. Besides, all the machinery and operators to do the excavation, we needed thousands of yards of concrete, lumber for footings, $33,000.00 for the first stage of Dual Block, rebar, etc.. We had to re-plot the property and have the town re-zone the property for a church. The town was a little reluctant to sanction us building a church. They sent notice to all our neighbors within a block. The neighbors formed a committee and appointed a spokesperson. He came and explained that everyone wasn't in favor of us building a church there. They were concerned that it would be another 'eyesore' like my tarpapered and wired, stucco-less garage.

So I, by this time, had some drawings done by an architect friend in Toronto, Ontario, who had volunteered to help us out, as his donation to the Church. I pulled them out and showed them to the community's spokesman. You could see the look on his face which revealed an obvious change of attitude and then he gave us a favorable report. One other neighbor, an outspoken Lutheran lady, let us know that she was in favor of the church, but wished it didn't have to block her view. She wouldn't be able to see her neighbors down the street to her right side. She actually attended church fairly often after we built.

The church was built 95% by volunteer labor -- men, women, teenagers, neighbors, passers-by, and a few work bees organized by the Woodlea Pentecostal church in Red Deer, the Sherwood Park Pentecostal church, and a group came out from the Sunnyside Pentecostal Camp at Sylvan Lake, etc.. I am sure, I won't remember all that came to help us, since the building project took two years. Don Bunting, of Action Electrical, gave us instructions on placing conduit etc. and made two or three plane trips down from Edmonton to pull wire, etc. and tie in our electrical plan.

My friend, parishioner and contractor, was going to be our General Contractor, but by the time we started building, he had been put on a job up in Athabasca, Alberta. So Pastor Lyle became the general contractor, by taking instructions over the phone from him. This kind of construction was way beyond my ability, so we discovered that God could even show us how to do stuff that we had never done before. You think maybe God knows all about building churches?

One of the volunteers was a trucking friend, who used his truck to haul all of the block down from Edmonton.

Another quaint couple who just stopped and parked in our yard for a few weeks, and volunteered his carpentry skills.

Another carpenter, who was attending Bible College and stayed with us in the summer of 1977, and was responsible for the finishing of the church windows. He also helped us design and build a spiral staircase around the chimney in the little old house, so that we could develop a 'Jack-and-Jill' bedroom in the attic for our two girls, Candace and Kimberlee. Eli was on his knees laying carpet.

The town wouldn't give us a building permit, based on an Ontario architect's drawings, without an Alberta Engineer's stamp, but they would give us a development permit so that we could get started. The town ran the new services to the edge of the church property and we got the excavations done.

My friend, Pastor Mel Jenkins, came down from Sherwood Park and gave us a few days to help with the lay-out and build all the footings and support pads. We set up a small cement mixer and mixed and poured the footings by the wheelbarrow full. We ordered two or three truckloads of gravel and pit run, to level off the basement floor in readiness for pouring. Just then the men were all going away for the weekend to Banff for a Men's Fellowship Retreat. Kay asked if there was anything we could leave for the women and the teenagers to do, so I lightly suggested that approximately thirty yards of rock and gravel all had to be spread around before we could pour the floor, and then left for Banff. Well, Sunday afternoon when we got back from Banff, Kay had organized a crew of kids and women and had all that rock and gravel leveled. wow!

I started laying the bottom row of Dual block. I borrowed my contractor friend's six foot level and put a carbide tip blade in my cheap little skill saw and with the use of an old hatchet, I set out to lay the first blocks of my life, with over-the-phone coaching from my contractor friend.

Dual Block, was a company in Edmonton that had developed an insulated block construction, inspired by the rubble clean-up in Germany, after the Second World War.

In Germany, they developed a process where they mixed the crushed rubble by hopper with a concrete mix and compressed it into a block mold.

Dual Block used sawdust for the aggregate in the concrete mix and made sawdust blocks by many thousands of pounds of pressure in a mold on a smooth floor. Then the mold lifted up, and moved on to form block after block on a smooth floor approximately 300 feet long. The blocks left behind were still wet, of course, and if kicked before they dried would just crumble. However, after they cured, they were strong and as hard as a cement block. A 1′ x 2′ x 8″ thick block would only weigh, approximately, 30 pounds, much lighter than a cement block, but, when constructed with the proper steel rebar placement, was rated, as a wall five and a half times stronger than a standard cement block wall. The obvious other benefit was the insulation factor. There was approximately two inches of a sawdust composite inside and outside of a four inch concrete and steel core.

So, we built the whole church out of Dual Block. You could place your hand on an inside sawdust block wall and an outside wall at minus twenty degrees Fahrenheit outside and not be able to notice any difference. It was a God-send, because even I could build with these blocks. They were shaped so that they fit together like kids blocks and only had to be shaved or trimmed with a skill saw, or a hatchet periodically to keep them from running, — you understand.

72

Faith for the Impossible– God Provides

───── ୧∕᠀∕୨ ─────

The miracle of building a sanctuary that seated approximately 500 people with no money in the bank are too many to tell. Time after time, as we needed an influx of major money, it would arrive on time from some unexpected source. We actually were naively numb to the many miracles that just kept us going, so that we didn't record them as miracles, but were living on a spiritual high of expectancy. Looking back, it's not hard to realize the many, many miracles of provision needed so that a small group of non-millionaires could build a building worth hundreds of thousands of dollars.

The memory of the days spent laying blocks, mostly by myself, because everybody was working during the day. Most help came from the Saturday work bees. From daylight to dark I would chip, cut, and lay blocks . . . fit the steel rebar in place and grout fill the blocks with cement. By the summer of 1976, we were ready for the main floor of the sanctuary to be poured. A group came out from the Pentecostal Camp, plus surrounding churches and poured the floor. More blocks now could be laid and we ordered the $6,000.00 worth of laminated arches for the main sanctuary. They were being shipped C.O.D. from Dring Canada in Manitoba, but we had no money in the bank to pay for them.

They were scheduled to arrive on Monday, if I remember right. Well, before they arrived three cheques arrived unexpectedly from three different sources, for $2,000.00 each. Praise the Lord!

The one cheque just seemed miraculous because of its timing, since we never appealed for funds but just prayed, so nobody would know our immediate needs. This cheque came from the Alberta District of the Pentecostal Assemblies of Canada. Some estate had just been settled in Saskatchewan and designated a certain sum for the Alberta District to divide up amongst new church building projects. $2,000.00 was sent to our Church building fund, just in time to help pay Dring Canada for the C.O.D. shipment of laminated beams.

Before the day was over, two more cheques for $2,000.00 arrived. The one cheque was from Las Vegas, Nevada — mystery for sure, since I didn't know anyone from there. The other cheque was from Montana — also a mystery, since we had no contact with anyone from there. We discovered later, that they were sent to us via these American churches because some American friends who were supportive of the vision needed their gift to be channeled through the American tax system. Again, that being as unique as it was, the miracle was the timing so that we could pay Dring Canada for the $6,000.00 C.O.D.

Another timely provision God arranged, was on the day the rafters had to be raised. We had a gathering of help from around the area and hired a crane to lift them into place. Each arch was engineered to be bolted together at the peak. We put all the big bolts in, while the arch was lying on the cement floor and then put the harness on each section to lift them by crane into place.

The very first arch was being lifted when they realized the calculation for the harness was wrong, and the joint at the peak broke and the bolts broke out. We were able to lower the beam back down to the floor, but were puzzled what we could do to repair that beam.

Just that week, one of the young men gave his heart to Jesus. He was a welder and had his rig on his truck parked on the street. He took a look at the problem and assured us, that he would weld a metal saddle for that joint that would fix it . . . Timing! By the time the other beams were fastened in place, the sixth beam had a metal saddle in place and was lifted into its place. To this day, you can look up at the beam in the balcony of that Church and view the timely provision of the invention that God provided just on time.

After hundreds (maybe thousands) of buckets of cement we had the mezzanine floor poured up behind the platform area, which housed two change rooms and a baptismal tank. I remember the day, I was working alone, laying block above the mezzanine floor. I turned around and looked out over this mammoth task, realized we had no money — maybe I was tired — it was seemingly overwhelming and I turned and looked out to the mountains in the west and burst into tears. I said, "God, what did you get me into? Did I really hear from you? This is a big building and we have no more money to finish it!" Just as if God sent a special ray of sunshine from the western sky, I had a jolt of spiritual electricity that seemed to be God saying, "I have supplied every need this far, and I will supply every need to finish it." I never had another doubt. The building was finished, with only about a $74,000.00 mortgage, which has since been paid off.

"Miracle" Church at the fourth place of ministry

73

Miracle in the Bush

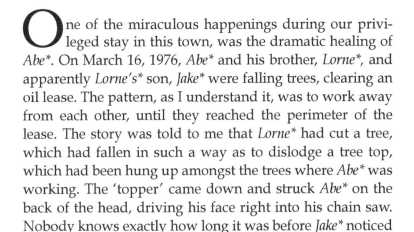

One of the miraculous happenings during our privileged stay in this town, was the dramatic healing of *Abe**. On March 16, 1976, *Abe** and his brother, *Lorne**, and apparently *Lorne's** son, *Jake** were falling trees, clearing an oil lease. The pattern, as I understand it, was to work away from each other, until they reached the perimeter of the lease. The story was told to me that *Lorne** had cut a tree, which had fallen in such a way as to dislodge a tree top, which had been hung up amongst the trees where *Abe** was working. The 'topper' came down and struck *Abe** on the back of the head, driving his face right into his chain saw. Nobody knows exactly how long it was before *Jake** noticed it and began to yell so loud that Lorne shut his saw down and ran to help.

They ran for help and a battery operator was going by and radioed for the ambulance. They were about an hour or so hauling *Abe** in waste deep snow to the road. By the time the ambulance got out there and back to town, approximately three hours had elapsed. The doctor took one look at him and discerned that his skull was caved in at the front, so he rough-stitched his head together and shipped him on to Edmonton emergency, without much hope that he would live. The doctor said, that if he did live, he would be nothing more than a vegetable.

*Abe's** wife, phoned the church for prayer! The church folk went to prayer. I'm sure, I can't do justice to *Abe's** story, but I'll tell it, as I remember it being told to me.

I don't remember whether the vision that *Abe** had, happened on the way to the hospital or during his stay there. However, by the time he arrived in Edmonton, the skull that had been caved in, was back out normally, so the doctors in Edmonton never did re-stitch his head. The jagged rough stitch that the first doctor had done, was all that ever was done. He remained in Edmonton for three weeks for observation and then was sent to the home hospital for one week.

Whenever the vision took place, it sounded something like this:

There was a long tunnel with a very bright light at the end of the tunnel. On one side of the tunnel was all manner of sin and darkness, and on the other side was all manner of Christian activity and right living. The implication was for *Abe** to make a decision. He decided to serve the Lord and woke up healed. Abe is as normal as *Abe** can be (my attempt at humor), to the time of this writing. Praise the Lord!

74

The Importance for us to know the TRUTH

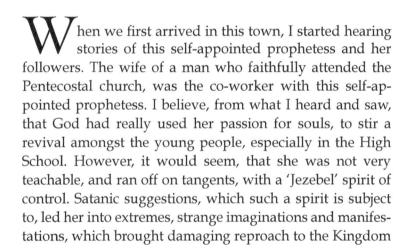

W hen we first arrived in this town, I started hearing stories of this self-appointed prophetess and her followers. The wife of a man who faithfully attended the Pentecostal church, was the co-worker with this self-appointed prophetess. I believe, from what I heard and saw, that God had really used her passion for souls, to stir a revival amongst the young people, especially in the High School. However, it would seem, that she was not very teachable, and ran off on tangents, with a 'Jezebel' spirit of control. Satanic suggestions, which such a spirit is subject to, led her into extremes, strange imaginations and manifestations, which brought damaging reproach to the Kingdom of God.

One manifestation which grew out of "zeal . . . but not according to knowledge" (Romans 10:2) was a campaign of fasting that swept through the High School. Great zeal, but not handled wisely, and several young people ended up in the hospital with bloating and ruptured villi. The town then passed some edict that banned the self-appointed prophetess from holding meetings in town. She ended up moving out to an acreage ten miles south of town and formed what was virtually a commune. Not Good!

She had already been prophesying people in and out of their marriages, point in case, her co-worker and husband. The issue seemed to be, to set you free from your 'flesh-mate' so you could marry your 'soul-mate'. Ungodly garbage! Same-o, same-o! Every self-styled, so-called prophet seems to fall into this same pattern; form, some special dispensation or social status to excuse immorality and selfishness and make right wrong and wrong, right?

Mabel* even was prophesied into believing, that she was pregnant with the 'man-child' of Revelation 12. Some of the folks in our church, who had been somewhat influenced by this group, were relating how sure *Mabel** was of this 'miracle' and was starting to show swelling in the abdomen. I think, now looking back on it, I would say that I blurted out prophetically with authority . . . even startling myself — with, "She is not pregnant! If she is swelling, she either has a tumor or has stuffed her clothing with a pillow! If she produces a baby, it will not be out of her womb, but borrowed, adopted or obtained from some other source!"

A dear sister, who had seen *Mabel** and talked with her, suggested that I should be careful making such a statement, because the story sure seemed to be true to her. I blurted out a repeat of the same statement, with more adamant excitement than the first time. It proved to be a true prophecy.

About the time of the proposed birth, there was feverish activity, trying to adopt a baby boy out of Manitoba. That never happened! The baby never materialized! The pillows were removed, and the story just quietly died. *Damnable garbage that Satan uses to deceive the believers and bring reproach on the genuine gospel!*

"For of this sort are they, which creep into houses, and lead captive silly women laden with sins, led away with divers lusts, ever learning, and never able to come to the knowledge of the truth." 2 Timothy 3:6 and 7.

307

Out of the 'commune' came devastating home and individual destruction. I fasted and prayed, asking God what I should do about this. It was effecting some of our friends and some of the people, that God brought across our path, with who we were sharing the gospel. After several days, I was so fired up, and sure that God would tell me what to say when I got there, that I jumped in my car to drive ten miles south and confront the self-appointed prophetess and the 'spirits' I was sure I would encounter.

I was driving, talking in tongues and virtually feeling like I was in another world. I left just enough time for the return trip and confrontation of the revelation of 'spirits'. When I came to myself, I was about a mile from the acreage and realized, it had taken the whole time allowed just to drive the nine miles. I wrestled momentarily and turned around and had to hurry, to get back to town for my next appointment. All the way back, I kept asking the Lord, what that was all about. He just gently calmed my spirit and assured me that that was not the way He was going to work.

Within a few days, four young ladies showed up at my door feeling that God had sent them to me from the 'commune' to confess their sins and repent. I swallowed the lump in my throat and exhorted them to understand, that I wasn't who they should confess to, but I would endeavor to be obedient to the leading of the Lord. They poured their hearts out and told me things that confirmed what I believed I had heard from the Lord already. I have no idea now what all they said, nor do I remember exactly what my response was, but we prayed together. There was some repentance. There was an obvious sense that God was doing a work, but I confess, I felt like I was sitting off to one side watching with awe and not understanding all that was going on. But God!

The next few days and nights, we received several phone calls from one of the young ladies, who was experiencing some mental and spiritual attacks. She was having visions of being burned in a fire, etc. The details of which I have forgotten, but God delivered her and she showed up in church, and faithfully attended and grew spiritually. Her husband made a decision for the Lord, but later turned back and left her. However, that lady is serving Jesus to this day.

Another of the young ladies is still serving Jesus along with her husband, but the other two never, as long as I knew them, got completely free from the influence of the 'commune'. The one young lady's husband left her, and she stayed with the other young lady and her husband for some time. I believe they all love Jesus and are endeavoring to serve Him, but are still influenced by some bad teaching and experiences. For the most part the rest of the group shut down and moved operations to another province.

75

Miracles on the Big Horn Reservation

———————⟨ formula ⟩———————

We had started drive-in-church, some years earlier on the first weekend in June, because that was the weekend that the annual Rodeo began. Our drive-in-church was on the I.G.A. parking lot and projected towards the Rodeo grounds about two blocks away.

On the Sunday night of June 1979, a truck-load of First Nation people drove on to the parking lot, thinking this was an extension of the Rodeo. They sat there through the whole service and then several of them gave their lives to Jesus. The driver agreed to come down to the church for lunch after the service.

My interpreter called me over to talk with him. He was a little shy to talk English to me, so she interpreted. He wanted to know, if I would come out to his Reservation and preach that kind of Christianity. I knew that they already had a Finnish couple living on the Reserve that were apparently Spirit filled and leading meetings there. The man shook his head and had my interpreter explain to me, that the Missionary on the Reserve was mixing Indian religion with Christian, and he wanted the kind of Christian preaching that we did on the street. After some discussion,

I agreed to hold meetings in the Band Hall every Thursday evening as long as the man made the arrangements.

July 1979 Drive-in Church

I phoned the Missionaries, and invited them to join me, because I would be like the Evangelist, but they would have to Pastor these people. After all, they lived on the Reserve and I didn't. The Missionaries didn't seem to appreciate me being there, and stirred up some opposition, but God continued to bless. As a matter of fact, I'm going to make a startling statement concerning those meetings on that Reservation. Without a question, they were ordained by God. In all of my ministry (at time of writing, approximately forty-seven years), I have never seen the consistent manifestation of God's power, as we saw at that Reservation.

From the first Thursday in June 1979, until the first weekend of October 1979, 100% of the people that asked for prayer were healed, including a horse. Let me attempt to recount a few of the miracles that God did in that time.

One of the elders, my interpreter's mother was very withered up into a bent over little lady with arthritis, so bad that her hands were uselessly crippled. She needed help to even move because of the pain, and was brought up to the front of the Band Hall for prayer. As I started to pray, her hands started to snap and straighten and her posture became erect, and I lost control of my English and was praying in tongues. I was ecstatic, weeping and talking in unlearned tongues, when my interpreter whispered in my ear, "Pastor, you're speaking in Stoney". I asked her afterwards and she explained to me, that I was praising God and saying how great He was!

One night an elder came hobbling up for prayer. He had a big lump on his one ankle. He put his foot up on the bench at the front and pulled his pant leg up. I said (what became almost a ritual), "So you know that I can't heal anybody. But do you believe that when I pray in Jesus' name He will heal you?" He kind of grunted "uh huh". I started to pray, and all of a sudden, this old man in his seventies, started to dance and shout and stomp that foot on the floor.

This man, to the day he died, used to call me 'The Big Man' and was convinced that whatever I prayed for, was going to happen. So much so, that he came in to visit my interpreter in town the next Thursday. He tried to explain to her, that he wanted her to ask 'The Big Man' if he would pray for his horse that night and wanted to know if that was proper. She brought him over to our house in the afternoon and explained the situation to which I promptly said, "Yes, we'll pray for your horse!"

Then I found out the circumstances. Three years before, he was riding this horse, when it stepped in a gopher hole and broke its leg. When the man got thrown from the horse, he also broke his ankle, but he had never wanted to shoot his favorite horse, so he had let it limp around the pasture for three years. That night, I had some of the young men gather around him to pray. He went home and laid hands on his horse and prayed. The horse was miraculously healed, after limping around on a broken leg for three years. Hallelujah! Isn't it great, to find people with such uncomplicated faith in God and His Word!

One other instance will help you to understand, why no preacher should ever take the credit for miracles.

This particular Thursday night, I felt strongly that I was to teach from God's Word and give some helpful instruction. The meeting went well, but it didn't seem conducive to calling people for prayer. I closed with a statement something like that. My interpreter came to me and said, "But Pastor, Charlie wants prayer." "Okay, we'll be happy to pray for Charlie", I said. Apparently Charlie had broken his leg around the knee and the doctors had been working with it, but finally said, that Charlie's leg was as good as it would get, and he would have to wear a brace on it for the rest of his life. So we gathered around Charlie, who was a pretty quiet man, I said, "Charlie, do you know that I can't heal anyone? But do you believe that when we pray in Jesus' Name that He will heal you?" Charlie nodded his head and grunted affirmatively. I knelt down to lay my hands on Charlie's leg and prayed 'the prayer of faith'. When I laid hands on Charlie's leg brace, my faith seemed to go right through the floor and I started planning in my mind, what to say to Charlie after we prayed, so that he wouldn't be discouraged if his healing didn't happen instantly like everybody else's had.

So, I proceeded to pray 'the prayer of faith' and stood up to try and encourage Charlie. What came out of my mouth wasn't as I had planned. Instead, I just asked Charlie, if there was something he could do now, that he couldn't do before? Charlie bent his knee and said, "That!" Then Charlie started to run around the Band Hall. He took that brace off, never to wear it again and rode in a Rodeo the following Saturday. Praise the Lord! We don't do miracles, but God still does!

Peter was somewhere in his nineties and virtually blind when he came for prayer, God healed him, so that he read his Bible without glasses until he died in his late nineties.

I was involved working on our new house, so I was in my coveralls and picking up the mail at the Post Office, when Charlie came in and told me that he and his wife had just come from the hospital and were taking their little baby home to die. The Doctor said there was no hope, since the baby was in the late stages of meningitis. I said, "Charlie, do you want to bring the baby to the church for prayer or should we just pray right here." He suggested that we go out to his van and lay hands on the baby there. His wife put the window down and Charlie and I reached through the window and prayed. God healed that little girl instantly.

I haven't seen Charlie and his wife for a few years, but the last report I had, was that that little baby grew up, and at 21 years of age was singing for Jesus! Hallelujah! How many know that we don't do miracles, but God still does!?

There were many healed of diabetes, gall bladder problems and other problems that weren't diagnosed, but left after prayer.

76

A Chain Reaction to a Changed Life

————◦⁄⁄◦————

Our children honored us by constantly bringing their school chums home to meet us. Kay and I always loved people and felt privileged to have our children feel free to bring their friends home.

One such little friend was a neighbor girl, *Betsy**. We knew her parents, but were not particularly close friends with them. I bought a car from her dad, and I knew that her mother was one of approximately a dozen ladies who attended the Anglican Church.

We were having an Evangelistic Crusade in the new church. *Betsy** came and gave her heart to Jesus and received a real baptism in the Holy Spirit. She proceeded to run home and attempt to explain to her mother what had happened. Well, *Betsy** had had a problem with her imagination and inability to speak the truth. When she tried to explain this spiritual happening to her fine, upstanding Anglican mother, her mother just put her off for lying again and *Betsy** was devastated and went sobbing to her bedroom. Her mother, *Susanne** sensed something different and thought to herself, "I know the Carberts, but I let my daughter go to that church and I have no idea what they teach or do in that church". So she determined to attend the next night with *Betsy*.

I don't remember much about that particular service except when I looked up, I saw *Susanne* about half-way up the one aisle swaying around in a circle, as if her feet were nailed down and she was doing a hula-hoop move which, under normal circumstances would have caused her to fall down. After several pivots, she finally went down under a powerful sense of God's presence and began to speak in other tongues. When she was able to get off the floor, I remember her first words were, "I know now why *Betsy* was having a hard time explaining to me what she experienced". *Susanne* was back the next night with her teenagers, one on each arm, leading them to the altar.

This began another chain reaction, as *Susanne* now wanted to leave the Anglican Church and join the Pentecostal Church. She was, I believe, a third generation Anglican. I knew her Pastor, and had some good talks with him when he was hospitalized. From my perspective, of course, the Anglican Church had died spiritually long ago and was just hanging on religiously, with about a dozen faithful people. I knew *Susanne* would never be satisfied with that, nor would it help her grow in the Lord.

I quickly counseled her to join us as often as she could, but stay faithful to the Anglican Church and pray for a spiritual revival over there. She agreed to do that. Then the Pastor resigned, and I think actually retired, so she came to us again and asked if she could now change churches. I advised her, that I would rather believe with her, that her new Pastor would be Spirit-filled, and maybe that would be the start of revival in the Anglican Church. But, of course, in the meantime I encouraged her to attend as many meetings as she could with the Pentecostal people. So she agreed to stay at the Anglican Church, but asked permission to join the Pentecostal Church, if they didn't get a Spirit-filled preacher as their new Pastor. So I agreed!

Well, God heard our prayers and sent the Western Director of Anglican Renewal to the church. Within a year, the church grew until they had to enlarge it. The mayor and his wife were Anglican and they both got on fire for God. The town manager and his wife both were saved and filled with the Holy Spirit. As a matter of encouragement to me, they, the town manager and his wife, on more than one occasion spoke up in our Sunday night service to thank us for hanging in there, until they got what we had. As far as I know, *Susanne** is still a faithful Spirit-filled Anglican.

77

God's Power Manifested in Setting the Captive Free

One Sunday evening service, in the new church building, we were ministering on "Ye shall receive power after that the Holy Spirit is come upon you . . ." Acts 1:8. Five men came forward to receive the Baptism of the Holy Spirit. None of them were from the Pentecostal persuasion. I think one or two of them were Christian Reformed, maybe one or two from the Christian and Missionary Alliance, etc. I don't really remember. Just as I stepped off the platform to lay hands on them and pray, a fairly large lady started running down the aisle screaming and fell face first and began writhing like a snake and flopping about like a fish.

I excused myself from the men, and encouraged them to keep praying. I ran down the aisle to hold her from banging her head on the pews as she flopped and wriggled down the aisle. My wife left the organ and joined me as we hung on to her and took authority over the demons in the name of Jesus. By the time we were finished praying, she was sitting on the floor leaning against the front pew. She wondered how she got there, but she was delivered. This is a miracle!!! We don't do miracles, but GOD STILL DOES!

(If my memory serves me right, I believe most, if not all of those waiting at the front for prayer were filled with the Holy Spirit.)

That lady had quite a history. She had been abused several ways and had experienced depression on more than one occasion to the point of attempted suicide. She and her husband had taken studies with the Mormon cult and were scheduled for water baptism. I was in the hospital visiting another lady in the next bed to her, when she kept butting in with questions or challenges to what I was saying. So I prayed with the other lady and turned my attention to *Lorna**. I said *"Lorna**, the Mormons are nice people and have some nice family programs, but when it comes to Bible doctrine or Theology they are extremely deceived. The first clue to that fact, is that though the Bible clearly states that "Jesus is God, manifest in the flesh, they don't believe that Jesus is God." Well, *Lorna** wanted to argue, so I suggested she ask her elders about it. Just then, the head nurse came in to check on her and guess who she was? The nurse was one of the leaders in the Mormon Church. *Lorna** put her right on the spot by repeating what I said. She assured her that I was right, and the Mormons don't believe that Jesus is God. So, when the nurse left, I gave *Lorna** Isaiah 9:6 to read and think about, and prayed with her and left.

Some months later, we held our annual business meeting. The meeting was going fairly late – maybe nine-thirty in the evening. *Lorna** and her husband were driving back and forth past the church wondering what was going on with all the lights on so late and all the cars in the parking lot. They finally got up the courage and came in and sat in the back pew. I recognized her, and encouraged her to feel welcome and carried on chairing the Church business meeting. There were a few issues that were being challenged by a few spoke-persons in an attack mode, but God enabled us somehow to patiently deal with them. At the end of the meeting *Lorna** spoke up and said, that the love that was shown in that meeting convinced her that she wanted to give her heart to Jesus. So we closed that annual business meeting and she and her husband came to the altar and gave their hearts to Jesus.

*Lorna** faced lots of challenges. Her husband eventually left her, but the last I heard, she kept her faith in Jesus as her Savior until the day she died.

There was another time, that we will probably never forget, when the devil tried to disrupt a service. The service was flowing with a great sense of God's presence. I slipped upstairs to the sound room for some reason and was just coming out of the sound room when a man named *Robert** let out a blood-curdling scream, and fell down between the pews. I ran down to him and we all took authority over the demons and he was delivered instantly. We were not able to walk along side of this man and we heard some months later that he committed suicide.

Two things we can learn from this case. As usual, in our experience, at least, and it seems to parallel Bible experiences, as soon as there is a great sense of God's presence, there is reaction or manifestation from the demonic, if it is present.

Secondly, we have absolute authority over the demonic in "Jesus name!" Mark 16:17; Matthew 10:8. So, when we order them to come out in Jesus' name, they have no option, they must come out. However, the Lord never gives us authority over a person's will. If the person refuses to deal with the problem that opened the door to the demons, then the last state of that person is worse than the first. (Luke 11:24-26).

78

A Life-threatening Experience

‒‒‒‒‒✒︎‒‒‒‒‒

Just after the new church was built and we still didn't have any doors on my office, I had an extremely interesting experience. I have never told this story to the family, when they read this story, it will be the first time that they will hear it. I believe, they all know me well enough to recognize the truth, even though they may not want to believe it. I'm going to change the names of most of the people involved to save any embarrassment.

The Sunday night service was just over and Kay had taken the children to the old house to put them to bed. I was at the desk in my office doing something, when the children came running in, all excited. Kay had sent them to get me, because a man who she recognized had pounded on the back door demanding to see me. Kay handled it well, and sent the children to get me, while the man went and squatted down in the bushes around the corner of the house. I came right over and the man jumped up with his six-pack of beer and brushed past me as he headed for the church office. I didn't have time to find out what it was all about, but followed him into my office. He plunked the case of beer on my desk. While I was asking him what was going on, he proceeded to grab a bottle out of the case with which to pry the cap off a second bottle. I grabbed the bottle out of his hand and explained to him, that the only thing he would be doing with that beer in the church, would be to pour it down the sink. I asked him again what was going on.

Let me give you a little background. He had given his heart to Jesus along with several of his relatives back in the 'garage-church'. He, along with several of his relatives had an alcoholic history. He was artistic, so I bought paint, brushes, a sheet of plywood and sundry other items to make a sign for the Good News Chapel (garage-church). He was coming along pretty good, played his guitar at prayer meetings, etc., when he fell off of the wagon and got some serious jail time for an altercation involving a stabbing. He spent his time in jail pumping weights and body building (three years, I think). When he arrived at my back door with his case of beer, he had just gotten out of jail and was on parole.

He proceeded to explain to me that he was so discouraged and defeated, that he was going to kill himself. He explained that he wanted to die with a friend, and he thought, that I was the only person that was his friend. So he was going to drink the beer, kill me and then himself.

(Now is the time for somebody to say, "With friends like that who needs an enemy".)

So when I refused to let him drink his beer, he suddenly reached down into his cowboy boot and pulled out a regular, well-honed butcher knife and explained his change of plans. Now, he decided he would have to kill me first, then drink his beer and kill himself.

Something supernatural then took place as a calm anointing started to express through my lips and actions. I calmly explained to my agonizing brother, that there were three reasons why he wouldn't be killing me that night:

1 — He wasn't ready in his present condition to die for killing me.

2 — He didn't have the prerogative to take my life since Revelation 1:18 says that Jesus holds the keys to death, and I didn't believe He would give them to my 'friend'.

3— Then I flippantly suggested, that he likely wasn't physically able to kill me (which may have been a little foolish and in the flesh), and then I made strong, possibly prophetic statement. I said, "So you won't be killing anybody tonight, but if you don't smarten up you're going to hurt yourself real bad."

With that he lunged at me, with both hands on the knife, endeavoring to thrust it into my body. Now this is where I feel certain that God intervened. This man, who had been 'pumping iron' for about three years, should have been able to accomplish his task. Somehow, I can still remember his red-faced effort as he tried so hard, to resist my grip and force that knife into my body, — somehow, I twisted the knife out of his hand, with just a little knick on the side of one hand. He stared at me in some measure of shock, grabbed the beer off the desk and ran out of the door. (I still have the butcher knife that probably belongs to his one sister.)

One of the men from the church apparently had been standing in the prayer room and had observed all this. When my friend ran past him on the way out, I looked up to see this wide-eyed brother standing there. I'm not sure that I could read anything on his face except overwhelming awe.

I grabbed a Kleenex, to dab the little bit of blood on my hand, and then took the phone to call the police. I knew that my 'friend' shouldn't have that beer and for sure shouldn't have that knife, because he was on parole. I explained to the police that he had just left my office in a terrible state of mind with a case of beer (I didn't mention the knife), and that I was concerned. I asked them, if there was any way that I could get a chance to talk to him if they picked him up. They assured me that they would endeavor to arrange it. The brother from the prayer room got in the car with me, and we drove up and down every street and alley looking for my 'friend', but never found him.

When we pulled back into the church parking lot, the police were there waiting. Their word to me was, that if I wanted to see my 'friend', I had better get over to his sister's place because he had already kicked a door in and broken a window, and if I couldn't handle him they would have to arrest him. The prayer-room brother got out to go home and I drove quickly over to my 'friend's' sister's place. As I came up the stairs, his twin nieces came running up the basement stairs crying saying "Uncle _____ is trying to kill himself".

Down the stairs I ran, only to find my 'friend' sitting on the concrete floor holding his head, with a bed sheet wrapped around his neck. He had stood on an old arm chair and tied the sheet around his neck and over the beam and jumped. The sheet tore and he fell and bumped his head on the concrete floor. Well, I had prophesied correctly and my sense of humor cut in and I laughingly shouted, "I told you so!"

Well, my 'friend' and I sat on the concrete floor talking and praying until about three o'clock in the morning, when he was relatively sober and prayed and re-dedicated his life to the Lord. To the best of my knowledge, he served the Lord right until he died in a car accident six months later, and I was invited to take his funeral.

79

Prison Ministry

The Ministerial had opportunities that we all shared besides the hospital chaplaincy. One was the ministry at the minimum security prison. Several preachers started taking turns, but gradually we ended up going every week, because the others gave up their turn to us. So Kay, myself or one of our men, took turns going out the fifty-six miles every Sunday night.

Sometimes the crowd would be as small as a dozen or so inmates out of the fifty-plus of the general population of the prison, but God began to reach hearts week after week.

One week the three 'heavies' came, and all made a decision for Christ in front of the rest of the prison population. 'Heavies' is a term you might hear around the prison scene, especially in a minimum security situation. The staff would count on the inmate leaders, 'heavies', to control the population in exchange for some favors. These three, and I hesitate to use their real names, were each unique individuals. We'll call them *George**, the biker; *Frank**, the bitter former Jehovah Witness and *Wilbert**, the weight lifter, fitness trainer, cook, compulsive liar, etc.. They were all professional cons, but made a genuine decision for Christ. The next week, I was ready to start the service, but there were only about five or six inmates there, until *George**, *Frank**

and *Wilbert** walked in and said, "Hey Rev! Is this all that's coming?" I assured them that it didn't matter, because I was about ready to start. *Wilbert** spoke up and said, "Give us a few minutes! We'll be right back".

Five minutes later, in walks about forty inmates with the 'heavies' barking out orders like, "you sit there . . . and you sit over there . . . and get ready to sing 'Amazing Grace'!" So, we sang 'Amazing Grace' and began a power-packed service. When the altar call was given for people to accept Christ, seventeen young men ended up at the altar. The first one was a six foot tall husky blonde man, who burst out of his seat sobbing and saying that his brother was a Christian preacher who had talked to him about the Lord and that he wanted to be a Christian like his brother. This young man married a Christian girl and attended a Pentecostal Bible College. I've lost track of him, but his step of faith was not only for his sake, but precipitated sixteen other young men making a decision for Christ that night. To see those men sobbing, tears flowing freely, as they took their public stand for Christ, in front of the rest of the prison population was extremely rewarding. Some of those men were transported fifty-six miles by the guards to attend Church and be baptized in water. They also brought van-loads to our 'Singing Christmas Tree' on a couple of occasions.

The man we called *George** was a long-bearded biker. One service he spoke up in the middle of the service and said, "Hey Rev! Are there motorbikes in heaven?" I assured him, we wouldn't feel the same need for motorbikes in heaven, and to the best of my knowledge, I didn't believe there would be motorbikes in heaven. He was quiet for a couple of minutes and then said, "If that's true, then I'm not so sure I want to go!" The rest of the guys laughed. I totally lost track of *George** but hope to see him in heaven.

Frank* had a tremendous change of attitude and seemed to just soak up the teaching about Jesus and the Bible. His problem had been, that whenever he got drinking, he would flip out and do something crazy. After his release, he got a job in town and started to live with a girlfriend.

Some of his old cronies talked him into a party and got him drinking. When he went home pretty drunk, he went to the wrong door and when a strange man came to the door, he presumed the man was with his girlfriend and flipped out in his normal violent way of solving his problems. The man called the police and *Frank** was charged with assault, and did some more time.

When he got out again, he made an attempt at serving the Lord, and even boarded with one of the church families. One night, his old cronies got him drinking again at an outdoor party in the town park. Approximately three o'clock in the morning, there was a banging on our door and some yelling. So I jumped out of bed, threw my housecoat on and ran down the stairs. I opened the door and there was *Frank**. He was shouting threats and some uncouth words, so I shouted back and told him to quiet down or I'd throw him out on his ear. He said, "I'm here to waste you, man!" "Well", I said, "how is that going to happen?" He said, "Do you know how much people hate you? I've just been offered five grand to waste you!"

Then, in my typical but strange sense of humor, I said, "I'm disappointed *Frank**, I should at least be worth ten grand."

He started to shout again and assure me that this was no joke. He was here to waste me and he intended to do just that. So, I gave him the reasons that I had used another time, when I was attacked under threat of my life:

1— you're not going to kill me, because you're not ready in your present condition, to die for killing me.
2— Revelation 1:18, says that Jesus holds the keys to death and I can't see him giving them to you.
3— "*Frank**, I could pin you in five seconds!" (I had taught wrestling for a few years).

He started jumping around as if to attack me saying, "Pitter patter, let's get at 'er!"

I was sitting on the couch by this time in my pajamas and housecoat. I said, "Are you serious, *Frank**?" You really want to have a go with me?"

"Yes, yes, yes . . . pitter patter, let's get at 'er!" He said.

So I stood up slowly, and *Frank** came flying at me. I slipped him into a half nelson chancery and pinned him in about two seconds and held him there. (For those who don't know about wrestling, that hold more or less puts his nose in my armpit and my arms under his neck and the middle of his back and my two hundred plus pounds pressing on his lungs. Every time he squirmed, I just tightened up until he had difficulty breathing. Both of his arms are tied up, so he can do nothing, but struggle himself into more difficulty.)

All of a sudden, he just went limp and gasped out, "Okay, so you can do that!"

I released him and he just ran out the door. I was concerned for him, because I knew, he would be in trouble with the law, the Lord and his future, if we didn't reach him now. I noted where he said the party was and I jumped into my old green station wagon and drove over to the park. It was a hot June night and I shut my lights off and crept into the park with my car windows all down. I could hear the voices talking fairly loudly, and as I pulled to a stop I heard *Frank** say, "I'm telling you guys, don't mess with him!"

I stepped out of my car.

There were probably six to eight guys standing near a picnic table loaded with bottles. I sat down at the next picnic table and *Frank** came over and talked with me for a while. I really don't remember the conversation in any detail. He was apologizing and a bit repentant and warned me to get out of there. I prayed with him and drove home.

The last I heard of *Frank** was that he had married and moved to the west coast and was in business for himself. May God grant His grace to *Frank** in such power and glory, that we'll see him in heaven.

80

Wilbert's Story

―――――〜✦〜―――――

W*ilbert** was a different stick. He had been a con for so long, that he had become a compulsive prevaricator. He couldn't tell the truth, mostly because he had lost the ability to know the truth from a lie. He believed his own lies so much, that he thought they were the truth.

We invited *Wilbert** to come and live with us, so that we could expose him to enough truth, to see him set free. "Ye shall know the truth and the truth shall make you free!" John 8:33.

The church was experiencing a revival spirit. *Wilbert** progressed fairly well right to the point where he would be talking, — stop — shed a tear or two and realize he wasn't telling the truth. But before that, he had a few battles. He could not resist cheating when we played games. He spun a few yarns before he started to deal with it.

One experience that has produced a chuckle from our family over the years, was spawned by the naivety of our son Gord, 'Trusting Gord,' just told *Wilbert** everything including where he kept his money in one of his dresser drawers. Just before Christmas, six hundred dollars was missing out of Gord's drawer. Well, there was suspicions, but no proof. Gord could have misplaced it or been mistaken. It wasn't worth falsely accusing and condemning, so nothing was said directly, but we all got about six hundred dollars-worth of gifts from *Wilbert** that Christmas. Gord actually got his own little T.V. (Ha! Ha!)

*Wilbert** helped us build a greenhouse for Kay's green thumb, and was busy teaching the church young people body building, etc.. He was naive when it came to trusting Christians, which should have been a good thing. At that particular time, there was a 'Jezebel' in the church (I'll explain the term later), who was subtly scheming to get her own way, by undermining the leadership (basically me). A 'Jezebel' or 'controlling spirit' is demonic! It follows a pattern:

1 — it must be in control of leadership with ambitions to <u>control.</u>
2 — if it is not able to control, it will try to <u>ignore</u> or dis-<u>card</u> the present leadership.
3 — if it cannot ignore or discard it will <u>attack</u> with lies and innuendos.

The person invariably, would need to be delivered from that spirit, by either spiritual discipline so that they might recognize the problem and repent, or ultimately they need exorcism.

The reason I raise this story now, is that this person approached *Wilbert** in his naiveté, and it blew him away. He could not get his new head around this concept. He had deceived and schemed most of his life, but when he found someone in the church, professing to be a mature Christian, acting like this, it shook his new found faith to the core. He came into my office confused and angry, somewhat devastated spiritually. Although I had occasion to bump into *Wilbert** once or twice later, he never seemed to come back to that sweet, child-like naiveté in his faith.

One of the cute encounters happened, when I was recovering from a car accident, and was dealing with a situation in the church, that necessitated me being away for a time. I took a job with my contractor friend up in Wabasca, Alberta, about seventy-five miles north of Slave Lake. It would take too long to describe Wabasca and the job, but there were only two places to eat. We chose the one restaurant for our supper meal. We walked in and sat at a table. I was facing the door into the kitchen and you would like to have seen the look on *Wilbert's** face as he came out of the kitchen, to take our orders and saw me sitting there. "Lyle, what are you doing here?" he said. I returned the question to him. Very interesting!

He served us and chatted with my friend and me. He said that he just took the job, because it was available. If he reads this story, he will find out that I perceived, that it was just a good place to hide from the social pressures. However, he still manifested some of his faith by setting me up, so that I was challenged to share Christ with the owners of the restaurant who had been deceived into Mormonism. I want to believe that *Wilbert* was exposed to enough of the power of God, that he'll always have a desire for God. (I still pray for you, *Wilbert**, and hope to see you again, here, there or in the air!)

81

The Baptism of the Holy Spirit

———⌑———

Concerning this 'Baptism in the Holy Ghost' which we preach, practice and enjoy. I was preaching along that line on a Sunday night. I had stepped off the platform and was moving back and forth amongst the pews as I preached. I remember stopping for a moment and saying something like this, "How many here have never received this baptism in the Holy Ghost, speaking in other tongues, but would like to?" Two people's hands shot up. One was a lady In her early seventies and the other was a younger lady whose background, if I remember right, was Jehovah's Witness.

The elderly, let's call her *Sally**, had a unique story of her own. She had grown up apparently in a strong holiness, legalistic influence. She married a man who became an abusive drunk, so she kicked him out and lived the rest of her days alone, with her son. She spent some years in a Baptist church and then attended the First Church of the Nazarene. When the Pentecostal Church was built, just around the corner from her house, she decided to attend there, because she had trouble walking up the hill to the Nazarene Church. All her church background she had been taught against this Pentecostal experience. She had been attending the Pentecostal Church for a few years, before this particular Sunday night.

When she raised her hand in response to my question (I think I was a little bit surprised), I perceived faith to receive and I felt the Holy Spirit leading me, to stop preaching and start praying. I turned and walked between the first and second pews, walked across, took the elderly lady's right hand in mine and she burst forth in a beautiful flowing language as the Holy Spirit gave utterance.

There are some, who don't believe, that the baptism of the Holy Spirit and speaking with 'other tongues' is available today, but that it ceased at the end of the First Century.

I then felt led to do the same with the younger lady, who was virtually unlearned in Pentecostal ways, but within less than a minute was fluently speaking in other tongues.

"Blessed are they which do hunger and thirst after righteousness: for they shall be filled" (Matthew 5:6).

I want to be sensitive, yet tell about the change this baptism in the Holy Spirit made in the elderly lady's life.

She had increasing discomfort, as she grew older and found it more difficult to walk to church. Different ones in the church offered to give her a ride to and from Church, which seemed to solve the problem. For whatever reason, this elderly lady became more and more abusive to deal with. If you helped her, you were 'too pushy!' If you didn't, then 'you didn't care!'

After she received the baptism of the Holy Spirit, she seemed to have an about face, concerning her attitude. Her past rigid teachings (which were not all that bad) didn't change much. She was raised to never place anything on top of the Bible. That didn't change! We still wouldn't roll the table tennis units out in the evenings until she was driven home, because she was offended that we would play ping pong in the basement of the church.

I believe, that when she passed away, she was loved by everyone in the church and greatly missed.

82

The Call to be An Encourager to Ministries

The next transition took a few years.

God told me, I was going to be elected to the executive of the Alberta District at the upcoming Conference and I was to accept. I had no desire to do so and felt that I wouldn't fit, but I accepted.

Sure enough, I was elected by due process and served as Presbyter for the Central Alberta section. God just wanted to educate me, I think. It certainly was an education and further gelling of my convictions concerning ministry gifts.

For some years I had been nurturing a burden for broken preachers and hurting churches. The stint on the executive further enhanced that burden.

Kay, of course, through her nine years as W.M.C. Director for Alberta Northwest Territories, had also developed a strong compassion for women in ministry, especially Pastor's wives. There came a time, when I felt very strongly, that God was saying, that the next church we planted would be our last, and then we should prepare to go on the road and just travel as God directed. He would lead us in such a way, that He could use us to bring healing to ministries and churches. Kay felt the same drawing, but neither of us could begin to make sense of the call.

How could that be? What could possibly qualify us for that calling? How could we live 24/7 on the road? Who would ever support such a calling? What would open the doors for us to be accepted? etc., etc.

Over the years, this whisper from God became louder and louder. I saw in a vision, that we would be stopping at places where God would bless and they would invite us to come on staff. We then were to shake the dust off our wheels and move on.

Other places would be so resistant, that they would like 'to tar and feather' us and run us out of town. We then, were to shake the dust off our wheels and move on.

Speaking of wheels — this brought another need for faith and education. I, as a man, could take off on the road sleeping in the back of a Volkswagen beetle. However, the Lord woke me up to the fact that, 24/7, 365 days of the year, even for a man, but especially for my wife, was not going to fulfill the plan of God in a Volkswagen beetle. So God started enlarging my vision and changing my thinking. We will tell the 'wheels' story later.

Meanwhile, back at home, we were still not feeling the release to leave this Pentecostal Assembly. From the first sense, that we would be going somewhere else soon, I started praying for direction on how to scripturally make the transition.

When I say 'scripturally', I mean this: the church must never be a democracy — the will of the people; the church must never be a dictatorship — the will of the leader; the church must always be a theocracy — the will of God.

Over the years, I had been assessing and studying church structure. The only times you find democracy in the WORD, was when the people wanted their own way instead of God's way. (Exodus 32; Isaiah 8:4-7; Matthew 27:21-26;

Revelation 20:7-9.) Democracy just might work, if ninety-five percent of the church attended prayer meeting and were taught how to know the will of God. (James 1:5-8.) Otherwise, you are bound to get a carnal majority winning the vote. Deacons were appointed not elected! (Acts 6:3, 4.)

An interesting ordination into ministry is recorded in Acts 13:1-4 — "When they had fasted and prayed, and laid hands on, then they sent them away."

The hiring and firing of preachers is pure carnality and 'blotch' in the function of the church. Besides, the unscriptural practice of an elected board of deacons becoming the board of directors, or the boss of this corporation, the church. Let me state an absolute for the church (Revelation 2:7, 11, 17, 29; 3:6, 13, 22).

God gave me a vision of driving the bus full of people. They chose this bus, because they wanted to go where it was going, and they trusted the driver to take them there. In order to change drivers, there would need to be some preparation of the new driver and the people on the bus.

If there was someone on the bus that felt called to drive and had ridden long enough to know the direction, then I would share the driving for a while. After a while, he could drive and I would ride along until he and I were comfortable in his ministry, and the people were comfortable with his leading. I could then step off of the bus to accomplish God's will in my life, and catch the bus again as God deemed necessary.

If someone joined us on the bus, because he felt God called him, he would then fit into his ministry after riding for a while, be it driver or whatever.

I kept focusing on finding someone, that felt called of God to shepherd these people. We had enviable experiences of young men that interned with us, but they all stepped off 'the bus' and felt called somewhere else.

After several years of 'driving the bus', with lots of new passengers and exciting experiences, we received a letter from a brother who felt God told him to come to pastor this church. I explained the bus scenario. He said he understood.

Without going into detail, it became obvious that he didn't. Thus began a power struggle, since he felt his job was to get rid of me and run his own show.

Now the brother was not the total problem. I had, well to make the explanation plain and uncomplicated, disobeyed the clear direction of the Lord in three aspects: (1) in dealing with a 'Jezebel' spirit in the church as God had directed, (2) in dealing with my personal problem, and (3) in dealing with this brother. In all three situations, for whatever foolish reasons, and I can think in hindsight of many, I listened to natural wisdom instead of clear direction which the Lord had faithfully given.

When I finally prayed through and decided I would now act obediently, I felt the Lord say, "You didn't strike while the iron was hot! Back off now, get a job out of town, and give this brother the rope to prove himself! Come back when I tell you!"

83

A Gospel Cabbie

———————

This was the beginning of fourteen months of driving Co-op Taxi in the city of Edmonton. That may seem like a strange leading and I felt the same way. However, let me endeavor to recite to you the taxi stories, as I am able to recall them, and you'll see the hand of the Lord through the wilderness.

One of the first shocking experiences for this uninformed, green, naive taxi driver went like this. One of the Co-op Taxi stands was at the Kingsway Motel. I pulled into line (about taxi number 8), and watched as a thin, emaciated, pasty faced, starry-eyed man with ruffled hair and a long black overcoat went from cab to cab trying to get a ride. They all turned him down. When he got to my car he didn't ask, but just got in the passenger's side and said, "Drive!"

I was curious about why the other cabs turned him down. He just called them all jerks and repeated loudly again, "Drive!" I thought I should make sure he had money for the fare so I quipped, "You got the money honey, I got the time." He pulled out his American Express card with some picture I.D.

I replied with, "Man if you want to go to New York, I'll take you!" A third time and a little louder he shouted, "Drive!" I suggested, he should give me an address and I could probably save him money by taking him the shortest way. He now became quite agitated and yelled, "Drive!"

So, I pulled away from the stand and started down Kingsway. I was wondering now if I had made a green-horn's mistake by taking this passenger. He had a bug-eyed stare and looked sick. He kept one of his hands under his black overcoat and kept mumbling something like, "I'm going to kill him . . . I'm going to kill him". This seemed like a time for prayer for wisdom. I didn't know where I was going, or what I was supposed to do.

I said, "You seem to be pretty sad and troubled. I spend my life helping people. Is there anything I can do to help you? Awkward silence.

"Is it a problem with a woman?" I asked.

Well that got his attention. He snapped around and stared for another awkward moment. I thought I heard him mumble, "Yes". Another awkward silence with his hand still stuck in his coat. I decided to drive with my left hand so my right hand would be free to protect myself. (I was 6'2", 245 pounds and fairly strong in my grip. I thought that if he had a gun or a knife in his hand I would grab his wrist and break his skinny little arm.) Meanwhile, I was praying up a storm for wisdom.

I began to talk. God seemed to be pouring some wise words of counsel through my lips. The man listened in rel-ative silence, with a little more of his mumbling until he interrupted with, "Go south-side!" "Okay! No problem!" I continued talking, and a compassion for the poor lost soul began to come over me.

We were driving along eighty-second avenue as he seemed to be looking for something or somebody. He inter-rupted again with "Take me back were you picked me up!" "Okay! No problem!"

On the way back to the Kingsway Motel he angrily said, "Isn't there a better cab than this? How about that one?", as he pointed to a black cab going the other way.

I said "Sir, you are in the best cab in the city with the best driver for your sake. That black cab is one of the worst in the city. If you have a problem with me or the cab just take the number of my car and phone in your complaint. The dispatch will straighten it out."

He repeated, "Take me back to the Kingsway!" "Okay! No problem. There will be a whole row of Co-op cabs there to choose from."

I stopped at the Kingsway Motel, number ten now. He paid me with American Express with a good tip on a pretty decent fare and went into the bar. I immediately called dispatch, to express my concern, that this man seemed so troubled. I was concerned that he would either commit suicide, or murder, or both. Bill, on dispatch counseled me to stay out of it, unless I wanted to lose the rest of my night sitting in a police station filling out reports, etc..

While I was still talking to Bill the man came out of the Kingsway and walked directly to my car and got back in. I excused myself on the radio, by saying that my passenger had returned. I then hung the microphone up but left the radio open so that dispatch would be able to hear whatever went on in the cab.

The man gave me an address that I didn't know, so he told me where to go . . . and I talked a little more directly about his need for a relationship with Jesus.

I had been told by Co-op, when they accepted me, knowing I was a preacher, that if they had one complaint about me preaching in the cab I would be gone.

I pulled up in front of the apartment as the man had directed me. He paid me in cash this time. I asked him if I could pray with him. He burst into tears and grabbed my hand and we prayed (with the radio open). When we finished praying, the man wept and wept as he gripped my hand and said, "Man, you don't know what you've done for me . . . you don't know what you've done for me." He went in to the apartment and I shut my radio off. Whether dispatch could hear all that or not I don't know, because I never heard a word about it.

I checked the papers the next day to see if a man had jumped off the bridge or something, but although I prayed for the man faithfully, and still do periodically, I never heard from him again.

Who knows the workings of the Lord? I just happen to believe, that there are no accidents in the Kingdom of God, just DIVINE appointments.

84

Christmas Eve Heartache for a Lost World

My first Christmas Eve shift, one of the busiest nights for taxis, presented me with one of my most painful experiences as a taxi driver, and an eye-opener.

I picked up three young women in the east end, who were heading downtown to prostitute alley. I had Christmas music playing, so they asked me if I would sing some Christmas carols for them. So I did, and they joined in with me a little. In between songs, I could hear the conversation in the back. The two older girls were trying to allay the fears of their thirteen year old sister who was sitting between them. They were taking her downtown on Christmas Eve to introduce her to the life of prostitution.

A little reality check for us Christians, who are sometimes so naively sheltered. It probably makes you weep, as it has done me, to be made aware of how the other half lives.

City cab drivers deal with a lot of prostitutes, pimps, and drug pushers during the night shift which I drove. The exposure is an awesome opportunity for a Christian cab driver. I rarely, if ever, picked up a prostitute in the cab, that I didn't get an opportunity to share Jesus with.

One of the questions I often opened with was, "Do you enjoy what you are doing?" The one young woman, I think eighteen years old, turned sideways on the seat and said loudly, "Are you kidding cabbie? Prostitution sucks!"

"Well why do you do it then?" I asked.

With the same tone of voice she said, "I need the money! Get me a job for $100.00 an hour and I'll change!"

I said, "You wouldn't need $100.00 an hour, if you didn't have to pay your pimp and buy your drugs!" Then I proceeded to share the plan that God had for her and offered to help her. She thanked me, but I never saw her again.

In all the months of driving, Wilf, my friend and fellow driver, and I were only able to help firsthand, one young woman off the streets. I don't remember her name, but she loved working with horses and Wilf had a contact at some stables that hired her to groom horses. Thank you Jesus! That's a start. Who knows how much of the good seed sown over fourteen months, actually found good soil and produced fruit that remained.

85

Christ Came to Redeem the Lost, Even the Prostitutes

———————⌒⌒———————

One beautiful young woman, who looked too classy to be a prostitute, but was, took my cab at approximately four in the morning. She talked very intelligently and friendly, but the address she gave me was a well-known front for drug dealing. I was about to pull over to the curb at this address, when she became agitated and told me to keep going around the block. I asked why and she explained that she had spotted a police car. So, around the block we drove and stopped right in front of the open door of the establishment. She stepped out and walked through the door. I watched carefully, because she hadn't left me any money and the meter was still running. Caution was necessary, especially in this part of town, because there was a tendency for passengers to run and not pay.

She just approached the counter as an oriental man stepped up to take her order. He went towards a back room and another man cuddled up to her, nibbling at her ear and fondling her. A third man tried to close the door in a hurry, but a rug jammed up the door and left it ajar enough for me to watch the proceedings. She purchased her drugs and the cuddling man pulled out a knife and demanded her drugs and her money. She yelled that she had a cab waiting and needed the money or the cab driver would call the police. They shoved a ten dollar bill into her hand and shoved her out the door sobbing. I, hero that I thought I was, jumped out of the car to help, but she yelled at me to get back in the car and get out of there.

She got in the car. Her classy dress was torn and they had nicked her side with the knife. She was sobbing and saying over and over, "Why would they do that? They were my friends." I offered to call the police, but she told me, that she couldn't do that because there was a warrant out for her arrest.

Well, all that set up a prime opportunity, to share the love of Jesus with her and pray that she would choose the road of blessing that He had for her, instead of this painful road to hell. I prayed with her and dropped her off at her apartment, but drove the rest of the night with the painful revelation first hand, of John 10:10, "The thief cometh not, but for to steal and to kill, and to destroy", and the opportunity of contrast as Jesus says, "I am come that they might have life, and that they might have it more abundantly."

One more story of a prostitute, and one more I think would be sufficient, is of a chubby young woman whose white, pleated mini skirt was not long enough when she was standing up, let alone when she was seated in the cab. I kept my eyes on the road, for she certainly was not discreet.

This story reveals another opportunity, for she was very receptive, as I shared the hope that God could offer her, if she would only trust him. She had already let me know, that she hated what she was doing, but felt doomed to this life of bondage. I had the opportunity to pray with her and she took a look at the meter, reached in the front of her underwear and pulled out a wad of bills.

Being somewhat fastidious, I suggested that she should just leave her fare on the seat between us. I just couldn't bring myself to touch that money. It stayed on the seat and I had the next few passengers take their change from that money. Oh me, oh my!

I picked up a young woman from the Yellowhead Hotel, who was going downtown to meet her boyfriend for breakfast. I asked her what she did for a living and she proudly told me that she was one of the best exotic dancers in the city. Well, I did my best to share Jesus with her, but she thought she was alright as she was. She didn't see anything wrong with her lifestyle. As a matter of fact, on the way to Humpty's to meet her boyfriend, we drove past some girls on 'prostitute alley'. My exotic dancer passenger sighed and said, "Oh, those poor girls!" I responded with, "What is the difference between what you do and what they do!?" She said, "We dancers show and tell, but those girls show and sell!" Straightest form of blind self-righteousness that I ever ran into!

86

A Divine Appointment in a Taxi

One of these divine appointments was made obvious to me, when I received a call to pick up a bar maid, named *Wendy**, at the Londonderry Bar and take her home. She was, apparently, a regular customer who always took a Co-op taxi home from work for about a $3.00 fare. I wasn't far away, so I showed up fairly quickly and met another Co-op cab leaving the bar. I pulled up to the curb, and a man came running up to my window, yelling some obscenities, about that so and so scooping me and that I should call dispatch and complain. I just informed him that I was here to pick up *Wendy**. He said that he was told to say that he was her. I just calmed him down and said that I couldn't leave without checking whether *Wendy** had gotten a ride.

I went into the bar and enquired after *Wendy**. Her friends assured me that she had gotten into a Co-op cab and was gone home. So, I readily invited my disturbed acquaintance to get in and quieted him down about the scoop, by informing him that he would probably be more than a $3.00 fare anyway.

He started talking a mile-a-minute about his predicament. I thought he looked familiar, but couldn't place him. He wanted to go down town to pick-up a prostitute, but he only had $10.00 cash in his pocket. I informed him that the

$10.00 would get him downtown and the prostitute was his business.

We arrived downtown at the rubby-dub, low-priced prostitute area and he decided to go get some more money, but — he had a little problem. His money was way out in the east end, which would cost him approximately $13.00 fare to get it. He wanted to know, if I would trust him by giving him a ride out there to get more money. That may seem to be no problem in your mind, but by now, I had run into a few scams and hesitated to jump at this suggestion.

He proceeded to explain his situation to me. He was, apparently, living with a woman in the east end, except on the weekends, when her sons were there, who didn't like him. She was handling his finances and he hadn't seen her since she cashed his last check. He said, that, if I would loan him a quarter he would make a phone call to her and I could listen in on the conversation. He was sure that she would agree to put the money in the mail box on the front of the house, if I would agree to drive him out there. Well, she did and I did!

Remember now, that this was a DIVINE appointment. As we were driving east, we just happened to pass a driveway with a gravel truck sitting in it. My passenger casually mentioned that he had driven truck for that guy in Red Lake, Ontario. "Red Lake!" I blurted out. "Oh come on cabbie, you don't have to make conversation by pretending to know where Red Lake is", he said. Suddenly, I realized why I thought this man looked familiar. I asked him his name. He told me. (I won't reveal his name for obvious reasons.) I asked him if he knew Earl Carbert. He did. So I said that I was Earl's son, Lyle. You could have lit the cab up with his eyes, as they opened wide and he turned and gripped my bicep and said, "Religious, muscles, Carbert! What are you doing here?" I was quick to inform him of the obvious, that God had arranged this encounter. The fact that I was even driving cab in Edmonton at the very time he needed one, the fact that he wasn't supposed to be my passenger,

*Wendy** was. The fact that out of approximately 3,000 cabs in the city of Edmonton he got me. WOW!

Obviously, this was going to be a unique ride. We talked all the way east and all the way back downtown, and then some more, back to his own place, a duplex where he lived alone on the weekends. I asked about his family, etc., because he had attended our Sunday school in Red Lake, Ontario. I also went to high school with his older sister. We, of course, talked about Jesus!

After he got his money in the east end, we headed downtown, with him feeling awkward about his lifestyle. He constantly apologized and would say something like, "You wouldn't do this would you!?" I assured him he had figured that out right. I'll spare you the sordid details, as he finally found a girl that he could hire cheaply and had me drive them to a flophouse, where he took all his valuables including his extra money and left them with me in the car, just in case he was walking into a setup to be robbed. My instructions were to wait in the parking lot and leave the meter running. I parked outside the window, where the lights went on and off, with my car securely locked. Bad neighborhood!

Approximately fifteen minutes later my passenger came out and was talking a mile-a-minute again, trying to excuse what he had done, etc. He gave me an address, pretty close to the Londonderry Bar, and I proceeded to drive him home. I picked him up around two in the morning and dropped him off around five-thirty with the meter running the whole time. I was well paid for approximately three hours of preaching. A divine appointment, in a different city, for a lost Sunday school pupil of thirty years previous.

87

Christ Reaches a Young Mother

———

M any times, over the four months, people ended up in my cab who either, I would recognize, or they would recognize me, or both. Some are serving the Lord today and I would be thrilled if God's divine appointments that he set up for me, were in the slightest way, part of the healing process.

Another most amazing story was of a beautiful young mother who became an alcoholic. Let's call her *Diane**.

Diane* had married quite young into a fairly well-to-do family. I'm not sure when the alcohol became a problem, but it had affected a couple of her four children through fetal alcohol syndrome. She apparently, had been through several dry out programs, but failed so often to turn her life around, that her young husband had pretty well despaired of her ever telling him the truth, etc.. Maybe you know the pattern of the addicted.

Diane's* sister became a Christian, and I believe her mother was. The sister came to try and help *Diane**, but was feeling somewhat overwhelmed by the extreme reversal in her behavior when she got drunk. When she was sober, she was clean, attractive, slender, blonde, and dressed well. When she was drunk, she became vile, unmanageable and embarrassing. Her sister knew how much *Diane** would despise her behavior, if she ever saw herself drunk. She came to see me, to ask for my help. She thought, that if I could get my hands on a video camera (they weren't very common back then), that she would secretly set it up in the living room of *Diane's** house and just turn it on when she was in one of her drunken, vile modes.

I had made some good friends in the school system and I knew they had a video camera. They gladly cooperated. Sure enough *Diane** 'tied one on' and her sister set the camera rolling. It would be too indecent and vile for anyone to see. Her sister waited until the next morning, and then subtly played back the video. Oh, was *Diane** angry, embarrassed, humiliated and a few more emotions. After she vented her anger, then her sister was able to lead her to the Lord.

*Diane** showed up Sunday morning for church with her four children, all five of them dressed to a 'T'. Her husband wouldn't come, as he told me later, because he thought she was just off on another of those short-lived manipulations, to impress him that she had changed. But not so! *Diane** and the children were faithfully in Sunday school and church for over a year and a half. She was growing spiritually and free from alcohol. Her husband, according to *Diane** and confirmed by him later, was constantly badgering her, to see if she would break down or possibly this was for real.

Approximately one and a half years later, *Diane** disappeared! Her husband came to my door somewhat troubled and asked if I would go with him to find her, and possibly bring her home. I agreed. As we were driving, we talked and talked and he confessed to me, that he had been giving her a hard time thinking she was playing a game. Now, he confessed, he was convinced of the change in her life and had even considered going to church with her.

He had an idea where we might find her, in the Calgary area with a Christian relative. We drove right there and, sure enough she was there. She wasn't ready to return with us, but she did come home a little later. I don't remember how long it was, but she disappeared again and I think her husband just gave up and didn't go after her.

I told you that story, because we lost all contact with *Diane**. I talked to her husband a few times, but he despaired of her ever coming back.

So, here I am in Edmonton some time later, driving taxi. Co-op Taxi had most of their stands in the northeast of Edmonton. I received a call and took the person out to the east end. I realized that it was bar emptying time and headed for the nearest bar, the Beverly Crest Motel. I was number two car with others pulling up behind me. The number one car pulled ahead to load and I pulled up in first position, right in front of the door.

An attractive young woman was coming out with a tall young fellow on her arm. She was scantily dressed with a mini skirt and a sparse halter top. I thought she looked familiar, but because of where I was, I couldn't imagine it could be *Diane** — but it was. Out of the approximately 3,000 cabs in Edmonton, I just happened, by divine appointment, to pull up to the Beverly Crest Motel, at the right time.

*Diane** and her friend climbed in the back. I kept looking forward as I grabbed my trip sheet and asked where they were going. *Diane** gasped audibly and cried out, "Pastor Carbert, what are you doing here?" Then she sobbed and apologized, and kept repeating to her friend what wonderful people the Carbert's were. She went on and on in her shock, as I kept telling her, that Kay and I had never stopped praying for her. Her friend finally said, "Do you two have something to talk about? Do you want me to get out?" Of course, I couldn't expect him to understand. I dropped them off at an address, gave her my card, and promised to visit with her.

Kay either came to Edmonton when she could, or I tried to make a trip home once a week. Kay was in the Edmonton area and we were excited to make contact with *Diane**. She did come back to the Lord, with a few struggles, but never got back with her husband or children.

She had a few good jobs, that took her as far east as Toronto and as far west as Vancouver. *Diane** died fairly young, but to the best of my knowledge, she was serving the Lord and we expect to see her in heaven. The last contact we had with the family, was when they came to redeem the heirloom banjo and silver tea set, that I had rescued from the pawn shop some years earlier, after we found her by 'divine appointment'.

There are more events, I hardly know where to start and stop with these 'divine appointments'. Maybe one more along this same line.

I picked up a man who had no cash, but said the lady at the house would pay. I arrived at the given address and, as my pattern was in such cases, I proceeded to go in the house with him. I was greeted with, "Pastor Carbert!" The lady of the house was the younger sister of a dear friend from the church. The young sister had drawn away from her walk with God and was obviously uncomfortable with me showing up at her door in the middle of the night.

Let's shorten this story, by praising the Lord with a very recent report that she's serving the Lord now.

88

Count Your Losses, Cabbie!

The taxi stories could go on for hours, since I had some attacks, or runners, or scams that I had to deal with every night for fourteen months.

Maybe, at the risk of getting side-tracked or boring you, I should give you some stories of God's protection, before I go back to the transition from our church to the next (which is why, I spent fourteen months driving taxi.).

I probably intensified the problems, by being too stingy, to let people run without paying. Most of the drivers just counted their losses and got busy with more calls, rather than waste time trying to catch the runners. I also reasoned, that if somebody didn't stop them, they would keep ripping drivers off as a pattern. I maybe, was a bit of a crusader, however foolish that seemed (and my character, calling, gifting would never give up — some call it stubborn — m-m-m-maybe).

I picked up a talkative twenty-three year old man, who was telling me, that he just got out of jail where he was 'pumping iron', and was in pretty good shape. The address he gave me should have made me cautious, but I really am quite trusting and push my negative thoughts to the back of my mind. I pulled up to this address where he told me to stop early, so my headlights wouldn't disturb anybody (second red flag). He jumped out of the taxi and said, "I'm not paying and you can't catch me old man!" He shouldn't have said that, because it made me act a little foolishly. I jumped out of the taxi and started to run after him. All the taxi lights on, the two front doors wide open, the motor running and in a bad area — what was I thinking — oh well.

He tore off down a dark back alley. I was hot on his trail. I could hear him more than I could see him, but I thought I saw him duck around the corner of a garage, so I did the same. As I circled the garage and came back on the alley, I saw him head down the alley again. I was gaining on him, so he took a desperate dive between two big spruce trees, and I dove also and landed on top of him. I put him in an arm lock, and started walking him back to the taxi, telling him the whole way, that I was taking him to jail.

The charge was transportation by fraud, $2,000.00 fine or two years in jail. He was talking a blue streak, but I wasn't yielding, so halfway back to the taxi he decided to fight me. Well, I'm not a little man and I had some wrestling moves he obviously wasn't expecting, so I put him in my favorite pinning hold, the half nelson chancery, putting him to the ground, and held him for a while. He got one arm loose and pulled my Co-op badge off ($5.00 worth), so I put my left elbow on his temple and said, "You've got about one second to decide if you want to live or die." He lay back and said, "Okay, okay, I give." I took him by the hair and an arm lock back to the taxi. I went to pull away and he said, "My girlfriend will pay. You see that basement window lit up just across the street, let me go there and I'll get the money." I said, "Yeah right! There's one born every minute, but I'm not one of them!" So he talked me into driving to that apartment building. He knocked on the window (I had him by the belt and the hair). His girlfriend looked up, and called him an unrepeatable name, and told us to come to the door. She guaranteed to pay me, but didn't get her check until Friday. Since I got her name, phone number and address, I agreed to leave him with her and collect on Friday.

I made six trips back to that address with a different reasonable excuse for five of the visits. On the sixth visit the apartment was empty — DUH! Count your losses, Lyle!

I picked up another similar character at a dumpy little hotel. He gave me the run-around to two or three wrong addresses, so I power locked him in the cab and started toward the police station. He got a little excited, and assured me, if I took him to his sister's place on Sixty Sixth Street that she would pay. I told him if he didn't come up with a better story than that, by the time I got to Sixty Sixth Street, I would turn north to the police station and not south to his sister's.

I think, I stopped at Ninety Seventh Street for a traffic light when he quietly unlocked his door and waited for the light to turn green and attempted to jump, when I was forced by traffic to go. I reached over and grabbed him by the collar just in time, put him in a headlock and threatened to break his neck if he didn't pull his feet in. He did! I hit the brakes and then the gas and the door slammed shut as I headed for the police station on One Hundred Thirty Seventh Avenue and Sixty Sixth Street.

I pulled up and grabbed him by the right shoulder of his jacket. Every time he tried to swing at me with his left hand, I shoved his right shoulder forward and he missed. I shoved him through the doors into the police station and the police laughingly said, "That's what we like to see — the John Wayne style."

They gave me a form to fill out, stating my charges and took him to one side. They frisked him, took his belt off, and his shoe laces out of his shoes and took him in a back room for questioning. The Sergeant came out in a few minutes and said, "Thanks cabbie, for bringing him in, but there's no money for you. We have three warrants for his arrest".

Count your losses Lyle! Maybe he'll think twice, before he tries anymore taxi scams!

Another little man gave me a phony address, a vacant lot, and apologized, because he gave me the wrong address, so redirected me and when I stopped he ran. I chased him! He was pretty fast, but when he went to turn a corner, he slipped and I caught him with my knees right in the middle of his back. I felt sorry for the little guy. I locked him in the cab and started for the police station on Ninety Seventh Street and One Hundred and Third Avenue. There is a 'rubby-dub' hotel right on the corner by the police station. This little guy talked me into letting him go into the hotel, where his friends would give him the money. I made him leave his nice overcoat in the cab and gave him five minutes or I would be coming in after him.

I parked where I could see him talking to a half dozen or so guys. They looked at me out the window and then talked some more. Five minutes passed so I locked the cab and walked into the hotel. I grabbed him by the arm and walked him out to the cab. Nobody interfered!

I drove around the corner to the police station. They did the same thing as the other station had done. This time they grilled him for quite a while and gave him a summons, to appear in court on a certain day and released him. On the way by me he said, "You'll never see me again! I'll be in Mexico by the time this court date takes place!" He was right! Count your losses, Lyle!

I was in Castledowns in Edmonton, dropping off a fare. I shut the meter off and immediately punched the computer for that zone, to see if there were any calls waiting. One call came on my screen, and it was only about six or seven houses away on the next street, so I was there in less than two minutes. I thought, because I was so early that I should go to the door and let them know I was there. I knocked! A man opened the door, and I announced my arrival. He slammed the door shut, so I went and sat in the cab for a couple of minutes.

I was just going to call dispatch to see what to do, when this man came storming out and sat in the front seat, slammed the car door and told me to wait. He was obviously aggravated! Then a woman came out (I presumed his wife) and got in the back. He gruffly told me to drop her off at an address a little ways across Castledowns and then go to the 'Limelight' bar.

When I pulled up to let the lady out, I followed policy by watching until the lady was safely inside. I just rolled slowly ahead so I could watch her. He suddenly burst into a rage and shouted, "I'm not going to be ripped off by any more cabs." He pulled a five inch hunting knife out of his pocket and shoved it under my chin. Once again God gave me the same calmness that I had, when a couple of other guys tried to kill me. I shouted, "Hold it! I'm not trying to rip you off, what's the problem?" He said, "Take off! Get out of here! I explained company policy and he had no interest in that, nor what happened to the 'blankety-blank' woman. I further explained that the reason I was pulling away slowly was because of the way the meters worked. If I sat still to wait for the lady it would cost him more, as the meter would keep running in the clock mode. If I pulled away slowly the meter would run according to distance and cost him less. He sat back in his seat and said, "You're not a cab driver! What are you, a narc?" I said, "No, I'm not a narc, but you don't want to know what I am!" Well, he went ballistic! Out came the knife and he stuck it under my chin again, and he was screaming, that if he didn't want to know what I was, he wouldn't ask. "Okay, okay", I said. "I'm not

ashamed of what I am, but I thought it might scare you —
I'm a preacher!"

He dropped back in his seat like he'd been slapped.
"What are you doing here?", he asked. I said that probably I was there for him, because he was obviously troubled. So I talked to him about Jesus all the way downtown
to the 'Limelight'. I even, at one point asked if I could have
a look at his hunting knife. He gave it to me with an obvious
wonderment of my motive. I checked it out for balance and
steel and handed it back to him. He pocketed it. I told him,
I had one very similar to it at home, except mine was a six
inch blade.

We arrived at the 'Limelight' bar. He paid me, gave me
a good tip and then stepped out of the cab. He took about
three steps and turned around. He opened the door, and
with a puzzled look on his face he repeatedly said, "A
preacher — a preacher — a preacher", paused, shut the
door and walked into the bar.

About four in the morning, I was in the downtown area
and picked up a call to the 'Limelight'. The bouncer was
heading home, so I asked him, for conversation sake, how
his night went. He said it was a good night, until a guy came
in and stabbed somebody. So I described the man I had let
off there, and the bouncer wondered how I knew what he
looked like. I explained that I had dropped him off there.
The bouncer just said, "Thanks lots!"

Who knows (only God), possibly count your privi-
leges Lyle!

Another little weasel of a guy, with a sleepy drunk
buddy, got in my cab for a short trip to another bar. He
started conning me as soon as we drove away. He wanted
me to take a pair of sunglasses for the fare. I pointed to the
meter and asked whether he thought it read in sunglasses
or dollars. He got real cranky and grabbed the seat belt to
try and strangle me. I stepped on the gas and turned a sharp

corner and hit the brakes. He went flying across the cab and banged his head on the far window. I jumped out of the cab and opened the back door and grabbed him by the arm, to pull him out of the cab by twisting his arm. He yelled for his drunk buddy to hold on to him, and so he did by grabbing him around the neck. I thought he was going to turn blue, because the guy was squeezing him so hard, so I let go of his arm and he kicked at me. Well, I had my right hip against the cab, so I grabbed him by the leg and yanked with all I had and out came both men on the pavement. Just then, a couple of well-dressed business men came running over to see what was going on. The little weasel jumped up and started complaining about me, but I spied a role of money in his jacket pocket. I grabbed that, took my fare and put the change back in his pocket, jumped in the taxi and left him standing there complaining. I called dispatch and explained what I did. Dispatch just answered, "Good for you!"

Well, Lyle — not much chance for eternal help, but at least you got your money!

God protected me many times! Night driving in Edmonton makes you aware of the messed up world of the crazy drunks.

Enough of that! I was privileged to pray and counsel a lot of people. Truckers with marital problems, prostitutes in bondage, drug users and dealers, etc. etc. etc. Four hundred and twenty shifts of twelve to eighteen hours.

89

Left for Dead, but Lived!

G od spoke to me in January to go back home, to deal with the issue. I procrastinated, because I didn't want to. God spoke quite strongly to me in February, and I more or less said yes, but didn't know how to make the necessary step.

March 4, 1988, I was left for dead, when I fell asleep at the wheel.

My future son-in-law had left his Pony Hyundai with me, to see if I could fix it.

I figured it was the alternator, so I picked one up in Edmonton and took it out to Devon and installed it. I took the Hyundai to Edmonton to check it out. I drove taxi all night and jumped in the Hyundai to head home at six in the morning. I was fighting sleep, as I had for many, many mornings in the past year. I remember turning south, from the Yellowhead highway onto highway #60 to Devon. It crossed my mind to check and see if I had my seat belt on. I don't remember any part of the highway south.

I apparently was about five miles north of Devon when I fell sound asleep. I crossed over through the oncoming traffic and flew off an approach. I drove along in the ditch, still asleep, and hit the next approach head on. I flew up in the air. I woke up staring down at the approach and knew my wheels weren't going to touch, but the top of my hood would.

I flipped 'kitty-wonkle' two or three times, then rolled a couple of times and went end over end coming to a halt, sliding on the roof. I had squeezed the steering wheel into an oval, snapped the steering column off, my left knee turned the instrument panel upward and the right knee folded the dash in a V shape. There was only one window not broken. It was the window in the driver's door. The car had virtually collapsed from the top of the driver's door, to the bottom of the windows on the passenger's side.

I came to rest lying on my back in a pool of blood on the ceiling of the car. I figured I had to get out of there, so I reached for the little finger latch on the driver's door. It clicked, but the door wouldn't open, so I spun around on my back and kicked the door open.

I thought the car had just stopped sliding and I was getting out. The truth was, I had lain in that pool of blood for half an hour. The farmer across the road saw the accident happen and ran right across the highway. He checked me for vital signs and could find none, so he went home and called the ambulance from Stony Plain and told them there was no hurry, because I was dead. So, when I kicked the door open, the poor farmer almost went into shock himself.

I will never forget the look on his face. He was dressed in matching brown shirt and pants and his eyes were staring wide-open. His words were, "You're alive?" I thought, that was a stupid question. I said, "Of course, I'm alive".

I started to climb out of the car, trying so carefully not to get dirt on my grey pants or drop any blood on my navy jacket. Ha, ha, ha! I had been lying in a pool of blood for thirty minutes. I stood up and saw a piece of paper blowing down the ditch and thought that I had better rescue that. I turned around, not even noticing the ambulance pull up, and there on a little knoll was all my papers and stuff out of the car gathered in a blanket. I couldn't figure how that could've happened.

A major thought crossed my mind and I said, "It's okay God. I got the message, and I'm going home to deal with this issue."

Meanwhile, one of the E.M.T.'s was running down the ditch to assist me while the other was pulling out the stretcher. They fired a whole lot of questions at me, such as: "What is your name? What day is this? How old are you? What time is it? [Of course, I looked at my watch which had stopped — thirty minutes ago]. When's your birthday?"

I guess I was in shock, because I was joking and wondering what all the fuss was about. They got me on the stretcher and asked if they could cut my clothes off. I said, "Whatever". The pain was starting to get to me. They put me on intravenous right away and began asking more questions, because they were sure I must have internal injuries. They put little x's all over my body where it looked like there might be internal bleeding. They took the shortest road to the Misericordia Hospital, but, man it felt rough. The pain was certainly starting to get to me.

The Misericordia Hospital was very busy. The halls were lined with stretchers and they left me in the waiting room with the sides up. I kept asking to get off my back, because it was so painful, but they kept putting me off. So, I let the one side down and they came running. I asked if I could please stand up to relieve some of the pain. The doctor came over and told them to put a gown on the front and the back and then said, "You can walk around, but try not to scare anyone!"

I shuffled very carefully over to a mirror and realized what the doctor meant. My head was half again its regular size, with the left side of my face swollen away out to the side. My left eye was closed with a cut and some blood. My head looked like a 'Bart Simpson' haircut, only it was with shards of glass, not hair.

At this time, Kay was in the city shopping for Kim's wedding. I didn't know how to get a hold of her. I phoned Joy Jenkins, to see if she knew where Kay was. She remembered what store Kay was shopping at and had her paged.

Kay, Lorraine and Angela Richmond, and Candace and Rikina (our daughter and granddaughter) showed up at the Hospital to take me back home. I had a few stitches and a lot of pain.

I carefully and stiffly lowered myself into the front passenger side of the car.

Kay drove as carefully as possible, but with every little bump or dip in the road . . . gave me great pain. Finally, we arrived home.

I could barely move, but I lay down in my 4' x 6' x 16" tub to soak all the blood off and ease the pain. They had used pliers and tweezers to pull the glass out of my head.

I went back in eleven days, to get the stitches out and that is when they took a closer look at the x-rays of my back. They sent me home, with the knowledge that I would likely never lift anything heavy again.

I was told by a sports injury specialist, that I might as well not expect to walk normal, for at least eighteen months. I was given a regimen to keep me from bending my back forward. They said, if I bent forward, it would be like bending a finger with a crack on the knuckle and it would damage my spine.

So, I sat in a special chair to keep my back arched and every two hours I was to carefully get on my belly on the floor and push up my shoulders without letting my belly lift off the floor.

My contractor friend knew that I was limited, and could do no manual labor, but thought it would be good to get me out of the house. He invited me to be the paint foreman, with no manual work, just to keep the inmates busy in the Peace River Jail.

Well, God miraculously healed me and by July fourth, I was lifting 4' x 8' sheets of one inch thick birch plywood, a whole lift, as a matter of fact, because I couldn't find any inmates. My contractor friend would walk by and we would shed a little tear of praise, for God's divine intervention. (At the time of this writing I am seventy-five years young and still playing hockey with no ill effects from my damaged back!) P.T.L.!

We then tried to be obedient to everything that God had told us to do. The problem had escalated in the church, to where it was obvious what had to be done. God is gracious and merciful, but we humans really struggle with healings of people's problems. The church problem was not handled scripturally and consequently, left some wounded and bleeding souls.

90

Warning to the Church

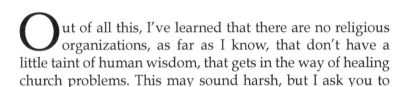

Out of all this, I've learned that there are no religious organizations, as far as I know, that don't have a little taint of human wisdom, that gets in the way of healing church problems. This may sound harsh, but I ask you to think on this for a time.

Once a church is formed, and becomes a denominational unit, the local church is, the denomination's 'raison d'être'. So it seems that denominations discard preachers fairly readily, to save the church, possibly hoping to rescue the preacher at a later date. Most church organizations form some sort of clinical counseling or pastoral care unit. But its success rate is terrible. The preachers that have been discarded, seldom come back to the ones that wounded them. The only ones those counseling programs help, are the ones who would make it on their own, with a little encouragement, because, possibly, they are married to the denomination.

For a year or so, we walked with the interim pastor, who was asked by the District Executive to oversee the church.

At this time, my contractor friend's company had a contract in town, where they needed some supervision, until my friend could finish up in Wabasca. They sent me to supervise, and then work as labor foreman, with my friend when he got there. (An answer to prayer for my friend, who was asking to be positioned back at home).

My friend got a phone call from a Pastor who was in between churches and wanted some work to keep the 'wolf away from the door'. I was walking past as the phone call came in, so he just said, "This is for you," and handed me the phone.

We had been praying for a Pastor for some time, who would feel called to this church. This man had been on our hearts about three years earlier, but he felt led to go somewhere else. That didn't turn out as he hoped, and here he was on the phone, looking to work on construction.

Apparently, as Kay was travelling for the Women's Ministry, she had visited this couple. When she found out that he was looking for work, she told him to call our construction site, because we were hiring. Thus the phone call.

I answered very business-like, asking for qualifications and intentions, only to find out, it was my friend, the Pastor. We offered him a job and room and board at our house. He accepted.

We were very careful, not to ever talk about the church situation, knowing in our hearts that this was a God-thing. Sure enough, within a month or so the church asked him to be their Pastor.

As soon as he was installed as Pastor, Kay and I felt the burden lift. The next weekend, we drove straight to the next point of God's leading and drove up and down every street and alley in tears, knowing in our hearts that we were to go there.

91

A Blind Man is Healed

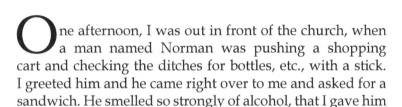

One afternoon, I was out in front of the church, when a man named Norman was pushing a shopping cart and checking the ditches for bottles, etc., with a stick. I greeted him and he came right over to me and asked for a sandwich. He smelled so strongly of alcohol, that I gave him my standard approach for such a condition.

I said, "Norman, I'm not a stingy man, eleven people just left my table. However, you just spent your money on booze that you should have spent on food. Now, for me to feed you would be like buying your booze and I can't do that! Come back tomorrow when you're sober".

Norman quickly pulled out a C.N.I.B card and told me his story.

He had been in an accident in 1965 (as I remember) and was left blind. He could only identify silhouettes of large objects in the bright sunshine. Thus, he had to collect bottles and beg for money, etc.

The truth was, that he collected bottles to get enough for another bottle of wine and lived off his C.N.I.B. pension.

I said, "Norman, I have a friend who can heal your blind eyes and you will never have to be a bum again."

Norman said, "Who is that?"

I said, "Jesus!"

"No, no, no, you don't understand", Norman said, "I'm blind!"

"Norman", I said, "This big building we're standing beside is a church. At seven-thirty tonight we're having a prayer meeting. If you go down to the back corner of the church and go in that door and up the stairs, you'll find our prayer room. You go right in and find a chair and we'll pray for you and Jesus will heal your eyes, and you'll never have to be a bum again." After explaining it again, we parted company. Then I thought of what I had said, "Jesus will heal your eyes" and I realized I didn't say, "may heal", but "will heal".

At quarter-past-seven, I went to the church and saw Norman's stick leaning against the church beside the door. I went in, and sure enough, Norman was sitting in a chair about half way down the back wall. I greeted him and made that same statement of faith again. "Jesus will heal your eyes."

As the people came in for prayer meeting, I introduced Norman to them, and repeated why he was there. I started playing my guitar and singing, when suddenly a shot of faith (1 Corinthians 12:9) hit me and I told Norman to pull his chair forward so we could gather around him and pray, and that "Jesus will heal your eyes." I heard what I said, and felt strange, as if I had really stuck my neck out.

Norman pulled his chair forward and I exhorted the people that if they could believe with me, they should join me by laying hands on Norman.

However, if they didn't feel at one with me in my "faith utterance", not to feel any guilt, but just remain seated and pray.

There were seventeen people in the meeting. Kay had gone into the sanctuary to pray with a lady and of the remaining number, four joined me to pray.

We didn't even finish praying, when Norman started to shout, "I can see — I can see — I can see all your faces, I can see!" Then he excitedly started kissing everybody in front of him. Before he got to me, I had my little four inch by five inch fine print King James Version Bible open to check his sight. He started reading haltingly.

A lady who had just been saved, formally of the Roman Catholic faith, had a large print Bible and graciously offered it to Norman to read, thinking his slow reading was because of his eyesight. Consider the fact, that he hadn't read anything for twenty years. When the Bible flipped open he started to read 2 Kings 6:17 " . . . Elisha prayed, and said, Lord, I pray thee, open his eyes that he may see, and the Lord opened the eyes of the young man; and he saw . . . ".

The prayer room erupted with praise, and one young lady who honestly wondered about the healing, stood up and burst into tears as she cried, "Forgive me, Lord, for doubting . . . I believe, I believe!"

One of the ladies in the meeting wanted to write an article for the local newspaper. She wrote it and gave it to me to edit. She published it, with a catchy title like, "Jesus still causes the blind to see".

A doctor, who had lived and practiced in this town, had retired in Victoria, British Columbia. When he saw the article in the local paper, he contacted us for confirmation, because he was gathering information for a book on medical miracles.

I thought I should follow this miracle with some more confirmation. I was downtown and saw Norman without his stick. He was coming out of the 'lower bar' with a brown paper bag in one arm and a woman on the other. I asked him to come and see me in my office when he had time. He assured me that he would be there at three o'clock that day. He never showed up, so I thought I would phone C.N.I.B. in Calgary for information.

I phoned, and was talking to a man named Ken. He said, "Yes, we know Norman. As a matter of fact he is due for his annual check-up any day now."

I said, "Ken, I am Pastor Lyle Carbert from the Pentecostal Assembly. We had occasion to meet Norman and I would like to tell you exactly what happened, even though you may find it hard to believe." So I told the story, and explained how we had checked it out with him reading. Ken said that if Norman read anything, it would be a miracle. So, I explained that the Doctor who had retired in Victoria had phoned and wanted Norman's information to put in his book of miracles. Ken said, that he couldn't give the information to me, but he could give it to the Doctor. He said he would pull Norman's file and call me back.

In about twenty minutes Ken called back. He started off, "Reverend, I heard what you told me and it was hard to believe, but let me tell you what happened here. I had just hung up the phone with you and Norman walked in the door. I greeted him and suggested that his eyesight might be better now, but he said that it was worse. So, I made no comment, but proceeded to pull his file. While I was getting his file, one of the ladies came to the office and asked what has happened to Norman since he bent over and picked up a coin off the floor."

We talked for a while and exchanged information, for the Doctor's information and hung up. I never saw or heard from Norman for quite some time.

We held services every Sunday evening at the Penitentiary, where we had many exciting experiences. One was when I walked in, took my guitar out of its case, turned around and saw Norman walk in with glasses and no cane. I went right down and asked him to give his testimony of healing. He was quite adamant, that he wasn't going to do that. So, I said, "Then I'll tell the story". He didn't want me to do that either, but I did.

Later, some of the new converts came and told me the problem. Norman had been showing his C.N.I.B. card around, showing that he was legally blind and then challenging guys to play pool with him. He was known in the 'pen', as the blind pool shark.

I've never heard from, or about Norman since then.

Jesus healed him even though he, as far as I could tell, never made a commitment to serve God.

I know, that may leave all kinds of theological questions for some. But like the man in the Bible in John 9, all he knew was "one thing I know, that, whereas I was blind, now I see."

92

A Million Dollar Coach for God's Work

The summer of 1989, Kay was still travelling with Women's Ministries. We went to this town to shop for a home. We found one that needed repairs and was priced right. The bank got in on the miracles, by giving us a mortgage with no job and no money, but it looked good on paper. Then I got a job on construction, took possession of the house and moved in with a table, chairs and a bed.

We planned a tent meeting with an Evangelist friend, which was our introduction to ministry in this town. We did our normal thing, and attended several churches in town with some interesting results.

Someone gave me a name and address of a man that was a Pentecostal brother. I decided, that I should go and visit him. When he opened the door he was in awe. I don't remember the whole story, but he apparently had a dream or a vision and I fit the picture.

We were having Sunday school and Church in our home in the mornings, until some parents were uncomfortable, with their children's discipline in a home, so, we rented the Community Center all day Sunday, where several souls got saved. In the summertime we had Drive-in Church on the parking lot with some interesting results.

This town has been the most different of all the places where we have ministered. The crowds would increase and then decrease — increase and decrease.

All the time that we were in this town, we were mindful of what the Lord had said about this being the last church we would plant and then hit the road with compassion for broken preachers and hurting churches.

Community Center, our first rental hall in this new town

We were constantly on the search for an old bus or motor home, that we could fix up for 24/7, 365 days of the year living. If you think about that, you realize that what may be sufficient for camping trips is quite different than a live-situation. If that doesn't register with you, I understand. It took years of listening to the Lord, and little by little, catching on by revelation, as to what was acceptable for my efficiency; for my wife's sanity; for a visual acceptance by the people, that the Lord would send us to, and especially, for the Lord's glory as we represented Him. After years of searching and planning, but never able to afford anything suitable, I had my 'faith' settle on some $300,000.00 motor home. I say faith in quotations, because I had no money and knew that it would have to be a miracle of God's provision.

I had mentioned my growing compassion and leading, towards broken preachers and hurting churches, to one or two preachers, who asked me what made me think I qualified for that. I had already dealt with that, although I couldn't put it into words myself. "If God gives me a horse, He will surely give me the oats to feed it!"

Consequently, I decided not to discuss it with anyone, except my friend, Bruce Ingebrigtson, who was giving me advice on old buses, etc. and offering me space, as available, to work on one at his shop in Salmon Arm, British Columbia.

Bruce had developed, over the years, a custom coach conversion business, which appealed to the high-end customers. Most of his coaches exceeded one million dollars. 'Bruce Coach' was considered, by many in that field, to be number one in North America, for quality custom coach conversion. Nobody in the industry was able to match, or duplicate the quality that 'Bruce Coach' was putting out.

So, I had the right person advising me on how to fix up an old bus, if I could find one. Bruce had worked from the bottom up and was just starting to come into a profit margin, but with his generous spirit and busy schedule, he offered me needed space and valuable advice for my faith venture.

I literally worked through years of searching, scores of old buses and hours of prayer, realizing this church would be my launching pad, for this new venture in ministry.

January 4, 1999, on a Monday morning, Kay was sharing with me the dream that she had. In the dream, she knew that something excitingly good was going to happen. At ten o'clock this same day, I received a phone call from Bruce. He said, "Well, old guy, you can quit looking for old buses, as a matter of fact you can quit looking for any buses, because I have a brand new one for you."

Silence!

I couldn't get my head around that. Bruce only built one million dollar coaches and up, and I couldn't think in that area. Bruce couldn't afford that. How could that be?!

My breathing seemed to stop. My tears started to leak out. Lyle Carbert was speechless (another miracle).

Bruce then continued to tell me the story:

A man from down in the United States, whom Bruce had built some coaches for, walked into Bruce's office and said, "Bruce do you know a preacher who could use a coach?"

Bruce, the only man I had shared my vision with (think about that), shared my story with this man. Bruce said the man almost did a little dance and said something like, "Get that man in a coach right now!"

The details of this miracle would be too long and unnecessary to relate. He gave us (well God gave us), a one point two million dollar ($1,200,000) coach, with more bells and whistles than you can possibly imagine. Maybe, you can stretch your mind to imagine Lyle and Kay Carbert with no money, shopping for a million dollar home on wheels (we had a choice of one of four)! Wow! Actually, Hallelujah! Praise the Lord!

We used that exact coach, for a couple of years on kind of a trial basis, but the saga of God's provision is still going on.

Allow me to reiterate!

A man, from another country, walks into Bruce's office (the only man in the world that knew my need), and has the passion and ability to be used of God to provide my need. Amazing! I now have a little concept of what that verse in Ephesians 3:20 might mean: "Now unto him that is able to do exceeding abundantly above all that we ask or think . . . " I thought my 'faith' was up to $300,000.00 and God just multiplied that by four. "Unto Him be glory". If God gives you a job to do, He will provide the right tools for the job!

93

Ministry in Mexico

W hile we were in this town, we entertained a couple of ladies from Mexico with a 'God turn' in their circumstances. Then a lady who pastored with her son, in Chihuahua, Chihuahua, Mexico. She had come to Calgary for a Conference, with her friend and travelling companion. While visiting with us, the Pastor, was quite insistent, that Kay and I should come to Chihuahua for a time of ministry, especially to the mission stations, in the Sierra Madre Mountains, amongst the Rarámuri Indians. We prayed about it, and made the arrangements, booked our flights and set the dates. God provided the funds (without us having to make any appeal for money).

You may think that was unnecessary, but let me share with you a conviction about faith. I am concerned for the direction that public ministry has taken. As I explained, concerning a brother who said he was living by faith but was panhandling, pure and simple, conning or begging, so now, I state again my concern for people with big ideas, begging for everybody else to pay for it. Faith, to me, means that you talk to God in your closet and he "shall reward thee openly" (Matthew 6:6). Hear me now! "If God gives you a job to do, He will provide the tools! If God gives you a horse, He will give you the oats to feed it."

A few days before we were to fly to Mexico, the Pastor's son phoned and said there was a slight dilemma in our plans. A church Conference had been called, right in the middle of our mission schedule, and he wondered, if we could change our schedule and come at a later date. I said that we would certainly try. I actually put the phone down, explained it to Kay, and walked toward the bathroom for my shower. I just got through the bathroom door, when I felt the Lord speak to me and say, "Don't change your schedule! Trust Me!" I turned right around and told Kay. She felt the same word, so we got on the phone right away, to explain how we felt. He said that he just hung up the phone and knew that I was going to phone him back and say that. He felt God told him to go with that word.

We arrived on schedule, and the son picked us up in his half ton mission truck at the airport. Suffice it to say, that we didn't have time or desire to go to any resorts. Time and space now must limit the rehearsing of all our experiences while in Mexico. The hotel on the first night, was an invaluable experience. The countless opportunities to hand out Canadian lollipops, or pencils, or whatever, with my attempt at Spanish, "Cristo te ama!" roughly translated "Jesus loves you!" The ministry at the mission in Laguna de Aboreachi, with Pastors Eliseo and Cuca Arvizu Castilo, where the Raŕamuri walked from the mountains barefoot or with homemade 'Goodyear' tire sandals.

The ones from the farthest distance walked seven hours and were on time, visited for a few hours after church and walked home again. It was dark when they started out (no flashlights), and dark when they arrived home. Awesome people, with uncanny endurance.

The amazing bus ride through the mountains; the army stop-check, facing loaded and cocked (I think) AK47's; the homes that were in the caves in the side of the mountains, with a section for the animals; Eliseo's eyes and expressions on the underground subway and the hotel elevators in Monterey; the favor shown us by Eliseo and Cuca, giving us the 'master bedroom' while they slept on the floor in a shed;

besides the honor of eggs and tomatoes with our beans; and the hundreds of people prayed for, of whom we can share a few confirmed healing miracles.

The Pastor's son said, we were going out for breakfast with a few ministers, but didn't clarify until after we arrived at the restaurant. I think he had invited most of the ministers in Chihuahua for breakfast. The meal was served, and then he stood up and introduced Kay and myself, and said, "Okay brother, give them a word!" He knew of my compassion for broken preachers and hurting churches and I suppose, expected me to be ready to preach, pray or die at a moment's notice.

94

Five-fold Ministry Explained

God quickened something in my spirit that I had never actually preached on before in my life.

I opened with, Jesus said, "For my yoke is easy, and my burden is light. How do you brethren feel about that for your ministry?" The silence was deafening! Some looks and body language said, that most of them didn't feel that applied to their ministry.

I then, led by the Spirit, launched into a message, fresh and God-breathed, on the five-fold ministry from Ephesians 4:11. I had never explained it that way before and was learning from the Holy Spirit as I shared.

Basically, it boiled down to the necessity for the church of Jesus Christ to be ministered to by all five of the ministry gifts that Jesus gave to the church, if it expects to be healthy and productive. Secondly, as long as one hired shepherd tries to fulfill all five ministry gifts, some of which he does not possess, he will be dealing with stress and burn out. Round pegs in square holes, etc. are never efficient.

For instance, if you have the gentle spirit of a Pastor, and the distinct need for the special strength of the Apostle or Prophet, you are going to bend and break under pressure, which your beautiful gift isn't prepared to handle. If you have a truly shepherd's heart, and you hit the road as an

Evangelist, you are going to leave your heart at every altar, which leaves unsolvable stress. If you are a true Evangelist, and decide to settle down in a pastorate, without walking alongside a Pastor, you will fill the church and lose them out the back door like still-born babies. It will look successful because of the crowds and fit the description of, "A mile wide but only an inch deep".

The ministry gifts are like the five fingers of your hand (and all the time I was preaching, God took me through the five fingers of my hand, and I'll say just enough here for a basic understanding of how God taught me).

The thumb, the strongest in tensile strength, is set apart in such a unique position to effectively react to or work with all of the other four fingers. The thumb I likened to the Apostle.

The index finger is right alongside the thumb, and between it and the outreach (longest) finger. The index finger is the Prophet, and works closest with the Apostle and the Evangelist. It does the pointing.

The middle finger is the longest finger, and speaks of the Evangelist, the outreach of the church. When the Prophet, Evangelist and Pastor are close together they can carry quite a load, but individually they best relate to the thumb (Apostle) and have little interaction sideways to the other gift.

The ring finger is the Pastor, somewhat in a more compassionate, loving (almost like the closeness of a marriage) relationship with the church. His first calling is caring.

The little finger is the Teacher, the caring Pastor either will have a strong teaching (feeding) ministry or, his caring responsibility for the strength of the flock will cause him to depend heavily upon this Teacher gift, which seems to even have less strength and recognition than any of the other gifts.

Most of the God-called leadership gifts major in one gift, but carry somewhat of a mantle in one or two others. However, these gifts have major differences that would make it foolish of us to presume to cover all five needs with one hired preacher.

Isn't that interesting? Be sure to give it scriptural consideration before you try throwing it out.

Out of this meeting, we were invited to minister in practically all the churches represented. We couldn't work them all in, but it led to one very full Sunday as our host drove us from church to church. The first one had us at an early service, so that we could get to the next one just in time for the preaching, followed by praying for people who lined up for prayer.

The reason I mention this, is to testify of a special meeting, just before we climbed into bed in the wee hours.

We had started early on Sunday and ministered in church, private sessions, and counseling, until late at night, then we headed back to the Pastor's house, thinking we would have a light snack and off to bed. When we arrived there, we found three or four people waiting for prayer. So we fellowshipped a while and began to pray for these people. If I remember correctly, the ailments included an injured shoulder, an injured knee, diabetes and a man with a blind eye.

I can't confirm any of the healings of all the people we prayed for in Mexico, except this blind man. Many said they were healed, including all these people at the Pastor's home.

We started to pray for the blind man. As we were praying, I saw him put his hand over his good eye and pick up his Bible with his other hand and started to read with his blind eye. He was pretty excited. Kay and I went to bed, and again just lay there in tears, thinking of the goodness of God.

We were scheduled to leave early Thursday morning, but because of the good things that were happening the Pastor asked us if we would have one more meeting in their church on the Wednesday night. We agreed, but didn't think there would be many people because of the lack of time to advertise. We need not have worried. The church was pretty full and even one demon possessed lady came in off the street and was delivered.

Everybody in the church knew this young man who was blind. When he got up to testify and demonstrate his healing by reading his Bible, the church erupted with praise. Wow!! (That's Canadian for the Hebrew word, Hallelujah!)

This story must soon end, we don't do miracles, but God continues to do them!

"Jesus Christ the same yesterday, today, and forever." (Hebrews 13:8)

"God is no respecter of persons" (Acts 10:34)

If one person is healed by God, all who are sick are qualifying candidates.

"But my God shall supply all your <u>need</u> according to His riches in glory by Christ Jesus." (Philippians 4:19). So, if you have a <u>need</u> you can rest assured that "his riches in glory" have not been impoverished and Jesus is "alive for evermore" (Revelation 1:18) to meet that <u>need</u>!

95

Ministry in Tobago

ill you allow me one more story of a divine appointment?

We visited Tobago with Dr. Ralph Dubienski, the dentist, his wife Glenda and some teens. On our return trip, the airport personnel seemed to have confused our <u>confirmed</u> (Ha, ha!) reservations and Kay had to sit up front in about row seven and I got stuck in the middle seat of three, about row twenty-seven. The man on my left hand was obviously feeling sick and troubled. I closed my eyes and asked God for His leading, and God gave me the words to speak. The man received my words and seemed to cling to them. I asked him if I could pray for him and believe for the 'touch of Jesus' to heal him. He responded affirmatively, so we prayed. I don't remember all the details, except that he was desperately sick, I believe.

I turned to the lady on my right and was able to pray with her as well.

I probably wouldn't have given it much thought, but when we arrived home there was an email from the man telling us of his check up in Toronto, and discovered he was healed and was given the best report he had ever had.

"No, we don't do miracles but God still does."

96

Miracle in a Hospital: Broken Leg Healed

———————⌇⌇———————

Oh, one more will do you good!

At Kay's and my fiftieth wedding anniversary, Saturday, September 12, 2009, there was a friend from London University days in 1956. On Sunday, my friend Gordon had a stroke that hospitalized him in the Foothills Hospital in Calgary, Alberta. Kay and I left his room to wait for some of his family to visit him.

We walked down to the main entrance to grab a muffin and some juice. Kay suggested, that I reserve two seats in the sitting area, and she would get the juice, coffee and muffins. I sat down in one chair and put my movie camera and stuff on the one next to me, on the right. On my left was a young lady with her leg in a cast up on the coffee table.

We started a friendly conversation, and she found out I was a preacher. She asked me since I was a preacher if I would pray for her leg. I readily accepted and waited for Kay to come with the goodies. When Kay arrived, the young lady was busy filling out some forms or something. We finished our little lunch, and she finished her conversation with the other lady and turned and asked if we could pray for her now.

Kay laid her hands on the cast, and I took the young lady's hand and we prayed. The young lady thanked us with tears and headed up to have an x-ray in preparation for the operation. I remember one thing I said while I was praying, "Lord, let the doctors be amazed at this healing!"

The next morning, we had an email from the young lady saying that the doctors were 'baffled' at the healing of her leg and they didn't have to operate. Apparently it was broken so badly that it would need an operation with pins to make it heal. God did it without pins!

97

Financial Miracle:
To the Penny!

One of the most unusual **miracles of God's provision** is as follows:

There was a time, while we were living in Cochrane, Alberta, that Kay and I both had pretty good incomes.

I was building wood fences, which paid very well. Kay was working for a logging company from British Columbia. The fencing season was usually from about mid-April until mid-November. So, fencing hadn't really started yet, in 1998. The logging company closed the office in Alberta, when the American lumber market went bad, and wanted Kay to move to B.C. to work. Well, that wasn't going to happen!

After some years of having more money than month, we suddenly found the bills piling up. We had lived by faith for so many years, that we just accepted our incomes as one of God's ways to meet our needs.

Thursday morning, Kay, in her typical administrative gifting, called me to look at her blue file folder with a current list of bills to be paid, which included our mortgage (due on Friday), and our tithe. Total $1,865.56. I told Kay that there was no way, without God, that we could come up with that kind of money. If I started a job that day I wouldn't get a check for another two weeks. I suggested that maybe the bank would allow us to miss one month on our mortgage payment. We had never missed a payment in our lives!

We prayed! I walked across Glendale Way to the mail box where there was only one envelope. It had been mailed in Cochrane, but contained a card to bless and encourage us and . . . (people to this day have difficulty believing the rest) — a bank money order (if that's what you call it), signed, of course, by the bank teller from the Hong Kong Bank of Canada, who processed it, for $1,865.56.

(I've talked about this story for years, and stated that figure as I remembered it. However, I didn't realize that we had proof of it until now. Kay went to our files of 'keepsakes' and found the card, with the deposit slip in it — $1,865.56).

With tears of thanksgiving, we praised the Lord and spent Friday in tears, paying the mortgage, and the other bills.

This is a most unusual, miraculous, God-thing. We have had many, many financial gifts over the years, which have been how God has provided for us in a variety of ways. We learned that even with a set stipend every week, we must never transfer our faith, or dependency, from God to any regular check.

This precise, to the penny, gift from an unknown giver was by any standard, an impossible happening. Nobody could have known our financial need. We have held to the principle, that if we are going to trust God for our need, then we must talk to HIM in the 'closet' and let HIM 'reward us openly'.

Even if this principle had been broken, it wouldn't have made a difference in this case. Kay had just finished totaling up the list of our bills, before I walked across to the mail box. That money order had to be made out and mailed at least three days before the bills were totaled up.

I think we felt the nod of God's encouragement, when we realized that we hadn't had any financial needs, for some time, because of both of our incomes. Nor, had we received any notable gifts for that time.

So, it seemed to us that God was letting us know, that He still knew our address and our need to the penny, and we could still trust HIM to 'SUPPLY ALL' our need. (Philippians 4:19).

Isn't HE GREAT?!

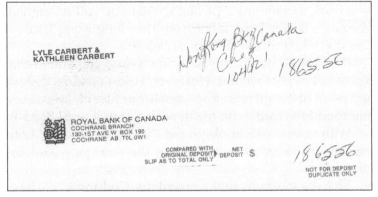

Paperwork for the impossible, miraculous gift of $1,865.56

"No, we don't do miracles
(As a matter of fact nobody does).

98

A Challenge and Encouragement

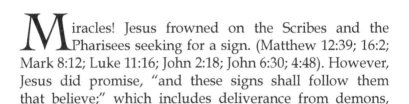

Miracles! Jesus frowned on the Scribes and the Pharisees seeking for a sign. (Matthew 12:39; 16:2; Mark 8:12; Luke 11:16; John 2:18; John 6:30; 4:48). However, Jesus did promise, "and these signs shall follow them that believe;" which includes deliverance from demons, speaking with new tongues, divine protection and healing.

The problem seems to be in motives and priorities. Wanting miracles for the sake of miracles is just curiosity. Wanting miracles to draw attention to ourselves is dangerous in accepting glory that belongs only to God!

Instead of seeking miracles, for any reason, we should be seeking and encouraging the very real and manifest sense of God's presence and learn to let God be God!

Of course, if we don't need the miraculous we don't need God. Any smart administrator can organize a church and make it run well without God. But if we expect the miraculous it will necessitate the very real presence of God and a surrender to His will.

One of the nine gifts of the Holy Spirit is Miracles.

MIRACLES DON'T MAKE FOR
SPIRITUAL MATURITY, BUT
THEY DO DEMONSTRATE
THE PRESENCE AND POWER OF GOD.

You see, whatever all the negative arguments may suggest, God is for real! Most so-called atheists are really agnostics that means they really don't know. A true atheist would have to state that there is no God or that God does not exist! Such a person would be rare. All atheists fit in to one of two categories, if not both, as a fool or a liar.

The Bible states in Psalm 53:1, "the fool hath said in his heart, there is no God." That statement makes sense to believers in God, who have opened their hearts to the faith that God has given to everyone (Romans 12:3). They can say "Amen" to what the Bible says in Psalm 19:1-6 "The heavens declare the glory of God; and the firmament sheweth his handywork. Day unto day uttereth speech and night unto night sheweth knowledge. There is no speech, nor language, where their voice is not heard. Their line is gone out through all the earth, and their words to the end of the world. In them hath he set a tabernacle for the sun which is as a bridegroom coming out of his chamber, and rejoiceth as a strong man to run a race. His going forth is from the end of the heaven, and his circuit unto the ends of it: and there is nothing hid from the heart thereof."

Or in Romans 1:16-25 "For I am not ashamed of the gospel of Christ: for it is the power of God unto salvation to everyone that believeth; to the Jew first, and also to the Greek. For therein is the righteousness of God revealed from faith to faith: as it is written, 'The just shall live by faith'. For the wrath of God is revealed from heaven against all ungodliness and unrighteousness of men, who hold the truth in unrighteousness; Because that which may be known of God is manifest in them: for God hath shewed it unto them. For the invisible things of him from the creation of the world are clearly seen, being understood by the things that are made, even his eternal power and Godhead; so that they are without excuse: Because that, when they knew God, they glorified him not as God, neither were thankful; but became vain in their imaginations, and their foolish heart was darkened. Professing themselves to be wise, they became fools, And changed the glory of the incorruptible God into

---

an image made like to corruptible man, and to birds, and four-footed beasts, and creeping things. Wherefore God also gave them up to uncleanness through the lusts of their own hearts, to dishonour their own bodies between themselves: Who changed the truth of God into a lie, and worshipped and served the creature more than the Creator, who is blessed for ever. Amen."

Anyone who has walked in the mountains, watched a humming bird, studied the human body from the brain to a pimple or compared the atom to the universe, and is not a fool, knows <u>in his heart</u> that there is a God!

Most so-called atheists are not fools, but liars! They lie to themselves first and choose the philosophy of the atheist so they won't have to be responsible to a personal God who created them for a purpose. They want to do what they please so they reject the obvious and choose to reason away what their heart knows instinctively to be true.

Possibly these true personal accounts which cannot be explained away will encourage you, the Reader, to go with faith to the God who loves you and made a phenomenal plan to save you from yourself, your sin and your folly.

NO, WE DON'T DO MIRACLES — BUT GOD STILL DOES

CPSIA information can be obtained at www.ICGtesting.com
Printed in the USA
BVOW08s0108090714

358534BV00005B/8/P

9 781498 402583